SHOAH
THROUGH
MUSLIM
EYES

The Holocaust: History and Literature, Ethics and Philosophy

SERIES EDITOR:
Michael Berenbaum (American Jewish University)

ACADEMIC
STUDIES
PRESS

SHOAH
THROUGH
MUSLIM
EYES

MEHNAZ M. AFRIDI

Boston
2017

Library of Congress Cataloging-in-Publication Data

Names: Afridi, Mehnaz Mona, author.

Title: Shoah through Muslim eyes / Mehnaz M. Afridi.

Description: Boston: Academic Studies Press, 2016.
Series: The Holocaust : history and literature, ethics and philosophy | Includes
bibliographical references and index.

Identifiers: LCCN 2016037755 (print) | LCCN 2016038999 (ebook)

ISBN 9781618113542 (hardcover)
ISBN 9781618113719 (pbk.)
ISBN 9781618113658 (e-book)

Subjects: LCSH: Islam—Relations—Judaism. | Judaism—Relations—Islam. |
Antisemitism—Islamic countries. | Holocaust, Jewish (1939-1945)—Islamic
countries—Public opinion. | Muslims—Attitudes.

Classification: LCC BP173.J8 A357 2016 (print)
           LCC BP173.J8 (ebook)
           DDC 297.2/82--dc23

LC record available at https://lccn.loc.gov/2016037755

ISBN 978-1-618113-54-2 (cloth)
ISBN 978-1-618113-65-8 (electronic)
ISBN 978-1-618113-71-9 (paperback)

Book design by Kryon Publishing Services
www.kryonpublishing.con

Published by Academic Studies Press in 2017
28 Montfern Avenue
Brighton, MA 02135, USA
press@academicstudiespress.com
www.academicstudiespress.com

To my Scott, my life, who spurred in me the drive for this book

Table of Contents

Acknowledgments

The list of the people who have inspired me and supported me in this project is very long. My colleagues at Manhattan College have been indelible to this project, especially the Department of Religious Studies and including the support of the college as a whole. Thanks to my interfaith partners, who trusted in my work and crossed boundaries of thinking with me, and encouraged one another regardless of one's faith or identity. The encouragement of Michael Berenbaum, Sander L. Gilman, Alan L. Berger and Reuven Firestone throughout this project was invaluable. The resources at the Museum of Tolerance in Los Angeles, USC *Shoah* Foundation, and the United States Holocaust Memorial Museum have made my research and interviews possible. I especially want to thank my friends who have been so patient about my work on the *Shoah*, especially David M. Buyze, Judith Clark, Art Kellner, and Melody Steffey—*thank you!*

I would also like to acknowledge the five survivors who invited me into their homes—to be interviewed and recorded for this book and my own research.

Finally, thank you to Ameey and my beloved Papa and my children, Alex and Ruya, who are always my inspiration.

Chapters One, Two, and Three contain revised and previously published material from my chapter "Jews and Muslims: Collaboration through Acknowledging the Shoah," which appeared in *Judaism, Christianity, and Islam: Collaboration and Conflict in the Age of Diaspora*, edited by Sander L. Gilman. It is reproduced here with permission of Hong Kong University Press.

Chapter 6 contains revised and previously published material from my 2014 article, "The Role of Muslims in the Holocaust." It is reproduced here with permission of Oxford University Press.

Introduction

My heart has become capable of every form: it is a pasture for gazelles and a convent for Christian monks.

And a temple for idols and pilgrims [Kaaba] and the [tablets of the Torah] and the book of the Koran.

I follow the religion of love: Whatever way Love's camels take, that is my religion and my faith.[1]

Shoah through Muslim Eyes is a journey that I began many years ago. This book and my scholarly interest in Jews, the *Shoah*, and Judaism were sparked by my desire to understand the "other." I decided to write this book as I began to interview survivors because I wanted not only to tell their stories, but also to join their stories with my experiences of antisemitism today. This book is written for everyone to read: it lies between a trade and a scholarly book purposely, and I hope my Muslim brothers and sisters will take my general criticism of Muslims as an act of being Muslim. As Muslims, we are taught to accept justice, truth, and equality. It is time that people of all faiths, and even the faithless, start listening to the voices that speak up for the "other"—those with a message to all of shared humanity. An example is the universal message that came to Muslims as believers of Abraham and his family, which is similar to that of Jews and Christians. As Muslims recite the following *durud shareef*:[2]

O Allah, let your blessings come upon Muhammad as You blessed Ibrahim and the family of Ibrahim.

1 Ibn al-Arabi, *The Tarjuman al-Ashwaq*, trans. Reynold A. Nicholson (sacred-texts.com: 1911), 67 [Islam World's Greatest Religion, Durood–e-ibrahim], retrieved May 1, 2016, https://islamgreatreligion.wordpress.com/2009/04/12/durood-e-ibrahim/.

2 The *durud shareef* is an invocation that Muslims recite while mentioning prophet Mohammad (PBUH) and it is always complimentary.

Truly You are the Praiseworthy and Glorious.

O Allah, bless Muhammad and the family of Muhammad as You blessed Ibrahim and the family of Ibrahim. Truly You are the Praiseworthy and Glorious.[3]

Contrary to its public perception in the contemporary world, the message of Islam has always been a universal one to me—encouraging tolerance, egalitarianism, and acceptance of other faiths and cultures. Growing up in many cultures opened up my eyes to the vast differences that can arise because of ignorance and generational intolerance, and how these very differences have been divisive. I can only say that if different people begin to see the suffering and injustice visited on others as their own, there may be some hope for the future of Jewish–Muslim relations.

Following the attack on the World Trade Center in New York on September 11, 2001, many Muslims—I among them—faced discrimination and were seen as believers in a violent religion and participants in terrorist groups. It was an unbearable time for some Muslims, who were attacked because of how they looked or what they wore. We became targets in the United States and Europe. This was a time of reflection and despair for many Muslims; I believe we are still very much, in a sense, seen as either apologetic or defensive. Many Islamic scholars and leaders spoke out, but their voices were buried under the louder and stronger extremists magnified by media sensationalism. Unfortunately, not much has changed. We still witness attacks both verbally and physically by those who believe that we do not belong in the United States. As a Muslim, when you live anywhere as a minority and watch the media talk about your faith and person as extremist and violent, it is deeply impactful. At times, I admittedly begin to wonder if Islam is buried under an oriental carpet with such diverse colors and divided patterns. However, I am surrounded by courageous people who have shown me that self-examination and justice are the path to peace in cooperation with others and living with oneself.

Almost five years ago, Manhattan College (where I teach and work) courageously appointed me to direct the Holocaust, Genocide, and

---

3 Ghulam Sarwar, *The Children's Book of Salah* (London: The Muslim Educational Trust, 1998), 36.

Interfaith Education Center. The college, a Catholic Lasallian institution, had enough confidence in me, my work, and my faith as a Muslim—and their own institutional values—to defy many people in New York and elsewhere who accused the college of hiring a "neo-nazi," "Palestinian lover," "terrorist," and "Jew-hater." For example, a child of *Shoah* survivors, law professor and writer Thane Rosenbaum, director of Fordham University's law school Forum on Law, Culture and Society, and moderator of an annual series of discussions on Jewish culture and politics at the 92nd Street Y[MHA], was puzzled by the center's decision to broaden its focus. "The moral travesty that was the Final Solution was not based on faith, and interfaith dialogue this [sic] would have made no difference to the Nazis," he said. He felt that while "Afridi's sensitivity to the Holocaust may be genuine, it would be better to allow a Jew to be guardian for this particular history. Jews have a right to be proprietary in this," he continued. "In a world of multiculturalism and identity politics, everyone owns everyone else's tragedy."[4]

The controversy over my position was understandable, yet I was very sad to learn that some Jews believed that no Muslim, no matter how well credentialed or committed, could be trusted. As a guardian of *Shoah* memory and my commitment to survivors, criticism stings, yet it also triggers self-examination. I delved deeply into my soul and asked myself what business I actually had teaching students about the *Shoah*. But all I could think of was how important the lessons of the *Shoah* had been to me and how many survivors had trusted me by sharing their own memories of pain and humiliation. Their act of sharing imposed a responsibility on me.

More important, I was frustrated at the appalling lack of understanding of the *Shoah* in Muslim communities and the growing contemporary antisemitism that I had witnessed. Perhaps I could serve as a bridge between the abyss that separates contemporary Jews and Muslims. Furthermore, Islam has taught me to be brave in matters of difference and justice; through the power of difference and acceptance, the Qur'an has opened up my being to all humanity as equal in the eyes of God. The following verse 5:48 comes to my mind as I think of the "other" in this case, the Jew.

---

4 Jonathan Mark, "Muslim Woman to Lead Holocaust Center," *Jewish Week*, accessed January 2014, http://bovinabloviator.blogspot.com/2011/03/manhattan-college-gets-religionsort-of.html.

We have revealed to you [Mohammad] the scripture in truth, confirming the scriptures that came before it and as a guardian over them: so judge between them according to what God has sent down. Do not follow whims, which deviate from the truth that has come to you. We have assigned a law [*shir'a*] and a path to each of you. If God had so willed, He would have made you one community, but He wanted to test you through that which He has given you, so race to do good: you will return to God and He will make clear to you the matters about which you differed.[5]

The very concept of difference in the Qur'an has beckoned me to seek others in community, whether "People of the Book" or others as part of the world in universal equality. The Qur'an has inspired me to think through the vulnerabilities of my own community (Muslims), and recognize weaknesses and failures. It is every person's business to stand up for justice and truth, to eradicate the hatred of one people, whether it is because of race, religion, or gender. Islam came with the message of the prophet Mohammad (PBUH [Peace be upon him]) containing the concepts of equality for minorities and women at a time when these concepts were not even in the vernacular in Mecca and Medina. I hope to revive these messages in light of the context of the *Shoah* and recognizing the suffering of the "other."

This book is a simple act of remembering who we are as human beings and how we should not and cannot intensify the hatred of others through the spreading of false rumors and lies about the other. Self-examination is essential in Islam; it is with this hope that I write this book. *Tazkiya* is a term in the Qur'an that is very important within Islam. It is the purification of the soul or examination of the self in various forms that involve both intellectual and physical exercises and contemplation. This is the way to remind oneself of one's reactions and hostilities against others, and work on the self, especially the ego.

Tazkiya literally means growth, one example of which can be seen as a tree. The tree is the result of the growth of a seed. When a seed

---

5 Muhammad Assad, trans., *The Message of the Qur'an* (Gibraltar: Dal-al-Andalus Publishers, 1980), 5:48.

finds a favorable environment, it starts growing till it becomes [a] green, verdant tree. The same is true of the purification of man. In this sense *Tazkiya* also conveys intellectual growth.[6]

My own intellectual growth stemmed from many supporters: Jews, Christians, Muslims, and others who whispered to me words of comfort and love as I took on a job so many deemed unsuited for a Muslim woman. The chances of a college seeking an Islamic *Shoah* scholar is in itself a message from God, a message that He sent so that I could put my work and love in a place of institutional value: Manhattan College.

The center that I direct, the Holocaust, Genocide, and Interfaith Education Center, is deeply committed to *Shoah* education. Through this commitment, I have been able to host many educational and emotionally moving events. The interfaith piece is flourishing, fostering new partnerships and social action with multifaith communities in New York. Interfaith work and studying the lessons of the *Shoah* are not unrelated: through both, we can hope to appreciate and respect difference and eradicate harmful differences through interpersonal contact and mutual understanding. The *Shoah* was undeniably most widely spread across Europe to Africa under the German government, Axis, and Vichy governments. We can neither deny the numbers of people murdered in the *Shoah* nor can we underestimate the enormous horror of this event and the suffering of Jews throughout this time. We must remember that we (humanity) must engage in challenging and painful memories to understand our present. I hope we will.

In the last few months of 2015 in the press, I have found some glimmers of hope in recognizing the *Shoah* and Jewish suffering within Muslim and Arab communities as significant. This article appeared in the *Jerusalem Post* most recently:

At school I hadn't read a single line about the Holocaust. In the 12th grade there were lessons about World War II, but still no mention of the Holocaust. In fact, there is no "Holocaust" in Palestinian history

---

6 Saniyasnain Khan, ed., *Tazkiyah Made Simple* (New Delhi: Goodword Books, 2014), 1–2.

books. I'm currently a law student at a Palestinian university, and still, the word "Holocaust" isn't mentioned anywhere. Yesterday, for the first time, I was privileged to meet a Holocaust survivor. She was standing with her daughter Suzi Nunes. An Israeli filmmaker called Yasmine Novak made a film about Suzi's mother's story called *The Lost Love Diaries*. It is the story of Suzi's mother, Elise, and a man called Bernie. They were torn apart by WWII, and 65 years later Elise decided to read Bernie's diaries and go on a journey to discover his fate. I don't usually watch romance films, but this one wasn't just a love story, or even just a movie. It documents the pain of the millions who suffered and died, and of those who survived. Even though my schools and university didn't teach me about the Holocaust, I read about it on the Internet, and checked some books. But I must admit that what I read wasn't good enough to give me a clear image. Holocaust education isn't only a Jewish issue, it is an issue for humanity.[7]

This article has, for perhaps the first time, examined the antisemitism (would like this as one word) that lurks in many Muslim communities, survivors who have spoken to a Muslim woman, and how the lack of education encourages an imbalanced perception of Jewish–Muslim relations—in this case, the suffering of Jews. My journey through Judaism—research on Muslims and the *Shoah* and its survivors—like that of many other scholars, intends to awaken a deep gulf between two faithful and important communities in the world: Jews and Muslims.

I have written this book in my mind a hundred times—imagining how I would word my thoughts, the horror of the *Shoah*, and grappling with the aftermath of writing such a book—I watched this book grow at different times and moments of my life. The past few years, I thought of how I could do a better job at communicating such a sensitive topic to Muslims and Jews, while maintaining my faith and belief in both communities. It has been quite a challenge; many times I hesitated to write, hesitating to think about the gaps between our cultures as I witnessed the brutal political and

7 Ahmed Maswadeh, "Why Should We, Palestinians, Learn about the Holocaust?," *Jerusalem Post*, retrieved November 9, 2015, http://www.jpost.com/Opinion/Why-should-we-Palestinians-learn-about-the-Holocaust-399168.

social polarization that I believe is exaggerated by leaders in power and armies with ammunition. So, years passed and I felt even more compelled to add a strong voice to the study of the *Shoah* and Islam that was not mutually exclusive.

The first two chapters of the book address the challenges that I face as a Muslim who wants to continue to address the issues of antisemitism and, more important, bring the *Shoah* to the Muslim world as a lesson for all humanity. The beginnings of the book examine many aspects of my own frustration with the dismissive nature of human beings in light of antisemitism and the relativism of the *Shoah*. The *Shoah* has brought me more knowledge about the world, intermingling of identities, displaced people, persecuted Jews, and Muslims during this period and the intimate connections of two Abrahamic faiths through rescue and common suffering.

My journey is threefold. The first part of this journey is the interest of such a study and passion because of my own unique upbringing, my own understanding of Islam as a religion of peace, justice, and acceptance. I have distinct memories of sharing sacred holidays as well as racism with my peers in many schools. As well, I was the one who experienced anti-Semitism in my own Muslim community and academic circles. The second part of this journey is my undertaking of the study of the *Shoah* and the interviews with survivors that I will hold deeply in my heart and mind. This led to the discovery of new stories, histories, and courage of survival that resonate to this day in this field of work. My visits with survivors in their homes, in museums, and hosting them in my house fostered my deep connection to them and their experiences. I consider myself very fortunate to have been welcomed into their lives. My new friend, Gisela Glaser, who is a survivor of Auschwitz and lives in the Bronx, New York, calls me from time to time to discuss the unending pain of losing her whole family, and tells me the same story as if it were the first time. "Mehnaz, my friend Ella and I were on the train, the wind was blowing and it was cold, Ella had a severe fever and she was sick with thirst. I had an idea, I took a small handkerchief and put my own urine on it and gave it to her so she should live. . . ." These are the stories that I live with and reflect on as I have written this book.

In Chapter One, I make the connections between the importance of accepting each other's narratives in creating dialogue and reconciliation.

I show how Muslim acknowledgment of the *Shoah* is connected to dismantling stereotypes of Jews and confronting antisemitism. I discuss the connections of Muslims to the *Shoah* through the metaphor of *Muselmann*, the stark reality of how, if Muslims were to acknowledge the history of the *Shoah*, I argue that there could be a deeper understanding of Jews, Jewish history, and Israel. Alongside this, I discuss how the *Naqba* is and was a pivotal moment in history for Palestinians and Muslims all around the world. These pages become a challenge to me as I reexamine my personal journey as a child (throughout) but also the frustrations I have held toward antisemitism within the Muslim context. In the opening of this book, I stressed how the testimony of a Muslim woman sheds light on the complexity of Jewish–Muslim relations. Islamic principles of justice and self-examination compelled me to write this book; I thus focus on the core meanings of Islamic justice and truth as the cornerstone of my thinking, both ethically and spiritually.

In Chapter Two, I examine how academia treats the issue of the *Shoah* in direct connection to Israel, problematizing the relationship of other genocides and the *Shoah*. These issues are current as we witness many scholars who are enveloped in the Israeli–Palestinian political conflict, which undermines the import of the *Shoah*. I deal with this issue and describe the Jewish experience in the United States and Israel post–*Shoah*. Delving into my experience while I was in Israel in 1995 and then at Dachau in 2007, I explore the parallels and similarities of the displacement of Jews and Muslims. The first two chapters are not chronologically coherent in terms of my life; rather, they are an interweaving of my experience from childhood to adulthood regarding Jews, Judaism, and Islam. This structure was more real for me and carries with it a weight that brings the reader back and forth from academic facts to personal nuances and experiences that speak to a general audience.

In Chapter Three, *Why Is the Shoah Unprecedented?*, a challenging subject, I make a case for why and how the *Shoah* is unprecedented without focusing on its uniqueness, for fear of offending millions of genocide victims, because this too has been an issue within academia. I argue that the *Shoah* was unprecedented in several ways: (1) Jews were sought worldwide by the Nazis, their allies, and collaborators, and killed. (2) Jews were seen as a danger to society both as human beings and as economic barriers. Their elimination was regarded as redemptive to German society. (3) Jews were massacred in a more process-oriented, technological, and mechanical manner than was the case with any other genocide. (4) Jews were easy targets of hatred because of their long-standing mythical history of having committed deicide against Christians, not to mention many myths of blood libel that are still discussed in many parts of the world, Christian and non-Christian. (5) Jews were not from one nation or country, where they could fight or take up arms; Jews had no single country in which to establish a stronghold to defend themselves against the Nazis. (6) Jews had been living in Europe as assimilated citizens for, in some cases, hundreds of years, and the *Shoah* was a war against a minority within several countries in which the minority itself had citizenship. (7) The event occurred in the heart of Europe, with vast implications for Western culture and civilization. (8) It was perpetrated by the most advanced, technologically sophisticated, scientifically developed country in the world. (9) It involved two of the great monotheistic religions of the world, Judaism and Christianity. (10) It used the full power of the state and its resources and involved 22 countries across the globe. All of these aspects are explained in this chapter, and I discuss why they are significant to our current perception of Jews, Judaism, Israel, and Zionism.

Chapter Four, the most poignant in terms of my first experiences of interviewing *Shoah* survivors, is transcribed with snippets about the feelings I had or descriptions of certain moments I felt with the survivor. This chapter explores the engagement—and, at times, tension—between survivors as Jews and me as a Muslim. The interviews are all varied because of their experiences and gender; however, I maintained the same format and questions for all of them so that I could understand whether they could identify any fact or experience about Muslims and the *Shoah*. This chapter is accidental in many ways; I was there to interview survivors because I just wanted to tell their stories as a Muslim woman. They inspired me to write this book by their presence and their own ignorance of Islam. I was surprised to learn how many of the survivors were skewed in their knowledge of Islam or Muslim culture. I discuss this perception in this chapter to examine how victims can also have deep prejudice and fear of the other at different historical moments and times.

Chapter Five, on antisemitism and Islam, discusses the history of antisemitism from Christianity to Islam. I discuss the ways in which Arabs and Muslims became antisemitic and were influenced by the propaganda of the Nazi Party. This chapter discusses the Qur'anic verses and scriptures that have been used to incite hatred against Jews. I address these verses and discuss the problems of interpretation. I examine the ways in which Muslims need to reexamine the motives and interpretations of the Qur'an. I analyze how Muslims view Jews and vice versa. I further make some parallels between how Muslims and Jews have been perceived and misunderstood at different moments and times in history. "Antisemitism is often discussed through the lens of propaganda literature in the context of the recent growth of European-style antisemitism in the Arab world, which derives in the main thrust from a need to ascribe to the Jews a role very different from their traditional role in Arab folklore, and much closer to that of European antisemitic prototypes."[8] Zionism is also discussed in detail to illustrate the misunderstandings about the movement and the unfair depiction of Zionists as Nazis or colonists, which has been a recent issue in Jewish–Muslim relations. I examine the deep anti-Muslim sentiment around the world today, but also resentment toward the Jewish community and some of the propaganda that creates fear and distance between these communities.

In my last chapter, Chapter Six, I examine the role that Muslims played during the *Shoah*. It explores historical and religious antisemitism in the Arab world and the consequences that led to the denial and relativism of the *Shoah*. The chapter contends that Muslims were also rescuers and victims with Jews in Arab countries under the Vichy government and shows how entrenched the colonial forces were in Arab/Muslim lands during World War II. The conclusion of the chapter points to literature and scholarly works that might bridge an understanding between Jews and Muslims through *Shoah* and postcolonial understanding. This book was a journey of

---

8 Bernard Lewis, "The New Anti-Semitism: First Religion, Then Race, Then What?" *The American Scholar* Dec. 1, 2005. Retrieved October 23, 2016 https://theamericanscholar.org/the-new-anti-semitism/#.WA005uArLlU

education; learning from museums, memoirs, history books, interviews, my trip to Dachau, and my own teaching; and work at Manhattan College. I grew through the years that this book has been gestating in my mind.

Finally, my last and ongoing journey is to speak out against antisemitism and anti-Muslim sentiment, to advocate for speaking out for another, to continue my work in the field of Jewish–Muslim relations in both issues of memory and contemporary life, and to be an integral part of the outreach programs and initiatives that are crucial to bringing all Abrahamic faiths together.

Chapter One

Why The *Shoah*?

"Idiots!" she exclaimed. "How can anyone deny the Holocaust in their mind, I am here, I am the living document."
Elisabeth Mann[1]

The language of awaiting—perhaps it is silent, but it does not separate speaking and silence; it makes of silence already a kind of speaking; already it says in silence the speaking that silence is. For mortal silence does not keep still.
Maurice Blanchot, *The Writing of the Disaster*[2]

M aurice Blanchot challenges his readers with the following question: How can we write after a disaster like the *Shoah?* His was one of the first books I read about the *Shoah*; he compelled me to examine how we cannot fully express the horror of the event in writing or in speech. However, this became a metaphor for me as I began to think about my own work and the silence about the *Shoah* in Muslim communities. "The language of awaiting—perhaps it is silent," as Blanchot writes, describes the expectation that I hold for many Muslims to speak up against the antisemitism in my religious community. He goes on to write: "it does not separate speaking and silence." This to me expresses how, even though humanity can be silent,

1 My interview with Elisabeth Mann, 2009.
2 Maurice Blanchot, *The Writing of the Disaster*, trans. Ann Smock (Lincoln and London: University of Nebraska Press, 1986), 59.

I must speak out. To write about a disaster when by its very nature it is not spoken of in my community cannot be kept waiting, as he says, "For mortal silence does not keep still." In other words, the horror of the *Shoah* and its silence or relativism within Muslim communities screams out at me. The silence implores me to write, talk, and take responsibility. As Blanchot writes: "The disaster—experience none can undergo—obliterates (while leaving perfectly intact) our relation to the world as presence or absence; it does not thereby free us, however, from this obsession with which it burdens us: Others."[3]

How can one deny the genocide and silent screams of so many lives lost during the *Shoah*? Do political differences make us inclined to separate ourselves from others to the point of denial and repression of one another's suffering? The denial of the *Shoah* is a crime against humanity. What is it about humans that becomes undeniably repulsive when they deny the deaths of millions, knowingly avoid the evidence, and remain painfully silent? The silence that I refer to is the tacit silence and casual acknowledgments within Muslim communities and countries that the *Shoah* is a subject that is not discussed, and if discussed must be seen as relative to other discussions of suffering. To deny the suffering and loss of another human being is a failure on the part of humanity. What lessons can we learn from the denial and the acknowledgment of the *Shoah*? To deny the *Shoah* is to deny the millions of lives their narratives of life, breath, and imprints on the world. God created these lives and others destroyed them; is it not our duty to preserve their memory and remember that millions were created to die at the hands of murderers because they were seen as subhuman?

> The Holocaust is not Europeans killing off "their Jews" (a calamity restricted to Europe, as is often heard), but a horrific event that must engage all humanity precisely because it is a crime against humanity. Perhaps it is the feebleness of this concept in Arab culture and thought which has precluded broad Arab under-standing of the Holocaust's centrality to Western culture and thought, and which may account for our continued puzzlement at

the "exorbitant" attention it gets in the Western media, [academia], and politics. In short, we fail to grasp the significance of the Holocaust to Western modernity because we still have difficulties engaging the issues raised by modernity, namely the ethical, juridical and political issue of human rights.[4]

This quotation by Anwar Chemseddine (a pseudonym used by a professor of English at a university in North Africa) illustrates that there is a need not only to recognize the *Shoah* in the Arab/Muslim context, but also to understand that it stands out as the archetype of a crime against humanity. The game of denial and relativism of others' suffering can lead to historical relativism and dangerous identification that separates groups and religious identities from one another. Another example of an intellectual speaking out for the recognition of the *Shoah* is Mohammed Dajani, the Palestinian professor who was forced out of his job at Al-Quds University. He received death threats and his car was set on fire after he took students to visit Auschwitz. The controversy escalated due to an educational trip and because the *Shoah* was read as an event of the past that was comparable to the *Naqba*.

> The visit to the concentration camp was part of a project to study the Holocaust and teach tolerance and empathy. "It is about understanding the other," Dajani told *the Guardian* during a conference in the Qatari capital, Doha. "You need to understand the other because reconciliation is the only option we have. And the sooner we do it the better. Empathizing with your enemy does not mean you sanction what your enemy is doing to you."[5]

---

4 Anwar Chemseddine, "The Arabs View of the Holocaust is Indeed Troubled," *Legacy Project*, accessed July 12, 2010, http://www.legacyproject.org/index.php?commentID=1&page=comment_detail&sympID=1. This article is not longer available on the Internet. However, a discussion of the article can be found in Robert Satloff's *Among the Righteous: Lost Stories from the Holocaust's Long Reach into Arab Lands* (New York: Public Affairs, 2006), 186.

5 "Palestinian Professor: No Regrets over Taking Students to Auschwitz," *The Guardian*, accessed July 15, 2014, http://www.theguardian.com/world/2014/jun/13/palestinian-professor-resigns-students-auschwitz.

Dajani here explains that to empathize or acknowledge others' suffering even if they are seen as an "enemy" today has nothing to do with historical fact and the continual memory and history of their suffering. The way in which we conceive of genocide and others' suffering influences the way in which we view history. We may challenge ourselves and others at times by asking the following question: Who were the oppressors and who were the victims? Which community destroyed others, and which abstained? Memory of the oppressor stays with us for generations and, over time, the memory of war and genocide is refreshed. This memory is important to all communities; however, in this case, Dajani pressures us by recalling, respecting, and acknowledging the suffering of the Jews during the *Shoah*. Dajani is exemplary in bringing an important moral lesson to us: if we accept your suffering, does that mean we suffer less? The Olympics of suffering is, in itself, the denial of other people's humanity. Dajani in no manner was denying the suffering of Palestinians, nor the *Naqba*, yet he wanted to engage through a deep understanding that we all suffer and we are victims at one time or another.

We have witnessed so many genocides (Armenia, the *Shoah*, Cambodia, Rwanda, Congo, Bosnia, and Darfur) in historical documents and journalistic accounts on television and radio, as well as Internet coverage and social media, yet we distance ourselves and focus on the ordinary events of the world. Genocide awareness seems to have little if no effect on present-day genocides occurring in Congo, Darfur, and Syria, even after all the overwhelming historical, journalistic, and media evidence. My students ask the following in my classes: What is the point of *Shoah* and genocide education? We can learn about them, but how can we stop this? To me, the educational purpose is to stop the prejudice and intolerance today so that people will speak out as agents of change in the future. I have encouraged many students to share their stories about their own witnessing of antisemitism and Islamophobia on a daily basis and how education has pressured them to intervene or educate their own peers, family members, and people on the street.

My students are always horrified by how fellow humans commit these horrendous crimes through repeated acts of genocide. They pressure me to explain why these atrocities occur, and surmise that the perpetrators must be psychotic, mentally ill, or under duress. However, when they discover that the perpetrators were ordinary citizens and "regular" people, the contemplation of the merging of evil and good becomes deeply disturbing. The students' revelations regarding "ordinary" evil and "normalizing" crime raises questions that are morally disturbing for them and the memory of the victims. Perhaps, through sharper attention to the religious, ethnic, political, and national conflicts that continue today, we can refocus on the horrors that have become banal, and may remain points of conflict within communities for years. The memory of evil remains to be simplified, and as Agamben notes:

> [Primo] Levi at Auschwitz concerns an area that is independent of every establishment of responsibility, an area in which Levi succeeded in isolating something like a new ethical element. Levi calls it the "gray zone." It is the zone in which the "long chain of conjunction between victim and executioner" comes loose, where the oppressed becomes oppressor and the executioner in turn appears as victim. A gray, incessant alchemy in which good and evil and, along with them, all the metals of traditional ethics reach their point of fusion.[6]

The melding of good and evil is difficult for most people to discuss, but it is a significant factor in exposing how communities create conflict rather than cooperation by living in either the "oppressed" or "oppressor" zone. My students have the most trouble deciphering the evil and how many perpetrators never questioned this gray zone. In the evidence of genocide and in this case, the *Shoah*, Giorgio Agamben notes that Primo Levi opens up questions of oppression and victimization. Levi demonstrates that the ethical dimensions of good and evil can change and meld together into the gray zone. In other words, how can we take responsibility if we are always on the good side and cannot see the evil?

Agamben's book is concerned with how we view Auschwitz (death camp where 1.1 million Jews were murdered) as an atrocity that was ethically wrong and how one can take on responsibility if one recognizes that we are all

---

6 Giorgio Agamben, *Remnants of Auschwitz: The Witness and the Archive,* trans. Daniel Heller-Roazen (New York: Zone Books, 1999), 21.

ethically responsible. What were the victims thinking and what types of images did they have in the most horrific circumstances?

As noted by many scholars, the Jews in camps had their own perceptions and images of the "other." For example, Agamben focuses significantly on the figure of *Muselmann*, a term used in many *Shoah* survivor testimonies, especially those who were at Auschwitz. It literally means "the Muslim"—the general consensus is that it was used to describe a prisoner who was giving up. Many have described the condition as "the living dead, defenseless, dying of malnutrition," "useless garbage," "the drowned," and "the one who submits."[7] The literal meaning of a Muslim is one who submits to the will of God totally and categorically. This term in *Shoah* literature became a challenge to me. Muslims prostrate themselves to God as they pray five times a day and surrender their mind and bodies in the act of prayer. The image of Muslims prostrating, bowing down and, in a sense, giving up all consciousness in the remembrance of God is again witnessed in the camps. Did Jews see Muslims as dead men, with no backbone, who were half-dead? I am not certain where the term originated, but it is most likely based on the figure of the Muslim praying, prostrating to God in prayer; "used mainly at Auschwitz, the term appears to derive from the typical attitude of certain deportees, that is, staying crouched on the ground, legs bent in Oriental fashion, faces rigid as masks."[8] This only became important to me as I wanted to give testimony as a Muslim to the *Shoah*. I am in no way suggesting that I am a witness, but that the figuration of the Muslim (even if negative) was present and absent at the most horrific death camp: Auschwitz. In other words, Jews were thinking of the oriental figure of the Muslim as they attempted to survive the most horrific existence. The use of the *Muselmann* metaphor seems to me an indication of what Europe had painted as the image of the Muslim with the colonial mindset and force of oppression. Few Jews incarcerated in Auschwitz ever had any direct contact with Muslims, as almost all were Europeans and Muslims were then a small, unknown population within Europe, especially within Eastern Europe. More important, looking through *Shoah* testimonies,

---

7 Ibid., 41–45. Also mentioned in "At the Borderline between Life and Death: A Study of the phenomenon of the Muselmann in the Concentration Camp," in *Auschwitz-Hefte*, vol. 1 (Weinheim & Basel: Beltz, 1987), 127.

8 Ibid., 45

one finds the figure of the *Muselmann* as the most base metaphor and, at the same time, the most poignant figure. Muslims were "other," and to see a bent-over body was in the consciousness of some European Jews in some camps. I was curious about this description as an image of the pious Muslim prostrating in submission within the Jewish imagination in some camps.[9]

> There is little agreement on the origin of the term *Muselmann*. As is often the case with jargon, the term is not lacking in synonyms. "The expression was in common use especially in Auschwitz, from where it spread to other camps as well … In Majdanek, the word was unknown. The living dead there were termed 'donkeys'; in Dachau they were 'cretins,' in Stutthof 'cripples,' in Matthausen 'swimmers,' in Neuengamme 'camels,' in Buchenwald 'tired sheikhs,' and in the women's camp known as Ravensbruck, *Musel-weiber* (female Muslims) or 'trinkets.'"[10]

Muselmann was a term that travelled in the camps along with the perception of the Muslim as "other," or the one that submits to God: "But while the Muslim's resignation consists in the conviction that the will of Allah is at work every moment and in even smallest events, the *Muselmann* of Auschwitz is instead defined by loss of all will and consciousness."[11] This is a disturbing and horrific thought, but it brings me to this project, which is about the presence of Muslims, whether negative or positive, in the camps, both imaginatively and literally in some cases (Chapter Six). How can Muslims understand that they too were part of the consciousness in death camps and were seen as the fatalistic ones that had no will, or even moved into a place of no human will? However, this may be a small observation of long-standing perceptions of Muslims in some Jewish perspectives at a very terrible time. The perception of Jews from the general Muslim perspective post 1920s to 1948 was in juxtaposition to how they were seen as the oppressor and conspirator. The image of Jews as oppressors is a modern one, although

---

9 "Muselmann," Shoah Resource Center, International Center of Holocaust Studies, accessed May 12, 2016, http://www.yadvashem.org/odot_pdf/Microsoft%20Word%20-%206474.pdf.

10 Agamben, *Remnants of Auschwitz*, 44.

11 Ibid., 45.

German propaganda and political interests in Muslim countries were mobilized during the First World War to influence relations against Jews.[12] However, these perceptions on both the Jewish and Muslim sides are still an issue today. If one holds these perceptions, what room do we have for the transformation of these images? Transformation will be especially difficult if one does not delve into another's suffering, or further denies it altogether.

From the *Shoah* in Nazi Germany to the current situations in Darfur, Sudan, I look at how the acceptance and acknowledgment of genocide, suffering, and historical reality can lead to positive collaboration in rethinking one another's identity. We might be able to work together if we can recognize each other's suffering. I argue that a deep and painful fear of another culture's past can lead to a rethinking and identification, which, in turn, can lead to positive collaboration. If we can accept one another's narratives even if they challenge our own identities and religious traditions, we may have a chance to see the fear and pain of the other.

The two groups that I examine in this book are Jews and Muslims,[13] and the discussion will focus on the *Shoah*. Note that I will use the term *Shoah* instead of Holocaust here to identify this genocide clearly. *Shoah* to me is more of an appropriate word than Holocaust for two reasons; the first is that it means "catastrophe," versus Holocaust, which means "burnt offering."[14] This relates to a theological meaning that resonates with a religious sacrifice. It is the pagan ritual of an animal sacrifice to God, in which the whole animal was burned as an offering; this sacrifice was practiced in the ancient Temple at Jerusalem. It was through Michael Berenbaum and my own work in religious studies, especially teaching

---

12 David Motadel, *Islam and Nazi Germany's War* (Cambridge, MA: The Belknap Press of Harvard University Press, 2014): see Part 1 of the book on pre-1948 historical information on how the Jews were already being seen as oppressors and how Nazi propaganda was used to mobilize Muslims against Jews and the British.

13 The terms "Jew" and "Muslim" throughout this book are used very broadly. For the purposes of this book, I have at times identified specifically who they are, but I intend to keep the conversation more general. I also do not, by any means, refer to Muslims and Jews as a whole; there are many exceptions I would like to make note of, but in this book I am not able to except for some. I am fully aware of the stereotyping of Jews and Muslims, which is also part of the discussion in my book. Thus, I would like to apologize to anyone who feels offended by my general usage. There are also other distinctions, such as Muslims/Arabs/Jews/Europeans and others, that are also used loosely in the context of the argument of the book.

14 *Encyclopedia of Mass Violence*, accessed May 12, 2016, http://www.massviolence.org/Shoah.

Judaism, that I discovered the many meanings of the word "Holocaust" and why it is important to me. The image of something being offered or sacrificed in a religious sense made me deeply uncomfortable; thus, I chose the word *Shoah*. As Berenbaum notes:

> Holocaust, Hebrew Sho'ah, Yiddish and Hebrew Ḥurban ("Destruction"), the systematic state-sponsored killing of six million Jewish men, women, and children and millions of others by Nazi Germany and its collaborators during World War II. The Germans called this "the final solution to the Jewish question." The word Holocaust is derived from the Greek holokauston, a translation of the Hebrew word 'olah, meaning a burnt sacrifice offered whole to God. This word was chosen because in the ultimate manifestation of the Nazi killing program—the extermination camps—the bodies of the victims were consumed whole in crematoria and open fires.[15]

The term *Holocaust* imparts a religious meaning to the destruction, which mollifies the event. The second reason I use the Hebrew word *Shoah*, which means "catastrophe," is to demarcate it from other genocides. In my research, I have come to believe that the Nazi murder of Jews is unprecedented, since the goal was to eradicate all Jews no matter where in the world they were as part of the "Final Solution to the Jewish Problem."

I also argue that long-standing identifications of perpetrators and victimhood are not always consistent with historical facts—an oppressor can become a victim and vice versa. This is one of the questions that I am faced with by Muslims who have equated Israelis (Zionists) with Nazis or the *Naqba* (catastrophe) to the *Shoah*. I believe that these two events should be seen as different moments and times of suffering for both Arabs and Jews; however, to deny either or vilify the catastrophe of the other as false creates a deeper rift. Dajani expands on this idea of vilifying the other by stating that we cannot ignore the history of the *Shoah* and its lessons. He states:

---

15 Michael Berenbaum, "Holocaust European History," accessed October 24, 2016 https://www.britannica.com/event/Holocaust

Implacable in the face of the uproar, he rejected accusations that he intended to promote the Zionist narrative of the conflict rather than respecting the primacy of the *Nakba* ("catastrophe" in Arabic)—the flight, expulsion and dispossession of hundreds of thousands of Palestinians that was the price of Israel's independence in 1948. "I felt it was important for us Palestinians to learn about this event first because it is historically wrong to deny it and also because it is morally wrong to ignore it," he said. "I felt I should not be a bystander but take a stand. I lived in a culture where the Holocaust was not viewed in depth and was used artificially, linking it to the Nakba. We never learned about its impact, its lessons, why it happened, to whom it happened. It was always in the background as if it was a taboo topic."[16]

The linking of the *Naqba* to the *Shoah* remains problematic and assumes that the two are the same or that one led to another. This becomes one of the points of contention that creates a rift that we have witnessed through other genocides in history. For example, there are many other historical facts pointing to a cycle of violence that we tend to ignore. For example, "consider how little we know about the Kurds who were encouraged … to take advantage of the helpless Armenians and who were later subjected to mass deportation (1915), or the Twa, a tiny minority in Rwanda who were suppressed by the Hutu and the Tutsi throughout history and who in 1994 were incited to take part in genocide."[17] History shows that victims and oppressors can switch roles, and no one race or religion can be free of responsibility in the face of genocide and war. We all make mistakes and commit atrocities, and we have to acknowledge this by accepting one another's suffering, whether in the past, present, or imminent future. More important, we must accept our own failure in taking action and speaking out when our own community is oppressing the "other." This acceptance may shed light on how we might see sin and culpability in terms of religion—in this case, Islam.

---

16 "Palestinian Professor: No Regrets over Taking Students to Auschwitz," *The Guardian*, accessed December 10, 2016, http://www.theguardian.com/world/2014/jun/13/palestinian-professor-resigns-students-auschwitz.

17 Anton Weiss-Wendt, "Problems in Comparative Genocide Scholarship," in *The Historiography of Genocide*, ed. Dan Stone (New York: Palgrave Macmillan, 2008), 44–70.

Thus, as a Muslim, it was important to me to speak with the victims of the *Shoah* and write in the context of my Muslim perspective. I wanted to hear the survivors' stories and venture into the depths of their lives and circumstances. Speaking to any victims of genocide is a challenge, but it is important to hear and learn from their stories, especially for students who confess that when a survivor visits our classroom, their own connection with the genocide grows deeper and they can humanize the atrocity.

My own education had an impact on me comparable to that of my students, but the omission or censorship I experienced was indelible to me—that is how my journey began. I realized that Judaism, Jews, and the *Shoah* were omitted from the educational curriculum at the school I attended in Dubai, United Arab Emirates. This led me to study Judaism and the *Shoah*. I was intrigued by the suspicious omission in my education of the words "Israel" and "Jews." I wanted to discover a place where Muslims and Jews may have some reconciliation on a religious and/or political level. I was unsure of how my journey would take flight, but I found myself starting by investigating the *Shoah*, which has led me in many directions. Such directions included learning more about Judaism and Islam, historical fact finding, and the relationship between Muslims and the *Shoah*. As Abdullah Antepli states:

> This includes Muslims understanding Israel and Zionism through the perspective of Jews who identify as Zionists. In return, this includes Jews' understanding of Islam not as an anti-Semitic, vengeful monolith, but rather as a complex, living tradition interpreted and practiced by diverse Muslim communities throughout the world, including in America. There is also a dire need for many Jews and Muslims to acknowledge each other's pain and suffering that this decades-long conflict had inflicted upon all of them.[18]

The acknowledgement of suffering needs to come from both Jews and Muslims, and as Israel was born in 1948—Palestinians suffered, they lost and were displaced. Many complexities came before and after 1948 but the vital point is

---

18 Abdullah Antepli, "After Abraham, Before Peace: Navigating the Divides," *Islamic Monthly*, accessed July 30, 2014, http://islamicommentary.org/2014/07/after-abraham-before-peace-navigating-the-divides/.

that there was a new cause of suffering. As Antepli notes that "Muslims understanding Israel and Zionism through the perspective of Jews" there should also be an understanding of loss and displacement of Palestinians through the perspective of Jews. In this vein, we must also read one another's sacred text through each other's perspective in order to grasp the theological and ethically meanings that underlie the birth of Israel and Islam.

How Did I Get Here?

Born in Pakistan to Indian refugee parents, I lived in Western Europe from the age of four until I moved to Dubai, then I moved to the United States in 1984. The people I encountered were of all faiths, and the principles of Islam that were taught to me by my parents mandated the acceptance of all people as equal. My interest and education in post-genocide identity perhaps stem from the hidden genocide and wars that my Muslim parents endured as refugees during the partition of India and Pakistan. In addition, being a minority in every country compelled me to try to understand the pain of others and dedicate my life to those who suffer under the oppression of racism and intolerance. I have yet to understand my own history; through understanding and speaking up for the "other"—in this case, the Jew—I am confident that this case study and intellectual path will open up wounds in me that my parents may have harbored as Muslim Indian refugees. So, began my journey looking into the eyes of *Shoah* survivors.

On February 27, 2010, I looked into the sky-blue eyes of Albert Rosa, an 85-year-old *Shoah* survivor, for three hours as he spoke about his experience at Auschwitz-Birkenau. As I left him, he told me with tears in his eyes that he wanted someone to write his life story, since he had very little formal education and would not be able to express in writing his feelings on the *Shoah*. He asked me, "How can I express in words how I felt when my sister was bludgeoned to death in front of me by a Nazi woman, or when I saw my elder brother hanging from a rope when I had tried to defend him?" I looked into his eyes, which had pierced me all day, and wondered how *I* could tell his story in words without losing the sense of the emotional and physical strength it had taken him to survive the horror of his life in the camps. He spoke of maggots crawling on his body as he was ordered to move the dead Jewish bodies, the gold he stole from the teeth of the dead, the urine he saved to nurse the wounds inflicted by a German Shepherd, the plant roots that he dug out with his fingers for nourishment, and the ashes he swallowed from the crematorium as he helped build Birkenau. How was I to give these events any life with mere words? These feelings of paralysis emerge as I write this testimony; how can I give the *Shoah* a life of its own without trespassing on politics, ethics, and the millions of victims? In some ways, I felt like abandoning this project because I feared that I could not do it justice. However, when I tried to repress my urge to work on this book, which is to me a simple acknowledgment of the victims and Jews of the *Shoah* by a Muslim, I simply could not—I became even more drawn to the project.

> But what of those who were not there? The Holocaust cannot be reduced to order, or even an overriding sense of meaning. The event defies meaning and negates hope. How then are we to approach it?[19]

Michael Berenbaum's question of "How then are we to approach it?" is one that I have asked myself for many years. The *Shoah* and its enormity have become a strange preoccupation, and I live in a strange space and time, pondering what it is about Jews and the *Shoah* that compels me to write this testimony. When I reflect on this question, I hear the voices, I see the deep eyes, I feel the strength, the pride, and the memories of men and women who have taken their lives in unimaginable directions so that they can sit and tell their stories to a stranger, a Muslim woman. When I left Albert's home, I gave him a hug because my words of gratitude seemed incomplete, and he smiled as he hugged me back. He said, "This is the first time in my life that I have hugged a Muslim woman." I told him that this should not be the last time, as "Muslim women are not so cold or segregated as people might think." Albert and I exchanged the first step in dialogue by humanizing one another.[20]

---

19 Michael Berenbaum, *The World Must Know: The History of the Holocaust as Told in the United States Holocaust Museum* (New York: Little Brown and Company, 1993), 220.

20 Albert Rosa was interviewed in 2007 at his home. I did not include a full transcript of his interview because he was very difficult to decipher due to his thick accent. I am also waiting for his daughter to send me a waiver for the full interview.

In addition to interviewing survivors, for the past few years, I have attended several interfaith events that speak about Jewish–Muslim relations or Israel and Palestine. My attendance at these events has led me to question my feelings on these topics. Events that talk about peace or education invariably seem to result in acute polarization. Any type of event like this is always filled with political fervor, and results in either the denigration of the state of Israel or the dispossession of Palestinians. Balance is rare; it seems that people have to take a strong position on the issue of Israel, many referring to it as occupied land, or as something that emerged out of the *Shoah*. I wanted to investigate this polarization further and grasp the history of Israel, the need for a Jewish state, and the culminating effect of this through my own questions regarding Zionism, Judaism, and antisemitism.

Having grown up in a diverse environment, I believe that people—regardless of race, religion, gender, or nation—can speak up to one another, and can speak up *for* one another. As a Muslim, I am obliged by my faith to speak out against all injustices, false rumors, and oppression. As the Qur'an states:

> O you who believe! Stand out firmly for justice, as witnesses to Allah, even if it be against yourselves, your parents, and your relatives, or whether it is against the rich or the poor. . . .
> (Qur'an 4:135)

> Let not the hatred of a people swerve you away from justice. Be just, for this is closest to righteousness. . . .
> (Qur'an 5:8)

> God does not forbid you from doing good and being just to those who have neither fought you over your faith nor evicted you from your homes. . . .
> (Qur'an 60:8)[21]

With Islamic principles in mind, and my own ethical responsibility, I still ask myself: Why this particular project? This project stems from the ethical

---

21 Muhammad Assad, trans., *The Message of the Qur'an* (Gibraltar: Dal-al-Andalus Publishers, 1980), 4:135, 5:8, 60:8.

responsibility that I have to speak out against false testimony and to witness directly the denial and relativization of the *Shoah*. As the Qur'an states, "Let not the hatred of a people swerve you away from justice." To hate a group of people or have prejudice against others is a fundamental human flaw; Islam recognizes this flaw when it speaks about justice and human rights.[22] Some might say that Israelis have dispossessed thousands of Palestinians, and according to Islam, Muslims are sanctioned to fight for justice for themselves—so why am I worried about justice for Jews? It is fair to fight for justice, but it is not just to terrorize and create a prejudice against a whole people—in this case, Jews. This project is about the *Shoah*—it is not centered on the politics of Israel/Palestine. I hope that through this book, Jews may be humanized in Muslim eyes, and that the *Shoah* may be given its unique place in the list of genocides committed over the course of human history.

There is, sadly, much suffering in the world. I have witnessed this suffering in my own country of birth, Pakistan, where women are mistreated, governments are corrupt, and the poor are deprived of opportunities and rights. Why, then, did the *Shoah* tale become so personal to me, the core of my personal journey? Perhaps I see the antisemitic antagonism that has seeped into Pakistan having some bearing on this project. Pakistan continues to burn Israeli flags and mistrust Jews. I feel a duty to Pakistanis and others around the world to seek another perspective. This is especially important to me because Islamic principles as I have been taught them and understood them simply do not permit this type of exploitation and racism. To me, as a Muslim woman, any espousal of hatred is forbidden under not only secular laws but also Islamic principles. However, we have witnessed violence and destruction from the pulpits of Muslim leaders, terrorists, and Islamists. This is, in itself, a cause for being a responsible Muslim in rebuking the false and violent face of Islam that has penetrated the world.

Pakistan, the country of my birth, has been through the oscillations of Islamic fanaticism and democratic secularity in which certain power elites wanted to dismiss non-Muslim minorities and harbor racism against the Hindus, Ahmediyyas, Christians, and now Shias. The identity of Pakistan seemed to have always fallen on the "purity" of being Muslim or even

---

22 This is my own interpretation of Islam. I discuss the problem of interpretation in Chapter Five.

maintaining a religious identity—or, in this case an ideology, called Islam—which became a necessity in the formation of Pakistani identity.[23]

For example, in Pakistan, Ahmediyyas, Christians, Sunnis, and Shias are not infrequently attacked in houses of worship. It is worth examining the treatment of minorities in the case of the Christian community in Gojra (province of Punjab), which has been marginalized, in order to understand the roots of intolerance of minorities:

> Following a flurry of unfortunate incidents that intellectual discourse aimed at identifying the factors which led to this tragedy involved mass scale persecution of the Christian community in Gojra and the misrepresentation of [Islamic] the religious teachings, it is high time we initiated. The principal purpose behind this exercise should be to fashion a cohesive and comprehensive strategy to educate [the] masses about the real teachings of Islam and preempt any similar untoward incident in future. It is also of equal importance to seek input of the representatives of all schools of thought and other sections of society like journalists, intellectuals, civil society activists, lawyers and professors, etc. Ideally, the Islamic Ideology Council is well-suited to spearhead this initiative and give it an institutionalized base for the production of effective results. The second phase of such an arrangement may be geared to engage the minorities living within Pakistan in a constructive dialogue aimed at allaying their apprehensions and fears.
>
> I am of the considered opinion that the long-term solution to such problems lies in changing the mindset through sustained engagement and projection of real teachings of Islam so that no bigoted mullah, having a limited understanding of Islam, could exploit the religious feelings of people for ulterior motives.[24]

---

23 Farahnaz Ispahani, *Purifying the Land of the Pure: Pakistan's Religious Minorities* (New York: HarperCollins, 2015). See this book for a thorough discussion on Pakistan and the history of relations with minorities.

24 Muhammad Ul Qadri, "Rights of Minorities in Islam," *Minhaj-ul-Quran International*, accessed December 20, 2013, http://www.minhaj.org/english/tid/8850/Rights-of-minorities-in-Islam/.

Not only Mohammed Tahir Ul-Qadri, but other scholars of Islam—such as Khaled Abou El-Fadl, Khaleel Mohammed, Seyyed Hossein Nasr, Omid Safi, Amir Hussain, Kecia Ali, Saba Mahmood, Zayn Kassam, John Esposito and others—have explained that Islam contains universal laws based on the idea of difference. Islam came with the message of racial and tribal equality in order for Prophet Mohammed (PBUH) to flourish all over the world. The idea of difference is inherently within Islamic ideals, which espouse that no race or nation is better than another. This is an ideal obviously not exemplified by extremists and regimes in many Muslim countries—as seen, for example, in Syria today—although it is still an Islamic prescription for ethical understanding. As Abou El-Fadl states:

> For instance, I'll give you one example. The Qur'an says, "We have made you nations and tribes so that you will come to know one another." And then elsewhere, it says, "And God has made you different and you shall remain different, and if God would have willed, all of you would have believed." Now, that text seems to be reaching for the supernal. It seems to be reaching for the sublime, not the contingent, because I think it is reasonable to say, if God has created us different to know one another—to know one another—then thinking in terms of states of siege is not consistent with achieving true knowledge of the other. Similarly, it seems to me that thinking in terms of the necessity of killing the other is not consistent with knowing the other. It stands to reason to say that, if you kill someone, you don't get to know them very well.[25]

However, the failure of Muslims to uphold these principles calls for reexamination of history and the present. We have been presented with the recent example of the Islamic State of Iraq and Syria (ISIS) in Iraq, who marked the homes of Christians as ones that need to convert or be killed. This behavior is unacceptable and points to the violence that infiltrates new

---

25 Khaled Abou El-Fadl, "Speaking, Killing and Loving in God's Name," *The Hedgehog Review* (Spring 2004), accessed January 15, 2015, http://www.scholarofthehouse.org/skiand-loingo.html.

extremist groups in many parts of the Muslim world.[26] The extremists' agenda has overshadowed many of the values that were set forth in the Qur'an and in the *Hadith* (stories about prophet Mohammad [PBUH]), which provides examples of what one should do in such circumstances of difference or with laws against non-Muslims. Many examples during the time of Prophet Mohammed (PBUH) demonstrate the need for laws for non-Muslims who were always surrounding Mecca and Medina. The Qur'an itself allows for marriages between Muslims and Jews/Christians, acceptance of their sacred texts, and the belief in the same god, as a few examples. However, many laws are overlooked in the clamor of extremist behavior and interfaith clashes in the many parts of the Muslim world. I would like to share one important account here from the *Hadith*:

> Once, a Muslim was accused of killing a non-Muslim, and was presented in the court of Ali, the Prophet's cousin and son-in-law. The evidence supported the accusation. When Ali ordered the Muslim to be killed according to *qisas* (Islamic jurisprudence), the relatives of the murderer made the brother of the murdered man forgive the murderer by paying him compensation money. When the Caliph came to know of it, he asked, "Perhaps these people may have coerced you into saying [that you forgive this murderer]." To this, the brother of the deceased replied in the negative, saying that killing the murderer would not bring back the deceased. Since the murderer's family was paying him blood money, it would help the family financially. The Caliph agreed to the deal, adding that the principle underlying the functioning of his government was that the blood of those of our non-Muslim subjects is equal to our blood and his blood money is like our blood money.[27]

One sees in both the media and commonly accepted beliefs of non-Muslims that Islam fails to recognize the rights of all religious minorities. One of the

---

26 "Iraq: ISIS Abducting, Killing, Expelling Minorities," *Human Rights Watch*, accessed July 20, 2014, http://www.hrw.org/news/2014/07/19/iraq-isis-abducting-killing-expelling-minorities.

27 Ya'qub Abu Yusuf and Abdul Hamid Siddiqui, eds., *Kitab-Ul-Kheraj* (Lahore: Islamic Book Center, 1979), 187.

most important Islamic laws asks non-Muslims and Muslims to share laws and common objectives. One of the major reasons for the rapid and early conversion to Islam from the eighth to tenth centuries was due to the egalitarian message and human rights for all, including women and slaves. However, some Muslims and Muslim countries have lost this theological and spiritual teaching of the prophet Mohammad (PBUH) and the Qur'an.

One might ask the following: How do these ideals of Islam hold true? In the rancor of the media in its many forms, we witness an ugly and terroristic face of Islam, yet the religious principles that I present are idealistic and peaceful. Why this discordance? There have been scholarly and newsworthy discussions of the "moderate" Muslim versus the extremist; however, what gets lost in these discussions is how the two categories negate the beliefs and behaviors of the majority of Muslims. For example, one might want to ask who is a moderate Jew or Christian? Is this a question that we can only ask of Muslims in light of contemporary extremist actions? It seems that being a moderate implies that Islam as a whole is, by definition, intolerant and aggressive—that the majority of Muslims are extremist, intolerant, radical, or violent. For example, why is it that non-Muslims call for moderate Muslim voices? Does that imply that there are only extremist Muslim voices? These questions are repeatedly posed in the media, conferences, and panels on Islam.

If I believe in the ethical principles and practices of Islam, is that an extremist point of view? Perhaps I am politically "moderate" in a given context, even though I have been seen to take extreme positions on religion, especially on how I read the Qur'an and its meaning in terms of other faiths, human rights, and justice. The term "moderate" becomes problematic to me as a Muslim. Perhaps we can reflect on this term as a bias, yet also see how Muslims have created an extremist picture or "fundamental" view of their lives through practices and violent acts that are inhumane. I would say that I am simply a Muslim influenced by my multicultural environment and upbringing within an Islamic frame. In a small but wonderful book entitled *Who Speaks For Islam?* by John L. Esposito and Dalia Mogahed, one can read about what ordinary Muslims think about faith and Islam around the world. It discusses extremism and Muslims in polls and definitions. For example, it states that, for Muslims:

Many regard religion as a primary marker of identity, a source of meaning and guidance, consolation and community, and essential to their progress. Majorities of both men and women in many predominantly Muslim countries want to see Islamic principles, *Sharia*, as a source of legislation. These respondents have much in common with the majority of Americans who wish to see the Bible as a source of legislation. Both groups emphasize the importance of family values and are deeply concerned about issues of social morality. In fact, what respondents in the Muslim world *and* a significant number of Americans say they admire least about Western civilization is an excessive libertinism in society.[28]

Although the Muslim majority may adhere to their faith peacefully, Muslims still need to reexamine these principles today in many Muslim countries inhabited by minorities who have been attacked because of religious difference, whether they are Jews, Christians, Zoroastrians, or Shias. Even though Islamic principles espouse humanitarian principles, we have a long way to go. Other religious traditions have publicly taken a stand; for instance, the Catholic Church issued in the documents of the Vatican II Council that Jews and Muslims have to be recognized as mutually spiritual religions and their respective heritage. The mission of the Center that I direct at Manhattan College states the following: "The Center's mission is to promote Jewish–Catholic–Muslim 'discussion and collaboration' as urged in 1965 by the Vatican's Nostra Aetate (In Our Time) and seconded in subsequent Papal actions and declarations. 'Since Christians and Jews have such a common spiritual heritage, this sacred Council wishes to encourage and further mutual understanding and appreciation.' Nostra Aetate also states that the Church 'regards with esteem also the Muslim,' and it urges all 'to work sincerely for mutual understanding'."[29]

Within Judaism, scholars have also seen a Reform movement that put into question the Jew in the modern period. The Reform movement

---

28 John L. Esposito and Dalia Mogahed, *Who Speaks for Islam? What A Billion Muslims Really Think* (New York: Gallup Press, 2007), 6.

29 http://www.hgimanhattan.com/home/, accessed October 21, 2016.

questioned how to live at the turn of the twenty-first century. One of the earlier examples can be seen within Rabbinic Judaism, which was so important in shaping Judaism as times and historical events forced Jews to accommodate and at the same time to maintain their identity. This was only possible when Judaism became a portable tradition after the destruction of the second Temple (A.D. 70), which is when the synagogue emerged and Jews were able to move yet still retain their practices. For example, in *In Ideas of Jewish History*, Michael A. Meyer observed, "For modern Jews, a conception of their past is no mere academic matter. It is vital to their self-definition."[30]

In the light of self-reflection within two major Abrahamic traditions, there also needs to be further reexamination of Islamic texts not only on the scholarly level, which is being done by many Islamic scholars, but this reexamination needs to apply the reinterpretation to Muslim societal, familial, and political laws. Instead, the Qur'anic injunctions and Hadith interpretations have been left to extremist interpretations. The extremist interpretations are the ones that most non-Muslims hear with the rise of groups such as Al-Qaeda, Taliban, Boko Haram, and ISIS. Even post 9/11, educating the general public on Islam has been very sparse, generating more stereotypical misunderstandings of Muslims rather than providing deep educational value.

Even though Islam also exhorts people to worship Allah Almighty, it does not coerce followers of other religions to accept Islam and change their own creeds. In practice today, this principle has been lost to radical responses to the "other" and has created a homogeneous need within many Muslim communities to act as the only messengers of God. An invitation to truth and the use of coercion are mutually exclusive things. The Qur'an has communicated the Islamic message of truth in these words: "(O Glorious Messenger!) Invite toward the path of your Lord with strategic wisdom and refined exhortation and (also) argue with them in a most decent manner. Surely your Lord knows him well who strayed away from His path and He also knows well the rightly guided."[31]

---

30 Michael A. Meyer, *Ideas of Jewish History* (New York: Behrman House Press, 1974; Detroit: Wayne State University Press, 1987), xi.
31 Assad, *Message of the Quran,* 16:125.

Furthermore, Islam has strictly disallowed the adoption of any methods of coercive behavior that affect the religious independence of the other party. As the Qur'an states: "There is no coercion in religion. Verily, guidance has manifestly been distinguished from error" (2:256).[32] Islamic principles of equality and peace have been lost to a significant minority in the Muslim world that adheres to combative and violent measures, which has resulted in a fallacious and anti-Islamic model. Herein is the issue between those of us who can speak out from the "awaiting silence" (this "awaiting silence" is from Blanchot, discussed in the Introduction) and those who adhere to their own community in shame, apathy, and ignorance of their own religion, which is embedded within their respective culture. Even as we seem to be witnessing an escalation of persecution of minorities in Muslim countries, "theologically non-Muslim minorities are free to undertake any business enterprise or profession in an Islamic state, and no restriction can be imposed on them in this regard."[33] Still, we see this violated in practice by those who claim to speak in the name of Islam.

> For non-Muslims, therefore, the relative stability over time of the basic law regarding their legal status assured them a considerable degree of continuity in this important matter. Further, Islamic judges remained faithful to the principle of noninterference in the adjudication of intra-Jewish issues unless brought before them voluntarily by the parties.[34]

Mark R. Cohen, a Jewish scholar of Islam, points out that the stability of minorities living under Islamic law allowed a certain freedom of noninterference. However, Cohen has also pointed out that Jews and Christians were allotted the *dhimmi* status within Muslim countries that marked them as second-class citizens who had to pay an extra poll tax. As Cohen states:

---

32 Ibid., Surah 2:256.

33 http://www.minhaj.org/english/tid/8850/Rights-of-minorities-in-Islam.html?fb_comment_id=10 150384312452221_23148008#f35872fe14f852, accessed October 20, 2016.

34 Mark R. Cohen, *Under Crescent and Cross: The Jews in the Middle Ages* (Princeton, NJ: Princeton University Press, 1994), 74.

In the pre-modern Muslim world Jews, like all non-Muslims, were second-class subjects, but they enjoyed a considerable amount of toleration, if we understand toleration in the context of the times. They were a "protected people," in Arabic, *dhimmis*, a status that guaranteed free practice of religion, untrammeled pursuit of livelihood, protection for houses of worship and schools, and recognition of communal institutions—provided that able, adult males paid an annual head-tax, accepted the hegemony of Islam, remained loyal to the regime, and acknowledged the superiority of the Muslims. There were deficits to being a *dhimmi*. The head-tax was often collected in a humiliating manner to symbolize the superiority of Islam, and it was burdensome for the poor. Special sartorial rules, originally intended to distinguish the majority non-Muslims from the minority of Muslim conquerors, could spell danger when exploited by hostile Muslims to identify and mistreat them. Protection, moreover, could be rescinded if *dhimmis* exceeded their humble position. This could happen, for instance, when a *dhimmi* rose to high office in Muslim government, violating the hierarchy that placed Muslims on top.[35]

In many instances, this was seen as a protected status from the point of view of the Islamic state. The laws that governed were Islamic, which caused problems for minorities regarding self-defense if attacked in some manner.

In the classical centuries of Islam persecution of *dhimmi*s was very rare: One single case has been recorded, that of the Fatimid caliph al-Hakim (r. 996–1021) who in 1009 ordered the destruction of the Holy Sepulcher in Jerusalem. In the late Middle Ages, however, there was a general hardening of attitudes against *dhimmi*s in Muslim countries. In the West, the Almohads adopted an intolerant policy, while in the East the government of the Mamluk state could

---

35 Mark Cohen, "When Jews and Muslims Got Along," *Huffington Post*, accessed January 15, 2015, http://www.huffingtonpost.com/mark-r-cohen/when-jews-and-muslims-got-along_b_4964469.html.

not resist the pressure of jurists, such as Ibn Taymiyya, who insisted on an increasingly vexatious interpretation of the law regarding *dhimmi*s. It was the legal system of the expanding Ottoman Empire that in the sixteenth century restored the classical Islamo-*dhimmi* symbiosis. This lasted until the middle of the nineteenth century, when under strong European pressure the provisions of Islamic law were increasingly replaced by new legislations that were intended to free the non-Muslims from their inferior status of "protected people" and to make them full citizens. Today most written constitutions of Muslim states confirm the principle of equality of all citizens irrespective of religion, sex, and race. Certain militant Islamic groups, however, advocate the reimposition of the *jizya* and the *dhimma* regulations.[36]

Islam attempted to allot full rights, justice, and near equality to minorities. These are the many rights that I was raised with, which I was taught were instituted during prophet Mohammad's (PBUH) time. Prophet Mohammad (PBUH) was a man who gave rights to women and slaves. The human rights that were allotted to minorities and women at that time have been swept in the malaise of Islamic practice today. With the imposition of certain dress codes, laws, and restrictions on minorities, especially women, comes the perception that extremists bring with them a reimposition of the *dhimmi* status and that they interpret this law literally in certain countries that are Islamic. For example, the return of the Caliphate that ISIL (Islamic State of Iraq and Levant) has claimed to be an Islamic creed is a fatal lapse and dangerous literalism that imposes harsher rules and laws than one finds in early Islam.[37] The crisis of modernity within some Muslim countries has led to a puritanical type of Islam in those countries.[38]

---

36 Patrick Franke, "Minorities: Dhimmis," in *Encyclopedia of Islam and the Muslim World*, ed. Richard C. Martin, vol. 2 (New York: Macmillan Reference USA, 2004), 451–52.
37 "Islamic Terror Attacks on Christians," accessed April 10, 2015, www.thereligionofpeace.com/Pages?ChristianAttacks.htm.
38 Many scholars of Islam have discussed this in recent scholarship, such as the works of Fazul ul-Rahman, Khaled Abou El-Fadl, Amina Wadud, Farid Esack, Zain Abdullah, Reza Aslan, John L.

Furthermore, the extremist lens from the Muslim world has swept away the memory of Muslims living peacefully with Jews and Christians or the early relations between Jews and Muslims. What we are faced with today is the contemporary perception of Jewish and Muslim mistrust. As Cohen further states:

> The great French sociologist Maurice Halbwachs wrote that collective memory is fashioned by the social frameworks of human experience. Changing social frameworks, especially the intensification of Arab–Israeli animosity, have caused many Jews to reject the more favorable interpretation of Jewish–Muslim relations and caused many Jews from Arab lands to replace memories of friendships with Muslims with a selective, bitter memory of enmity, exclusion, and persecution. In many ways this is a transplanted version of the bitter memory of Christian Jew-hatred and of the Holocaust that haunts Israelis and diaspora Jews when faced with the prospect of having to trust Muslims. Muslims need to be aware of this; anti-Semitism in an Islamic mode is, simply stated, politically unproductive.[39]

Even though it may be a challenge for some to have positive memories and perceptions of the first Muslims and the stories of early Islam, as well as the challenges of spreading its message of justice, it is a message that is still silent and awaiting. This is what compelled me to directly speak with survivors and discuss the *Shoah*.

I sat with Elisabeth Mann alone in the Hertz Theater at the Museum of Tolerance, Los Angeles, riveted by her story as a *Shoah* survivor. It was deeply emotional, and one of the most difficult moments of my life, as she sobbed and I lay my hand on her knee. She said to me, "Mehnaz, I hope you don't take offense to this, but I'd like to say something to you." I told her nothing

---

Esposito, Amir Hussain, Omid Safi, Kecia Ali, Richard Martin, Zayn Kassam, Bruce Lawrence, Edward Curtis, and many more. I urge you to read the works of these scholars and their interpretations of the Qur'an, which are poignant and reformist.

39 Cohen, "When Jews and Muslims Got Along."

could offend me, and she continued with hesitation. She said that she believed in souls that linger on for thousands of years, and that she thought I might have had a Jewish soul thousands of years ago. I smiled, and said, "Perhaps"—but as a Muslim, I was not surprised at the thought that my soul might have been Jewish. After all, we spring from the same source: Abraham. To me it did not matter. All that mattered was that she trusted me and felt free to talk with me. I felt like I could have listened to her for days as we walked arm in arm outside the theater.

Chapter Two

My Journey through Academia, Jerusalem, and Dachau

O ne of the many events that encapsulate my desire to testify to the *Shoah* occurred in November 2006. I had been invited to New York City to participate in the Women's Islamic Initiative in Spirituality and Equity (WISE). This is a wonderful organization—I am still actively involved with them and support their work on women and Islam, including a new project on confronting violence and extremism. Therefore, I want to be clear that the incident had nothing to do with the organization, but rather with one of the invited Muslim women who participated. On the agenda was a discussion of the role of the *shura*[1] council in diverse Muslim countries, and whether Muslim women could create the first Muslim women's *shura* council, with power over both Islamic and civil laws in Muslim countries where the *Sharia* (Islamic law) is practiced in certain family matters. A hundred or more Muslim women from North America, Europe, Africa, Asia, Eastern Europe, and several Arab countries participated. It was an amazing array of women with extraordinary talents in nonprofit, business, governmental, and academic organizations. On the last day, I was asked to moderate an interfaith panel. Moments before my introduction, as I prepared to take the podium, I was approached by a woman from McGill University who asked me, "Mehnaz, since you study contemporary Judaism and Islam, isn't it true that *only* two million Jews died during the Holocaust?"

---

1 In Arabic, "shura" means "consultation."

I was stunned and appalled by this young woman's question. A highly educated individual, earlier in the day she had battled in favor of human rights and just laws for Muslim women. I knew that she spoke four languages and was highly skilled in debating the Qur'an and its interpretation. Yet she had posed this question to me. I was speechless. With only a few seconds to go until I was due at the podium, I told her that she should talk with me immediately after my panel. Unfortunately, she did not talk with me, nor did I get her contact information. This story epitomizes both the many nods of casual acknowledgment toward the deaths of two million Jews and the unwavering refusal to accept that six million were murdered. The debate about the numbers of Jews killed during the *Shoah* requires some attention. It is astonishing that, to some, two million Jewish murders seemed to this scholar an ordinary fact, and not at all an unsettling one, whereas six million murders strains the mind too much to accept it.[2] This incident is not the first of its sort that I have encountered; numerous times I have been asked how it was possible that six million Jews were killed during the *Shoah*, especially since they had been assimilated into European culture. Weren't they aware of what was going on around them? How did they not rebel? What is so unique about the *Shoah*? And why are the Palestinians now suffering the consequences of European crimes, fighting for a homeland in Israel? Where are the facts?

Many Muslims believe that the Europeans in power in the post–World War II period, mainly the British and then the United States, gave Jews a state as some sort of compensation for the *Shoah*. Israel is seen as a state that was illegally created in what was Palestine to appease the guilt of Western powers. This reading of the State of Israel emerged immediately in 1948 when the state was created. Muslims felt betrayed by the western powers, and felt that Israel had been given aid to assert a non-Arab/Muslim presence in the Middle East. Thus, the question of power remains highly problematic. Muslims/Arabs believe that Jews have a strong influence on the United States

---

2 In Deborah Lipstadt's *Denying the Holocaust: The Growing Assault on Truth and Memory,* one can find a thorough discussion of *The Myth of the Six Million,* published by Noontide Press in 1969, a consortium of the antisemitic lobby. Many such books, pamphlets, and writings of Holocaust denial emerged after World War II. Antisemitism had much earlier beginnings in European and American right-wing lobbies.

with a strong lobby in Washington, DC and a long-standing presence in Europe.

Recently, a Muslim woman who is very active in pursuing human rights for all Muslims and non-Muslims responded to my idea for this book with the following remarks: "Are you going to discuss how the Jews have taken on the Nazi psychology and how sad it is that the Jews, once victims of genocide, are inflicting the same on the Palestinians ... ?" I am inundated with these questions and more. If my dinner table could speak, it could tell of how many Muslims, Christians, and others have accused Jews of worldwide control and how skeptical they are about the *Shoah*. My table has been deserted by many—I wish that this table could bear witness to the ignorance of the horrifying belief that Jews today embody the old European stereotype of murderers, conspirators, misers, and political puppet masters of the US government. I am horrified on several accounts: first, that somehow two million dead eases the idea of mass murder because the number is four million less than widely known; second, that this is so readily accepted; and third, how the *Shoah* has somehow become less tragic when viewed simply as a historical event with no extraordinary consequences. As Robert Satloff points out in his pivotal book *Among The Righteous: Lost Stories from the Holocaust's Long Reach into Arab Lands*: "The blatant refusal of Arabs to have anything to do with the Holocaust or even accept the number 6 million becomes symptomatic of how Arabs see Jewish history and Western alliances with Jews."[3] He also quotes from the doctoral thesis of Mahmoud Abbas (Yasser Arafat's successor as chair of the Palestinian Liberation Organization and now the president of the Palestinian Authority), in which Abbas asserts that "after the war it was announced that six million Jews were among the victims, and that the war of annihilation had been aimed first of all against the Jews, and only then against the rest of the people of Europe. The truth of the matter is that no one can verify this number, or completely deny it."[4] Satloff points out the relativism of the *Shoah* among Muslims, and further elaborates this point, on which the core of my book rests: "The purpose of Abbas's dissertation written in the Soviet Union, like many others produced

---

3 Robert Satloff, *Among the Righteous: Lost Stories from the Holocaust's Long Reach into Arab Lands* (New York: Public Affairs, 2006), 164.
4 Ibid.

by Arab 'scholars' of the last half-century, was to inject relativism into the discussion of the Holocaust. Yes, Jews suffered, this argument goes, but in a century that produced genocides in Cambodia, Bosnia, and Rwanda, the mass killings of Jews during World War II was hardly unique."[5] In addition, Satloff's book discusses the role of Muslims in Morocco and Tangiers who saved Jewish lives, but also those who became perpetrators and bystanders in their own lands. His research points to more evidence of Muslims' personal and direct knowledge of the *Shoah*, though not in its worst manifestations, as in these countries Jews were incarcerated in prison camps similar to concentration camps, but not in death camps. He states his goal in writing this book: "I [Satloff] decided that the most useful response I could offer to 9/11 was to combat Arab ignorance of the Holocaust. The question was how to do it. An adversarial approach, I soon realized, was the wrong way to engage Arabs if I truly wanted to change attitudes on a taboo topic. To do that, I needed to make the Holocaust accessible to Arabs; I needed to make the Holocaust an Arab story."[6]

My task is analogous: How can I make this story not just an Arab story, but a Muslim story in relationship to the *Shoah*? As I delved into mounds of research, I found many stories of Muslims who were directly connected to the *Shoah*—those who helped, those who were incarcerated in camps with Jews, and those who turned away. These Muslims have been silent, and need another Muslim to help them voice their own part in the *Shoah*, as Norman H. Gershman has done in his riveting book, *Besa: Muslims Who Saved Jews in World War II*, in which he discusses Albanian and Slavic Muslims who risked their lives to save Jews in their countries. The book tells short stories through photographs that illuminate the character of Muslims who saved Jews. Many of the narratives relate the rescuers' firm and deep belief in Islam, which, in turn, led to their acceptance of Jews and Judaism.

The reality of the *Shoah* for Muslims is skewed by Muslim politics and several long-standing myths—that Jews are exaggerating numbers, Jews want to take control of Muslim lands, Jews are the enemies of Islam, and Jews were indeed killed like others during World War II, but not six million

---

5 Ibid., 165.
6 Ibid., 5.

of them. The "cover" of war shields these numbers. Similarly, Turks today will argue that the Armenian genocide was not genocide, but that Armenians were simply casualties of a war aimed at defending Turks against Armenian rebellions and their allegiance to the Russians during World War I. Many Muslims feel that the Jews "used" the *Shoah* to colonize Palestine, and that Jews were given unrelenting support from Europe and the United States because of the *Shoah* and the guilt from both European perpetrators and bystanders as well as the power of the American Jewish community. At a United Nations anti-racism conference in April 2009, headlines such as "Ahmadinejad Accuses Israel of Genocide, Europeans Walk Out" leapt out from newspapers around the world. Former Iranian president Mahmoud Ahmadinejad (2005–2013) asserted that Israel, the United States, and Europe were committing genocide against the Palestinian people[7] (UN speech, September 18, 2009). Without delving too deeply into this, I can say that I do believe that Israel's current policies toward the Palestinian people in the West Bank and Gaza are problematic. Many Muslims, Jews, and other people who support Israel's right to exist strongly criticize many of its current policies. However, for a Muslim leader such as Ahmadinejad to organize a conference and call it the International Conference to Review the Global Vision of the Holocaust, with the express purpose of denying the *Shoah*, is reprehensible. The attendees at the conference included such notorious *Shoah* deniers as David Duke and Yisroel Dovid Weiss of Neturei Karta (Ultra-Orthodox Jews against Zionism). Discussion was to revolve around free and open opinions about the *Shoah*. An interesting fact that went unnoticed was that Khaled Kasab Mahameed, an Israeli Arab who established the Arab Institute for Holocaust Research and Education in Nazareth in 2004, was not allowed to attend because he holds Israeli citizenship. Mahameed was quoted as saying:

The Holocaust did happen and … Iranian President Mahmoud Ahmadinejad's position of Holocaust denial is wrong. Everything

---

7 "'Death to the Dictator' Chant Protestors as Ahmadinejad Denies Holocaust," *The Guardian*, September 18, 2009, accessed June 14, 2010, http://www.theguardian.com/world/2009/sep/18/opposition-protests-iran-quds-day.

that happened must be internalized and the facts must not be denied. ... It is the obligation of all Arabs and all Muslims to understand the significance of the Holocaust. If their goal is to understand their adversary, they must understand the Holocaust ... The *naqba* [disaster] the Palestinians experienced in 1948 [with the establishment of the Israeli state] is small compared to the Holocaust, but the political implications of the Holocaust have made its terrors a burden on the Palestinian people alone ... The Holocaust has all the reasons for the creation of the Arab-Israeli conflict, but also has potential to bring peace.[8]

I believe that Mahameed's thinking is crucial to understanding the ongoing antisemitism within some Muslim communities and Islamophobia within some Jewish communities, while offering hope of breaking the mutual distrust through acknowledgment of the *Shoah*. Even though the conflict between Palestinians and Jewish settlers is marked by events predating the establishment of the state of Israel, the memory of most Muslims lies in 1948. However, there are seminal events before 1948 leading up to the current conflict. As Jews began to migrate to Palestine, especially in the 1920s and 1930s, the Arabs who were already under the British mandate were struggling for independence. The Jews' massive influx—bringing property and skills acquired in Europe, growing the practice of agriculture, and considering Palestine as their "home" and a safe haven—met with significant resistance from Arabs, both Christians and Muslims. The two years that the settlers mark as divisive in the tension between the Jews and Arabs are 1929 and 1936.

In March 1920, the first Arab-Jewish confrontation erupted in Northern Galilee. In April 1920, there were riots in Jerusalem. In August 1929, there were massacres in Hebron and Safed. Yet all these incidences were short, sporadic bursts of violence. They came suddenly and passed suddenly ... The sustained violence of 1936 was different. It created an unprecedented all-engulfing conflict in

---

8 Yoav Stern, "Founder of Holocaust Museum in Nazareth Invited to Tehran," *Haaretz*, November 17, 2006, accessed December 12, 2006, http://www.haaretz.com/hasen/spages/789142.html.

Palestine. And because it was coupled with a Palestinian general strike and a Palestinian national institution building drive, it could not be mistaken for anything other than what it was: a collective uprising of a national Arab-Palestinian movement.[9]

Mahameed's and Shavit's voices can help to bridge the historical gap between Muslim and Jew through acknowledgment of each other's suffering, education, and understanding.

What is required is a deconstruction of stereotypes of Jews in the Muslim world, and vice versa, so that Jews and Muslims will no longer rely on negative images of each other. We must realize that it will take more than dialogue, interfaith events, and lectures to solve the problem. Openness and education within each community may shed some light for future generations. More important, accepting each other's history and suffering, though a significant challenge, will have a deeper impact on the political realities and circumstances of Jews and Muslims.

Since 9/11, there has been an outpouring of literature about the *Shoah* and its connection to Jewish-Muslim relations, which is indelible, as evidenced by the important scholarship relating to Muslims and the *Shoah*. This includes Satloff's work, mentioned earlier; Jeffrey Herf's *Nazi Propaganda for the Arab World*; Fariborz Mokhtari's *In the Lion's Shadow: The Iranian Schindler and His Homeland in the Second World War*; and Karen Ruelle and Deborah Desais's *The Grand Mosque of Paris: A Story of How Muslims Rescued Jews During the Holocaust*. Novels such as *The German Mujahid*, by Boualem Sansal, demonstrate that there are deep divides between generations and an important connection between the *Shoah* and colonialism. This connection is rarely made in contemporary novels and works. Some Israeli authors, however, have shown the connections of the past and present in the context of Israeli and Arab relations, for example, in *The Liberated Bride*, a novel by A. B. Yehoshua, and *In the Land of Israel*, a novel by Amos Oz. These novels present the way in which complex relationships develop between Israelis and Palestinians. The questions that are posed by the main character, Yochanan Rivlin, in *The Liberated Bride* circle back to Sansal's own work on the identity of the Algerian

---

9 Ari Shavit, *My Promised Land: The Triumph and Tragedy of Israel* (New York: Penguin Random House, 2013), 73.

and the past. For example, Rivlin, a professor who teaches Arab history, is fascinated by Algeria and the 1990s as he asks the following question:

> "And what does the memory of colonialism continue to sear the Arab mind more than that of Asian and African peoples with similar experiences? Is it the Arab world's relative proximity to the West, or the memory of its former dominance in part of Europe, i.e. in the "lost paradise" of Andalusia, that makes the pain and frustration of a remembered colonialism so great?"[10]

The frustrated memory of the Arab that Yehoshua speaks of is the memory of colonialism and oppression. Yet, on the other hand, Sansal expresses through Rachel's diary his desire to understand the condition of a *Shoah* survivor: "How is it possible to live after the camps? Is there life after Auschwitz? ... I didn't understand, I don't understand. It is a mystery to me."[11] The memory of colonialism and the *Shoah* are not comparable by any means, yet the desire to understand one another's suffering becomes significant in both these novels.

Yehoshua and Oz are renowned authors in Israel despite the fact that they present the narrative of the "other" with a degree of sympathy, and have retained some popularity and freedom to express their perspectives while critical of Israelis. In Oz's *In the Land of Israel*, a book of interviews and narratives, one finds the voice of the Arabs/Palestinians especially in one poignant section—"Just a Peace," in which he interviews three Arab men at a café and one of them states:

> "Before the '48 war, what did the Jews say? They said they wanted peace and that's all. Just give them a peace of their own and they'd be happy and have done with it. They talked pitifully. That was smart! Arabs had no sense then. They told Jews, We have the power, time is on our side, the Englishman is on our side, we have it all. The Jews won't get peace or anything else. Let them march into the sea. Now it's the other way around. The Arab will tell you today

---

10   A. B. Yehoshua, *The Liberated Bride* (New York: Harcourt, 2003) trans. Hillel Halkin, 308.
11   Sansal, *The German Mujahid,* 208.

that he's pitiful, that he wants only to be given a peace and nothing else, and the Israeli will tell him, I've got the power. I've got it all—why should he give the Arab a peace?

I am confused: peace? ... Now I decipher it: piece."[12]

Oz's conversation with the three Arabs provides a perspective that might be controversial, but it is the reality of such work and interviews that allow the Arab perspective to enter mainstream conversations between Israelis. His confusion between "peace" and "piece" is also indicative of how he hears them through his own perspective as an Israeli. This type of literature can open up both sides' thinking about one another in ways that are vital to the conflict and perceptions of one another.

Sansal's novel is another example of how Muslim countries—in this case, Algeria—have censored scholarship on the *Shoah*, as in his book. And as seen in the case of Mohammed Dajani, who left his home for safety and security issues due to having taken his students to Auschwitz. The act of censorship reveals that the themes that lie within the novel are dangerous, like the moral lessons of the *Shoah* and modern Islamic fundamentalism in Algeria of the early 1990s. Sansal's novel accentuates the *Shoah* and the guilt that comes with being associated with it, as with his father. Islamic fundamentalism and the *Shoah* are both read here alongside one another, which create a controversy for both Muslims and extremist Muslims. The following conversation takes place as Malrich, son of an SS guard, meets a friend of his father's from the past.

I would have been only too happy to wander through his brain, I'm sure I would have found charming grottos and ravines the bastard did not know he had, there's clearly no end to cretinism, what I had seen was only the tip of the iceberg. I felt ... like ... nothing. You don't kill madmen, you don't exterminate the handicapped, you pray for them. But for all his madness, his sickness, he managed to hurt me with a line: "You're your father's son alright!" It was like an electric shock to my heart. I thought of him as his father's son,

---

12 Amos Oz, *The Land of Israel*, trans. Maurice Goldberg-Bartura (New York: Harcourt Brace Jovano-vich, 1983), 80–81.

offspring of Jean 92, good Samaritan to Nazi fugitives, savior of murderers, and he had reminded me that I was my father's son, offspring of SS Gruppenführer Hans Schiller, the angel of death.[13]

Malrich's confession of not knowing anything about the *Shoah* is the most telling feature of the novel—"which, he admits, he "didn't know anything about … I'd heard bits and pieces, things the imam said about the Jews and other stuff I'd picked up here and there."[14]

Sansal creates a dichotomy that shows that both brothers are foreshadowed by their father's role in the *Shoah*. In her analysis of the novel, Emma Garman shows how one brother, Rachel "literally tries to turn himself into a concentration camp victim, growing more emaciated and haunted until, head shaved and wearing striped pajamas, he gasses himself on the anniversary of his father's death, "the day Hans Schiller [the brothers' father] finally eluded the justice of men."[15] In contrast, Malrich, Garman shows, "directs his shame outward to save his beloved 'Sensitive Urban Area, Category 1' housing project, which has slowly but surely been taken over by Islamists who are creating 'a concentration camp,' with an atmosphere of 'all conquering Islam.'" Telling his friends that "we're going to live, we're going to fight," Malrich considers it his legacy and his duty first to declare war on the "Nazi jihadist fuckers," and then to "tell the truth, all over the world."[16]

Through a thorough understanding of the suffering and truth of the *Shoah*, Malrich sees many issues with his own community's suffering— different from that of the *Shoah*, but a suffering that is real and interminable in his mind. The turn that Sansal makes in terms of Islamic fundamentalism and Nazis is ironic here; one witnesses this metaphor for both Israelis and Islamic extremists. The Nazis are seen as the lowest and most common denominator in a way that demonstrates that there is no shallower moral base that one can get to but calling one another a Nazi.

---

13 Boualem Sansal, *The German Mujahid* (Cathedral City, CA: Brunswick Press, 2009), 101.

14 Ibid., 68.

15 Emma Garman, "'The German Mujahid,' by Boualem Sansal," Retrieved October 24, 2016 http:// www.wordswithoutborders.org/dispatches/article/the-german-mujahid-by-boualem-sansal

16 Ibid.

This brings me to the question: Why do Muslims deny the *Shoah* and have no historical understanding of Judaism, Jews, or the history of Zionism? One of the fundamental flaws in understanding the *Shoah* in the majority of Muslim countries is the lack of education and censorship of the very word "Israel" in history and geography books. When I was living in Dubai in the 1980s, I attended a primary school that was based on the Lebanese French baccalaureate system. We were witnesses to censorship and the hatred toward Israel and Jews. Our Arab Christian and Muslim supervisors (security) would march into our history and geography classes with scissors or thick markers. They would approach every desk and cut or cross out the word "Israel" from our textbooks. These books were European-authored textbooks, and recognized Israel and Jews. As a young child, I was curious as to why they would make such a production of this event, taking time from class to do it, rather than creating a textbook that held Muslim/Arab perspectives about Israel.

But Muslims are not taught history in the way that people are taught in the United States or Europe. Muslims are educated in many ways that do not share the perspective of European or American models, and also have to encompass what is important to each country's curriculum. It goes without saying that in the United States, where I now live, we have had to change the way we narrate our own colonial history in view of things such as Native American genocide,[17] enslavement of Africans, Vietnam, and the Civil Rights movement. No similar move has been made in many Muslim curricula. History is interpreted differently by different peoples. Since the seventeenth century, the European and American historical lens has dominated the media and educational realm. Tamim Ansary, in *Destiny Disrupted: A History of the World through Islamic Eyes,* makes this precise point when he writes about his own perception of Islamic and Western history:

> Here are two enormous worlds side by side; what's remarkable is how little notice they have taken of each other. If the Western and Islamic worlds were two individual human beings, we might see symptoms of repression here. We might ask: "What happened between these two? Were they lovers? Is there some history of

---

17 I am in no way suggesting that the United States has come to a full change or transformation. However, the recognition or acknowledgment of suffering of others is significant in this context.

abuse?" But there is, I think, another, less sensational explanation. Throughout much of history, the West and the core of what is now the Islamic world have been like two separate universes, each preoccupied with its own internal affairs, each assuming itself to be the center of human history, each living out different narratives—until the late seventeenth century when the two narratives began to intersect. At that point, one or the other had to give way because the two narratives were crosscurrents to each other. The West being more powerful, its current prevailed and churned the other one under.[18]

Ansary's point is that Islam, alongside the "West," has been consumed by its own internal voices and significance, and the two have failed to consider one another in their historical lenses, or in this case, curricula.

Shoah education took a very long time to surface in the United States and Europe. Elie Wiesel broke his silence about the *Shoah* in the late 1950s when he wrote his memoir, *Night*; it was published in the United States then, but it took other events to bring the *Shoah* to the fore: the Eichmann Trial in 1961[19] and the Six Day War in 1967.[20]

Survivors who had immigrated to the United States were afraid to discuss the *Shoah*. Renee Firestone (a survivor from Auschwitz) recounts how they had to keep silent in the 1950s and 1960s: "There was a group of us, survivors that would meet and have meals together and in seeing a fresh loaf of bread, we would look at one another and whisper 'look, here is a full loaf of bread.' It was very difficult to speak about those days. Americans wanted to move forward, not backward. Even Jewish-Americans who had not been through the *Shoah* wanted to think of positive things, not negative experiences of Jews." History books and curricula were pressured to include the *Shoah* as a distinct event from the history of World War II.

18 Tamim Ansary, *Destiny Disrupted: A History of the World through Islamic Eyes* (New York: Public Affairs, 2009), xxi.
19 "Eichmann Trial," United States Holocaust Memorial Museum, accessed July 2, 2104, http://www.ushmm.org/wlc/en/article.php?ModuleId=10005179.
20 "Six Day War," *Encyclopedia Britannica*, accessed July 2, 2014, http://www.britannica.com/EBchecked/topic/850855/Six-Day-War.

The types of organized and structured institutions created by Jewish-Americans and Shoah survivors resulted after several years in an acute awareness in the American and European educational system. The prominence of the Holocaust in American Jewish identity is particularly noteworthy since throughout the 1950s and most of the 1960s it was barely on the Jewish communal or theological agenda. In contrast to today, there were virtually no courses on the topic. There were no more than a few commemorations of *Yom HaShoah*, or books, conferences, speeches, and museums dedicated to exploring the history and significance of the Holocaust. An examination of Jewish periodicals reveals few articles on the Holocaust. These Holocaust commemorations which were held were generally attended only by survivors. Non-survivors who attended remembered feeling like they "were crashing a funeral." Survivors who came to this country in the later 1940s and the 1950s were often discouraged from discussing their experiences. They were told Americans were not interested.[21]

However, Hasia Diner, in *We Remember with Reverence and Love: American Jews and the Myth of Silence after the Holocaust: 1945–1962*, portrays another story of memorializing and understanding how American Jews, organically and through an array of organizations, told their story of the *Shoah*. Diner points out that "memorial practices get made over time, and no one, scholars or others, ought to anachronistically expect them to be born whole and in final form. Because the memorial works of the postwar period differed from those of later decades does not mean that they did not exist."[22]

Diner makes a point to revisit the ways in which American Jews did commemorate and remember the *Shoah*; she also points out that the events in the United States had a deep impact on how and when Jewish-American voices were being heard. An interesting point that she raises in her book is

---

21 Deborah Lipstadt, *America and the Memory of the Holocaust, 1950–65*, *Modern Judaism*, vol. 16 (New York: Oxford University Press, 1996), 1.

22 Hasia Diner, *We Remember with Reverence and Love: American Jews and the Myth of Silence after the Holocaust, 1945–1962* (New York: New York University Press, 2009), 17.

how, indeed, many scholars discuss the post–World War II era as a period of amnesia for the many survivors and their children. However, this interpretation by these scholars is debatable and factually unfounded, since the manner of remembering the *Shoah* needs to be considered in the sociopolitical context of 1950s and 1960s America, as Diner states:

> Postwar projects and texts can only be understood in their own terms and not in how they measure up to those of other, different times. The American Jews of the period 1945–1962 had no doubt that their words and actions vis-à-vis the European calamity constituted appropriate ways of remembering the one-third of their people who had been liquidated by the Germans. They did not avoid the tragedy, but, rather, as they could, they made their communities places to enshrine it and act on it.[23]

Furthermore, the political climate in the United States was about optimism; for example, the General Electric slogan was "progress is our most important product." Effecting such change takes time—someone has to break the silence and tell the truth. It was Wiesel's memoir that brought the *Shoah* to literature through the eyes of a survivor.

> Although Wiesel made a vow to keep silent for ten years after the war, during that time he read widely and thought constantly about the Holocaust . . . Conscious of the need to bear witness, he did not know how to approach a subject so overwhelming in its magnitude that words could only distort it. Nonetheless, the ten years of silent reflection prepared him for his meeting in 1954 with the French Catholic writer Francois Mauriac, who encouraged the young journalist to write about his journey into darkness. Mauriac became a kind of patron to him, a protector, a friend.[24]

Elie Wiesel wrote the book *Night*, which millions have read from high school to college students, a book that I teach in my classes and that testifies directly

---

23 Ibid.
24 Ellen S. Fine, *Legacy of Night: The Literary Universe of Elie Wiesel* (Albany: State University of New York Press: 1982), 7.

to the horrors that befell him and others in Nazi concentration camps. His writing not only testifies to the horrendous acts in the camps, but pressures us to question the larger moral lessons of the *Shoah*: What was the meaning of the massacres? Is this the end of Jewish history? Where was God? These questions are powerful, and his writings show that we cannot always find meaning or reason in these acts of terror, even through God and Judaism.

Elie Wiesel passed away in 2016; his death compelled so many to continue his message of tolerance and peace. He was a man who would never let the world forget about atrocities committed in all places, and I remember he spoke out strongly against the Bosnian genocide. He said to then President Clinton at the dedication of the U.S. Holocaust Museum, "Mr. President, I cannot not tell you something. I have been in the former Yugoslavia last fall. I cannot sleep since for what I have seen. As a Jew, I am saying that we must do something to stop the bloodshed in that country. People fight each other, and children die. Why? Something, anything must be done."[25]

When people were silent, he was a strong voice in condemning the atrocities that came after the *Shoah*. Elie Wiesel was born on September 30, 1928 in Romania. In 1944, at age fifteen, Wiesel and his family were deported to Auschwitz.

A Nobel Peace Prize winner and Boston University professor, Wiesel worked on behalf of oppressed people for much of his adult life. His personal experience of the Holocaust led him to use his talents as an author, teacher, and storyteller to defend human rights and peace throughout the world. A native of Sighet, Transylvania (Romania, from 1940–1945 Hungary), Wiesel and his family were deported by the Nazis to Auschwitz when he was 15 years old. His mother and younger sister perished there, his two older sisters survived. Wiesel and his father were later transported to Buchenwald, where his father died.[26]

---

25 Paul, Kujawsky. "Bosnia Genocide Unrolls in Scrolls of Shame." *Jewish Journal,* accessed October 22, 2016 http://www.jewishjournal.com/opinion/article/bosnia_genocide_unrolls_in_scroll_of_shame_20080806

26 "Elie Wiesel: The Museum Deeply Mourns the Passing of Elie Wiesel, Holocaust Survivor, Nobel Laureate, and International Leader of the Holocaust Remembrance Movement." United States Holocaust Memorial Museum, Retrieved October 28, 2016 https://www.ushmm.org/wlc/en/article.php?ModuleId=10007176

Wiesel wrote the following in *Night*, which is spoken and echoed all over the world when discussing the memory of the *Shoah* and the impact on the victims. The idea of "never shall we forget" is reverberated throughout by survivors and Jews. This insistence of "never shall I forget" has to do more about keeping the memory alive of those who were murdered and challenging us to prevent future genocides.

> Never shall I forget that night, the first night in camp, which has turned my life into one long night, seven times cursed and seven times sealed.
>
> Never shall I forget that smoke.
>
> Never shall I forget the little faces of the children, whose bodies I saw turned into wreaths of smoke beneath a silent blue sky.
>
> Never shall I forget those flames which consumed my faith forever.
>
> Never shall I forget that nocturnal silence which deprived me, for all eternity, of the desire to live. Never shall I forget those moments which murdered my God and my soul and turned my dreams to dust.
>
> Never shall I forget these things, even if I am condemned to live as long as God Himself.
>
> Never.[27]

Elie Wiesel passed away in the summer of 2016. I was deeply saddened by his death, but, more important, was sad that I never met him and only had an opportunity to listen to him lecture a few times. He was a man of courage, bravery, and honesty. The purpose of post-*Shoah* narratives and literature is to continue with the testimony and not allow others to forget. However, if some educational curricula have omitted genocidal events from our history books or our communities, this prospect seems very bleak. How do we continue to tell one another's stories so that we humanize rather than

---

27 Elie Wiesel, *Night* (New York: Bantam Books, 1982), 32.

dehumanize the other? This is an important question for my own work and for the Muslim community. Dajani and Satloff discuss this eloquently:

> But Palestinians, and Arabs more generally, know little about the Holocaust and what they do know is often skewed by the perverted prism of Arab popular culture, from the ranting of religious extremists to the distortions of certain satellite television channels to the many ill-informed authors. What happened to the Jews during World War II is not taught in Arab schools or universities, either as part of world history or as a lesson in genocide awareness or as an atrocity that ought not to be repeated. Arabs have nothing to fear from opening their eyes to this chapter of human history. As the Koran says: "And say: My Lord, advance me in knowledge." If Arabs knew more about the Holocaust in particular and genocide in general, perhaps Arab voices would be more forceful in trying to stop similar atrocities.[28]

Another challenging issue regarding the majority of Muslim educational curricula is the refusal to study any religion other than Islam. This lack of any focus on secular humanities and cultural history has created a vacuum for many young Muslims, especially those who come to the United States for higher education (some of whom have been my students) and are immediately skeptical of critical thinking regarding Islamic history, or of acceptance of other faiths. This problem creates a distance between Muslims and other faiths, allowing Muslims to interpret Jewish and Christian thought and belief strictly through the lens of Islam. As a student of Judaism and Protestant theology, I was enriched by these faiths and was given another perspective outside my own, which had come from reading the Qur'an. Reading one another's sacred texts and history can help avert damage and misunderstanding between us. Studying one another's texts offers all of us new ways to build bridges. It is also

---

28 Daoudi Mohammed S. Dajani and Robert Satloff, "Why Palestinians Should Learn about the Holocaust," *The New York Times,* accessed November 2013, http://www.nytimes.com/2011/03/30/opinion/30iht-edsatloff30.html?_r=0.

spiritually important for Muslims to read the sacred texts of Judaism and Christianity since, theologically, both Jews and Christians are considered the "people of the book" and their scriptures are respected by Islam.

Living in the United States is a different experience in terms of diversity—it is a more multireligious society than most Muslim countries. Even though the United States was settled by the Protestants and Protestantism was the dominant religion, from the 1950s onward it was accepted to speak of Catholics, Protestants, and Jews, according to Will Herberg.[29] They were represented at presidential inaugurations and civic ceremonies; in recent years, Muslims and Asian religious leaders have been added to this mix. The lens of the United States has grown in a multireligious society and is represented as a country that accepts all faiths and customs. This image and political dimension of diversity prepares American students in such a way that they almost unknowingly absorb the diversity of religious faith and the respect accorded to diverse religions.

For example, when I received my bachelor's degree in English and Religious Studies from Syracuse University in Syracuse, New York, my father attended my graduation and asked the chair of my department, "How can one *study* religion? Is religion not all-encompassing?" My chair was stunned, and did not know what to say. My father was a banker, and supportive of my studies, but he could not grapple with the idea that his daughter was interested in the phenomenon of God. "How can you study *God*?" he would ask. The idea that religion has history, culture, and a rich array of contextual nuances escaped his thinking; the world in which he grew up taught him to accept God and Islam without hesitation. My father and family were never taught about the skeptics within Islamic history and literature or about the nonbelievers. Much of their own history and philosophy was omitted by the religious, cultural, and educational environment in which they were raised. Yet, true and full Islamic history provides reasoning, scientific inquiry, and skepticism. One has only to look at the historical exchanges between Avicenna and Maimonides[30] to grasp the breadth of diversity and reliance on the mind

---

29 Will Herberg, *Protestant—Catholic—Jew: An Essay in American Religious Sociology* (Chicago: University of Chicago Press, 1960).

30 "The Influence of Islamic Thought on Maimonides," *Stanford Encyclopedia of Philosophy*, accessed October 2013, http://plato.stanford.edu/entries/maimonides-islamic/.

during Islam's Golden Age (mid-seventh to thirteenth century). The lack of education and diversity in these curricula creates vacuums and myths that have helped me understand why there is antisemitism and *Shoah* denial in non-Jewish communities.

My own experience in talking with many Muslims and non-Muslims is that there is an uncanny insistence that the *Shoah* is not a unique event, and that Jews fabricated six million deaths as a means to obtain Israel for themselves. As an academic who is on many group e-mail listservs, I have also found that the discussion of the Jewish *Shoah* takes on another light. The *Shoah* is seen as a genocide that is privileged above all other genocides and at times dismissed through academia. The depth and strength of Jewish and Holocaust Studies in some universities are looked on as privileged areas that either ignore or value the *Shoah* more than other genocides. This has been an ongoing discussion and issue within the academy. Arthur R. Butz, an associate professor of electrical engineering and computer science, has been sharing his views about the *Shoah* since 1976, when he published *The Hoax of the Twentieth Century: The Case against the Presumed Extermination of European Jewry*. He shares the stage with others such as the French writers Robert Faurisson, Ernst Zundel, and Pierre Guillame, who have also published on the *Shoah*. These academics and writers have not only denied the *Shoah* but, even more cunningly, have encouraged students and others to relativize and question the documentation of the *Shoah*. However, in American academia, the problem is more with the privileging of the *Shoah* versus other genocides. I have consciously chosen to refer to the Jewish Holocaust as the *Shoah* for this very reason.

I have witnessed some interesting discussions about the privileging of the *Shoah* that need to be explored. This thinking relies on the idea that Jews have had too much attention and have too much power in the twentieth and twenty-first centuries, and that other genocides are equally important and significant. I am not saying, for my part, that other genocides are not as important as the *Shoah*, but what stuns me is that Jews are somehow vilified for giving a strong and unified voice to their own calamity, that *they* have originated the term "Holocaust"—*Shoah* in Hebrew—and have seen these terms become common currency in other languages and cultures. The following e-mail exchange gives a taste of this (all identifiers removed):

First e-mailer: Holocaust is the term used specifically to refer to the genocide of Jews in WWII, the enormity of the massacre deserves a specific name. Whether 1 or 6 million the pain is the same to the families who have lost the dear ones. However, the 6 million numbers [sic] is too large a number not to be identified distinctly [sic].

The term Genocides can be used for all other atrocities.

Second e-mailer: "Holocaust is the term used specifically to refer to the genocide of Jews in WWII" is not a justification for its continued use that way. The enormity of the massacre is beyond doubt. But that does not justify a specific name for it. Indeed, I am not sure whether you are familiar or not, but in terms of scale, there have been other genocides much bigger than the Nazi Holocaust.

I also find no justification for separating [the] Nazi Holocaust from all other genocides. This is clearly diminishing all other genocides. There is another reason why such specialness must not be allowed. Treat any people as special and you might face the prospect that such special status would be abused to victimize others. Unfortunately, instead of being a prospect, it has become a reality.

If I have to call upon my fellow Muslims that they should not think that their suffering in the world in the hand of others is not unique [sic], it would be unprincipled to acknowledge that somehow others are special. In this world if we cannot accept the entire humanity on this equal footing, every group will consider themselves special and when they attain power they may abuse others, as in the case of Israel.[31]

This exchange is quite common among academics; it is this precise point that creates a deep gulf between many Muslims and Jews. In Chapter Three, I argue that the *Shoah* is unprecedented, and that the slaughter of Jews in every country, including Arab countries, is terrifyingly so. One has only to look at the history of different cases of genocide to see the glaring

---

31 Listserv correspondence, anonymized for confidentiality, August 2, 2009.

difference. This statement does not denigrate murders of Native Americans, Cambodians, Darfurians, Rwandans, or Bosnians—indeed, it should be considered even more seriously in light of the *Shoah*. Many survivor testimonies from the *Shoah* overwhelmingly deliver the message that we must not forget, and must tell the stories of such atrocities so that they will never happen again.

My Hope and Optimism

I hope that my fellow Muslims will read this book and understand that my closeness to Islam was, in fact, intensified and inspired by studying Judaism. My respect for and understanding of Judaism were inspired through a teaching assistantship at Syracuse University under Alan Berger in a post-*Shoah* studies course. I was enrolled in a master's program, interested in critical theory and post-colonialism, and had never studied anything Jewish except for reading texts by Jewish authors. As a Muslim in Pakistan, the country of my birth, I was always caught between accepting Jews and rejecting Jews on the basis of anti-Israel political feelings within my family. From 1990 to today, my increasing clarity about Judaism has encouraged me to feel even closer to my own faith, Islam, in ways that I would have never otherwise discovered. I began to see many parallels between both faiths, and a congruence of identity questions as I lived as a minority in non-Muslim communities. As a student, I was engaged in postmodern understanding of identity and culture; I thus had been given the tools to think critically about the world, but I lacked historical and religious foundations. I decided to pursue religious studies in both Judaism and Islam. From this initial path, I began to journey into my own personal past as a Muslim child growing up in Europe. This has brought me to a better understanding of Jewish identity, but, more important, it has also taught me what racism, prejudice, and hatred can do. In Chapter Five, I discuss both my personal experiences and the historical face of antisemitism, the roots of such hatred, the transference of such hatred among Muslim extremist groups, and the general Muslim consensus regarding Jews in general. I also compare modern Antisemitism to Islamophobia. How can Muslims learn from the Jews living in Europe and North America?

I deliberated about writing a book on genocide for some years. I began to frame the book in my mind as covering multiple genocides: Armenia, the *Shoah*, Bosnia, and Darfur. I reflected on Samantha Powers's gripping and informative book, *A Problem from Hell: America and the Age of Genocide,* noting that her focus was on America and how genocide was ignored, silenced, and, at times, denied there. I wanted that kind of sharp focus, to give specificity to genocide. I wanted to speak about the ebbing and flowing anger and turmoil within me as I experienced antisemitism in many Muslim communities. I also wanted to explain to myself and others that genocide is still happening and is an ongoing human problem. Hannah Arendt coined the term "the banality of evil," and, in many ways, it is this banality of the evildoer that has moved me to write. As Arendt described Adolf Eichmann as a man who was banal but committed evil as sin, Christopher Browning states:

> Since his capture in Argentina in May 1960 and his subsequent trial and execution in Israel, Adolf Eichmann has remained one of the most enduring symbols of Holocaust evil, though the precise nature of that evil has been hotly contested. To Hannah Arendt the character of Eichmann posed a "dilemma between the unspeakable horror of the deeds and the undeniable ludicrousness of the man who perpetrated them" that could only be solved by understanding him as an exemplar of the "banality of evil."[32]

Considering how many times I have taught courses on genocide, I found myself discussing the *Shoah* as unprecedented more than ever. More important, as a Muslim, I wanted to speak out and bear witness to Jewish victimization. I wanted to confirm the six million deaths in an act of respect and as a signal of acceptance of a heinous crime committed against Jews because of their faith—actually, because of the faith of their grandparents. I felt that, in the tense cultural and religious climate in which we live, the *Shoah* would be my best first testimony to human slaughter. As a Muslim, I have found the past few years difficult in light of the war on terrorism and

---

32 Christopher R. Browning, *Collected Memories: Holocaust History and Postwar Testimony* (Madison: The University of Wisconsin Press, 2003), 1.

events in Iraq, Afghanistan, Syria, and Pakistan. However, what remains even more painful for me as a Muslim is the denial of the *Shoah* among Muslims and Muslim nations. To know that war and genocide have existed all over the world virtually since the inception of recorded history is horrible enough; but to deny such acts of human slaughter is to deny human life for all. This conviction stems from my understanding of Islam and Judaism; we cannot let false rumors harm others, especially since the Jews planted the seeds of Islam, for the Torah is also a message from God that we share as people of the book, and we have shared a community between us from the time of Abraham to the time of Moses. As the Qur'an states:

> It is He Who sent down to thee (step by step), in truth, the Book, confirming what went before it; and He sent down the Law (of Moses) and the Gospel (of Jesus) before this, as a guide to mankind, and He sent down the criterion (of judgment between right and wrong) (3:3).

> This day [the day of the Prophet's "Farewell Address" on which the last verse of the Qur'an was revealed] have I made perfect for you your religion, and have completed My favor toward you, and am satisfied with Islam for you as your religion (5:3).

> In truth We have sent the Qur'an to you, confirming all the previous heavenly books that were revealed before you and bearing witness to them (5:48).[33]

In writing this book, I do not seek to speak to *Shoah* deniers, but to Muslims and non-Muslims who see the *Shoah* as merely a political incident in the twentieth century. Deborah Lipstadt asserts: "If Holocaust denial has demonstrated anything, it is the fragility of memory, truth, reason, and history."[34] If my fellow Muslims were to accept the *Shoah*, Israel, and Judaism fully, we would be in a better place both spiritually and politically. If a Muslim

---

33 Assad, *Message of the Quran*.
34 Deborah Lipstadt, *Denying the Holocaust: The Growing Assault on Truth and Memory* (New York: Plume Books, 1994), 216.

believes that Jews are our enemies, then that individual must be listening to the extremist factions that blatantly and openly call for the extermination of Jews.

While I was a student in the Department of Religion at Syracuse University and teaching assistant to Dr. Alan Berger, he asked me if I ever wanted to visit Israel. I was taken aback at his question, because the word "Israel" was virtually taboo to me, having grown up as I did with Pakistani Muslims. As it was the 1980s, I also knew that there were two countries that I was prohibited to visit by my government, and those were Israel and South Africa. My passport said clearly that I was not allowed to enter these countries. I asked Dr. Berger how I would get to Israel and what would I do there. He told me about a small grant offered by the Hebrew University that would underwrite five weeks of study. He handed me the paperwork for the grant, and left. As I walked back to my dorm room, I felt nervous but excited at the prospect of being able to visit the Dome of the Rock and Haram al-Sharif—after all, these were important Muslim places of worship, and I remembered fondly the postcards that I had received from my Swiss Christian godmother when she visited Jerusalem. I also wanted to see what Israel was like, who Israelis were, and how Palestinians were treated.

I became obsessed with the idea of traveling to Israel and embarked on my journey to the country in 1995, much to my family's and friends' chagrin. People constantly warned me of the dangers, the climate, the attitude toward Muslims, and the risk I was about to take with a tiny piece of white paper from the Israeli consulate in New York that granted me entry into Israel. I was told that I could not be helped if anything were to go wrong, because I had a mere green card from the United States, and held Pakistani citizenship. I was actually excited at the potential prospect of being dispossessed, like Palestinians and many Jews. I had been reading a book by Edmond Jabès, a Jew who had lived in Egypt all his life but was exiled to Paris in 1952 for being Jewish. *The Book of Questions* inspired me to understand how exile, longing, home, and identity were part of Jewish theology, politics, and the psychological condition before, during, and after the *Shoah*. I came to understand that Jews were always in the condition of exile until their redemption by God. Jabès's universe is defined by homelessness; in his book, he tells the story of two *Shoah* victims, Sarah and Yukel, through poetry, prose, and rabbinic nuance:

"Yukel, which is the land you call Jewish, which every Jew claims as his own without ever having lived there?"

"It is the land where I have dug my well."

"Yukel, which is this water of our land, so good against thirst that no other water can compare?"

"It is water fifty centuries have forgotten in the hollow of our hands."[35]

Jabès's words came alive as I entered Jerusalem. I saw the hollowness, the land, the ephemeral identities pitted against each other at the Western Wall, and the water that holds no form but pours and pours from a well in the desert.

My trip to Jerusalem changed my life. I was able to be with students at Hebrew University who were from all walks of life, countries, and socioeconomic backgrounds, although all of them were Jews or Christians. My ability to visit the Dome of the Rock with the gatekeeper's permission was granted anytime because I was a Muslim from Pakistan. Palestinians favored Pakistan for being an ally and supporting the Palestinian cause; thus, I was seen as an ally and friend. I was able to frequent places with the Hebrew University students, since everyone assumed I was just another Jew from America. My physical dress and appearance did not mark me as any different from the other Christian and Jewish students. This duality and freedom gave me access to the personal feelings and perceptions of many Israelis and Palestinians, whether it concerned peace, hatred, memories of seemingly interminable war, or even their love for one another. This is a complex relationship that has been undermined by political parties on both sides through renewing cycles of violence and dehumanization. I thought that my time in Jerusalem would be valuable, but I did not realize how deeply I would become invested in this struggle and the misperceptions of both sides.

When I reflect on Jerusalem, I believe that the most important literature devoted to the issues and pain on either side is that produced by Yehuda Amichai and Mahmoud Darwish, the beloved poets of the

---

35 Edmond Jabès, *The Book of Questions: Volume One; The Book of Yukel, Return to the Book,* trans. Rosemarie Waldrop (Middletown, CT: Wesleyan University Press, 1991), 59.

Israelis and Palestinians, respectively, who bear witness to the deep similarities in both Israelis and Palestinians. As an article in the *Guardian* said (June 8, 2002): "Darwish has called the conflict a 'struggle between two memories … So we have a competition: who is the owner of the language of this land? Who loves it more? Who writes it better?" For his part, Amichai has written, in the poem "Jerusalem," of when Jerusalem was a divided city between 1948 and 1967, when Jews were not permitted on the Jordanian side[36]:

> *On a roof in the Old City*
> *Laundry hanging in the late afternoon sunlight:*
> *The white sheet of a woman, who is my enemy,*
> *The towel of a man, who is my enemy,*
> *To wipe off the sweat of his brow.*
> *In the sky of the Old City*
> *A kite.*
> *At the other end of the string,*
> *A child*
> *I can't see*
> *Because of the wall.*
> *We have put up many flags,*
> *They have put up many flags.*
> *To make us think that they're happy.*
> *To make them think we're happy.*[37]

The sentiments of these poets impart a vision of love and peace coupled with the longing of each poet for the other's humanity. With this thinking, I imagine that Muslims and Jews can take from these words the absence of peace and yearning for its presence. In Jerusalem, I had some deeply moving experiences that have shaped me in my approach to the conflict between Israel and Palestine.

---

36 "Poet of the Arab World," *The Guardian*, accessed November 20, 2013, http://www.theguardian.com/books/2002/jun/08/featuresreviews.guardianreview19

37 Yehuda Amichai, *The Selected Poetry of Yehuda Amichai*, trans. Chana Bloch and Stephen Mitchell (Berkeley, CA: University of California Press, 1996), 32.

The beginning of this journey and testimony began in Munich. It began at the Dachau concentration camp just outside Munich with my husband and three-month-old daughter in 2006. The experience of being at Dachau transported me away from Jews, Muslims, Christians, Germans, and Nazis, and toward the baby in my arms who was at the beginning of her life, at one of the centers of the death. In Chapter Four, I discuss my interviews with three *Shoah* survivors, letting their experience speak for itself. The book *Job: The Story of a Holocaust Survivor,* a memoir by Joseph Freeman, compelled me to interview survivors. I began to ask myself over and over again why Muslims wanted to deny these voices of pain and hope. Joseph Freeman was another survivor who inspired me as I read his memoir. He was born in Poland in 1915; before he immigrated to the United States, he, like many, survived several different camps, including Dachau. His story and others became a lens through which I began to see how organized the Nazi agenda was and how the SS guards forced the Jews into workers who maintained the very infrastructure of the camps that were to exterminate them.

As I reflect on the *Shoah*, I also think of a place in Darfur where genocide is ongoing. I feel chills down my spine when I think of what is occurring in Darfur today—Arab Muslims murdering African Muslims for land and control—and I am also reminded that Muslims are sitting on the sidelines as the Jews and the United States provide humanitarian aid. I can imagine that an African Muslim today could relate to Joseph Freeman's words when he described a scene from seventy years ago: "There was no water in the camp. After weeks without washing, shaving, or changing our clothes, we smelled and looked nearly inhuman. At night insects attacked us, and the rain poured in from the still unfinished roof. We lay in water. Our clothes froze against our skin. Many died from the cold."[38]

What, then, are we Muslims going to do about Darfur? Are we going to let millions be displaced and killed? No, this is a human problem. As one victim expressed at the end of the documentary *The Devil Came on Horseback*, about the genocide in Darfur, "Where are the Muslims? We are Muslims, and no Muslim has helped us, only America. Thank you America." Darfur is

---

38 Joseph Freeman, *Job: The Story of a Holocaust Survivor* (St. Paul: Paragon House, 1996), 67.

a painful example for me; I am Muslim, and I ask, where is the support from Muslim countries? Why are we not stepping up and issuing against Sudan the threats that the West continues to issue?

On the other hand, there is a strong lobby dedicated to fighting radical Islam and antisemitism. In February 2010, the Clarion Fund distributed the first of a trilogy of films, *Fitna*, which caused a stir for what many saw as its misrepresentation of Islam as completely radical. The second film, *The Third Jihad*, warns viewers of what Muslims are planning against the West. The third film, *Antisemitism on American Campuses*, discusses the discrimination, double standards, and demonization of the state of Israel on Canadian and American university campuses. These films are distributed widely to synagogues, campuses, and non-Muslim audiences. The Clarion Fund is committed to making people aware of the dangers of Islamic radicalism, which is important. However, distribution of such films to audiences that do not have sufficient background, education, or another perspective on Islam as a religion that supports human rights, equality, and justice is potentially dangerous. The positive image of Islam is thus buried by extreme points of view, including media coverage of Israeli mistreatment of Palestinians, and staged images of Jews wearing swastikas and SS uniforms. The same types of films and other media demonizing Jews circulate in Muslim communities and countries in which Muslims have no accurate knowledge about Jews, fanning the flames of hatred. Both perspectives damage the possibility for dialogue, peace, and understanding.

My study of Jews and Muslims in Los Angeles and New York has led me to numerous interfaith encounters with these groups, and I find myself at synagogues frequently, discussing the commonalities of their respective faiths and the challenge of how we perceive one another. Jews frequently find my perspective marginal, and I spend many hours trying to establish dialogue about who Muslims are and what the Qur'an teaches us as a religion—the message of peace. The face of Islam has been distorted by extremist Muslims; as contemporary, moderate Muslims, we have a deep responsibility to counter that distortion. Jews have experienced antisemitism for over 2,000 years because of their beliefs and traditions. Antisemitism lurks everywhere, and Islamophobia is just as pervasive; these sentiments are destroying any hope of peace or reconciliation between Jews and Muslims. I want to carry this voice of hope into the world with confidence, knowing that many moments of my life have demonstrated how, even if we can't agree on everything, we can indeed deconstruct the deeply ingrained superficial images that we have of one another. I have a deep calling as a Muslim to speak out against any injustice shown to anyone, and I feel that Muslims need to speak up when they witness antisemitism.

As a Muslim woman, I have thought extensively about Jews—I believe that Jews want to understand Islam and want to see Muslims offer a perspective through a self-critical lens that can shatter the monolithic negative image of Islam today. My relationships with Jews in Los Angeles and New York are founded on mutual goals of peace, Muslim acceptance of Israel as a state, and of the *Shoah* as a unique event in history. I am sad to note that my acceptance of Israel as a country and the *Shoah* as an unprecedented event has isolated me from many Muslims who dismiss me as a "Jew lover" or believe that my criticism of Muslims' attitude toward Jews has been shaped by my American experience. This has compelled me to write a book that is a testimony to Islamic principles of justice that force me to speak out against the misperceptions of Jews in Muslim countries. When I was at Dachau in the summer of 2007, I wrote a piece that was published in the *Los Angeles Jewish Journal,* "A Muslim's Journey to Dachau"; my family's response was disappointing, as they accused me of not focusing on the "holocaust" between Hindus and Muslims during the partition of India and Pakistan. These personal experiences of witnessing antisemitism and denial of the *Shoah* are the focus of this book. My message is clear: we must accept and understand all histories, and as Muslims we must speak for truth and justice, which are the true *Jihad.*

Chapter Three

Why Is the *Shoah* Unprecedented?

Have you seen, in fields of snow, frozen Jews, row on row? Blue marble forms lying, not breathing, not dying.

Somewhere a flicker of a frozen soul—glint of fish in an icy swell. All brood. Speech and silence are one. Night snow encases the sun.

A smile glows immobile from a rose lip's chill. Baby and mother, side by side. Odd that her nipple's dried.

Fist, fixed in ice, of a naked old man: the powers undone in his hand. I've sampled death in all guises. Nothing surprises.

Yet a frost in July in this heat—a crazy assault in the street. I and blue carrion, face to face. Frozen Jews in a snowy space.

Marble shrouds my skin. Words ebb. Light grows thin. I'm frozen, I'm rooted in place like the naked old man enfeebled by ice.[1]
Avrom Sutzkever, "*Frozen Jews*"[1]

This poem exudes a certain pain and vividness that many of the *Shoah* survivors with whom I spoke experienced in the cold and cruel "death marches" that they endured. When the Nazis heard that the allies were coming in to fight Germany from 1944 to 1945, there were grueling death marches. The climate was severe and the prisoners were sick, malnourished, and some close to death. The Allied armies were close but the SS was still committed to transporting the victims to labor camps; some collapsed from

1   Avrom Sutzkever, "Frozen Jews," accessed May 2, 2016, http://www.auschwitz.dk/id6.htm.

hunger, cold, and disease, or died along the way. There was immense pressure on the Germans from all sides as the Soviets were coming from the east, and the British, French, and Americans from the west. Even under this pressure, the Germans still thought that they could use the prisoners for labor—this was the desperation at the end of the war that the Germans exhibited. How could these men that were half-dead be useful for labor? How far could these soldiers go knowing that they were surrounded by allies? These prisoners were taken by train or on foot in extreme conditions. Many were women; by then there were few children left in the camps. Men died from exhaustion and exposure; those who survived were killed if they showed any sign of weakness or disease. The first line of Avrom Sutzkever's poem captures this dehumanization, depicting humans as marble, neither alive nor dead. "Have you seen, in fields of snow, frozen Jews, row on row? Blue marble forms lying, not breathing, not dying." This poem resonates with the many narratives that I have read about the deep suffering of *Shoah* victims. It pains me, but also serves as a focal point for meditating on the stark reality of human suffering and loss during the *Shoah*.

Why is the *Shoah* unprecedented? Why does it give such extraordinary pause when wars have taken lives in greater numbers and have been similarly ghastly? Why should the *Shoah* be remembered with such force and vivacity? Reflecting on these questions of the uniqueness of the *Shoah* for some time, and challenged by others on why and how I chose this journey, I will begin with some personal reflections on how I came to understand the Jewish Holocaust as a genocide with an inimitable place in the long list of genocides. However, without privileging the destruction of Jews over others during the *Shoah*, I came to this journey and juncture because of complete emotional exhaustion and frustration. As I have discussed in previous chapters, my education on post-*Shoah* studies was a focal point in grappling with the enormity of Germany, a highly civilized culture, setting the goal of destroying all Jews; it was also an eye-opening lesson about religion, race, and evil. My own work in Islam and contemporary literature is about showing the diversity and peaceful messages within Islam in order to counteract the many negative misperceptions of Islam in the West. More important, in my work on Islam, I wanted to revive aspects of ordinary Muslim lives, especially in the works of Naguib Mahfouz, Orhan Pamuk, and Mohsin Hamid. As I worked on my dissertation on "Naguib Mahfouz and Modern Islamic Identity," which discussed different ways of reading Islam and literature, I realized that Islam was not the only religion misperceived in a negative light—so was Judaism, especially the image of the Jews. I was stunned by the antisemitism from professional, educated, and extremist Muslims. I began to wonder if the diversity of Muslims[2] had only one point of commonality: Antisemitism? In other words, my challenge of deconstructing the image of the terroristic and violent Muslim became more difficult as I directly and indirectly witnessed the other side of Muslims, which spoke of mythological suspicion of Jews, conspiracy of Jews, and hatred of Jews, Zionism, and Israel in various Muslim communities (I discuss this in depth in Chapter Five).

I was frustrated and exhausted by the antisemitism, and decided to deconstruct some of the perceptions that were held about Jews by Muslims through my journey of studying the *Shoah*, Judaism, and Zionism.

There are many scholars who argue that genocide is genocide no matter what, and I tend to agree. However, the *Shoah* to me holds a unique place because of the lack of dialogue of the event in Muslim societies and the subsequent misperception that holds true to so many—that because of the *Shoah*, Israel and Jews have carte-blanche in geopolitical affairs. In my own research, I studied Judaism with Susan E. Shapiro and did research on the history of nineteenth- to twentieth-century Germany with Dr. Sander L. Gilman. I took workshops on the *Shoah*, researching testimonies at the USC *Shoah* Foundation, interviewing survivors, and trying to focus on what would create a better understanding or positive collaboration between Jews and Muslims in America. This book emerged from being frustrated, but it is now a book that seeks clarity, self-critique, and justice. I believe that if one can come closer to members of another faith and understand their suffering, then perhaps we can move beyond the binaries of hatred and segregation. Islam is to me a peaceful way of life, yet the practice and realities that surround us today indicate that Islam is in crisis internally and externally. From 9/11 to Iraq, Syria, Pakistan, ISIS, and Nigeria (2015), we witness the extremists that are in

---

2 By no means are all Muslims antisemites, nor do they want to eradicate Jews or Judaism; however, the point here is to demonstrate that in all my travels and contacts with Muslims, there is always a conversation about the mythology of Jews, which I discuss throughout the book. Furthermore, I also discuss Zionism in Chapter Five in light of these issues of prejudice and racism.

power and in battle on a loud stage with any other ideology but the Islamic extremist agenda. This is disturbing to me as a Muslim, as it is to other Muslims. However, this book hopes to at least highlight a major issue in the rhetoric of Muslims about the Jews, Israel, and Zionism.

My interviews with survivors (Chapter Four) were not only informative—I began to hear and see the pain of the loss and suffering in way I had never before. My impetus in interviewing survivors was to have firsthand accounts of victims and rescued Jews who could talk with me about antisemitism and their own journeys as people who suffered severely and somehow became ambassadors of peace for all human beings.

There are many reasons for arguing that the *Shoah* is unique:

(1) Jews were sought out worldwide, as far as the Nazis, their allies, and collaborators could search for them, and killed.

(2) Jews were seen as a danger to society both as human beings and as economic barriers. Their elimination was regarded as redemptive to German society.

(3) Jews were massacred in a more process-oriented, technological, and mechanical manner than was the case with any other genocide.

(4) Jews were easy targets of hatred because of their long-standing mythical history of having committed deicide against Christians, not to mention many myths of blood libel that are still discussed in many parts of the world, Christian and non-Christian.

(5) Jews were not from one nation or country, where they could fight or take arms; Jews had no single country in which to establish a stronghold to defend themselves against the Nazis.

(6) Jews had been living in Europe as assimilated citizens for, in some cases, hundreds of years, and the *Shoah* was a war against a minority within several countries in which the minority itself had citizenship.

(7) The event occurred in the heart of Europe, with vast implications for western culture and civilization.

(8) It was perpetrated by the most advanced, technologically sophisticated, scientifically developed country in the world.

(9) It involved two of the great monotheistic religions of the world—Judaism and Christianity.

(10) It used the full power of the state and its resources, and involved 22 countries across the globe.

In the field of Holocaust Studies, there have been many arguments about the uniqueness or the universal message of the *Shoah* and how we should understand the place of the *Shoah* in human history. These debates have been held by Jewish scholars, educators, multiple ethnicities, communities, museums, and memorials. For example, in 2013, David Cameron, Prime Minister of the United Kingdom, created a Holocaust commission to develop a plan for a memorial that could present a stronger message about the Holocaust to the British people while simultaneously offering an educational lesson of morality and diversity.[3] I was invited by this very commission, based in New York, to consult on ideas on how to build such a memorial in London. The conversation among about fifteen Holocaust Center leaders and the commission also came to this question: What is the place of the *Shoah* and how will people in a diverse city such as London relate to it? Will it be about Jews, Judaism, Gypsies, and Poles, and will it reach the growing minorities, especially Muslims? The meeting was turned into a conversation about how to remember the *Shoah* and include all others within these moral lessons. The message and lessons of the *Shoah* are both unique and universal. As a non-Jew, I explored these many arguments by Jewish scholars and non-Jews to expand my own knowledge of the stigma attached to Jews about them being a "chosen people" by God. The theological fact of Jews being chosen and accepted by non-Jews reflects that they are an elitist group. However, the chosenness came from God in a complicated manner. Jews were essentially chosen to spread justice and "Tikuun Olam" in the world; I believe that it was burdensome for Jews, and still can be today.

There are many arguments on how to memorialize the *Shoah*, and the debate is not only about the Jews themselves, but also, how to remember the unprecedented event for Jewish history, politics, and faith.

---

3 Miranda Prynne, "Holocaust Commission launched by Prime Minister," *The Telegraph,* accessed October 29, 2016 http://www.telegraph.co.uk/history/10599278/Holocaust-Commission-launched-by-Prime-Minister.html

The chief protagonists for alternate conceptions, Elie Wiesel and Simon Wiesenthal, are both survivors, both European Jews, both men of towering stature who have brought the Holocaust to the world's attention. Yet these two men differ markedly in their personal histories, their legacy and destiny. Simon Wiesenthal defines the word "Holocaust" as the systematic murder of 11 million people, of whom 6 million were Jews killed because of their Jewishness, and 5 million were non-Jews—Gypsies, Jehovah's Witnesses, homosexuals, political prisoners, Poles, Ukrainians, the handicapped and the mentally ill—killed for a variety of reasons in an apparent destruction designed for mass extermination ... Wiesenthal maintains that although all Jews were victims, the Holocaust transcended the confines of the Jewish community. ... For Wiesel the Holocaust is a sacred mystery that can be approached but never understood ... Wiesel fears that Wiesenthal's definition of the Holocaust may trigger an irreversible process that will erase [the] memory of 6 million Jews. He contends that people will speak first of 11 million people, 6 million of whom were Jews than of 11 million people, some of whom were Jews; and finally of 11 million people, deleting any reference to Jews.[4]

In these examples, there is a matter of including or excluding a certain memory of the *Shoah*; however, Wiesel, who survived Auschwitz during the Hungarian deportation—437,402 Jews were deported primarily to Auschwitz on 147 trains between May 15 and July 8, 1944—was immersed in an environment that only destroyed Jews, whereas Wiesenthal was at Mauthausen, where Jews constituted a minority of those imprisoned. The context of both survivors influences the memory of their own suffering and the *Shoah*.

Some of the debates focus on intent and ideology, methodology of the crime, enslavement of human beings, limiting the role of the *Shoah* within Jewish history, the ultimate evil of Western civilization, God's role, and the

---

4   Michael Berenbaum, *After Tragedy and Triumph: Modern Jewish Thought and the American Experience* (Cambridge, UK: Cambridge University Press, 1990), 19–20.

Germans' intent to annihilate the Jews. Yehuda Bauer has advanced several reasons as to why the *Shoah* is "unprecedented."

> As far as the Holocaust is concerned, though, one has to add that there is one element in the genocide of the Jews that is unprecedented even in the methods adopted: for the first time in human history, an industry was established that produced something that had never been produced before, namely corpses. In Auschwitz-Birkenau, Treblinka, Sobibor, Belzec and Chelmno, live Jews went in at one end, and corpses came out at the other end. There is therefore a caveat regarding the means employed in genocide, and the Holocaust stands out as something entirely new in this regard.[5]

In my own teaching, in my course "Religion and the Holocaust," I remind my students of how Jewish history and theology changed for many after the *Shoah*. Questions of faith and God, the absurdity of life, the evil of human beings, redemption, punishment, and survival are only some of the important themes that Jews and some non-Jews have been challenged to address. These issues have prompted various responses from Orthodox, Reform, Conservative, Reconstructionist, and secular Jews. Survivors that I interviewed have different responses to faith after the *Shoah*—some became more religious and some moved away from faith altogether. The *Shoah* is unique in challenging Judaism as a faith that affirmed the covenantal relationship with God, and this was a pact that was seen by some as a betrayal or punitive act from God.

> The question of the uniqueness of the Holocaust has been raised by those seeking to grapple with its theological implications. For the theologian Richard Rubenstein, the event was shattering, with implications for understanding of God, Israel, and Torah. And while the philosopher Emil Fackenheim was unwilling to share Rubenstein's conclusions, theological or otherwise, they did fully share the belief that they had lived through an epochal event with

---

5   Yehuda Bauer, "Holocaust and Genocide Today," *Yad Vashem*, accessed October 6, 2013, http://www.yadvashem.org/yv/en/education/international_projects/chairmanship/yehuda_bauer_genocide_today.pdf.

the power to shape a new national and religious reality. The event of the Holocaust was so unique that it required a new theology, new perceptions of God and humanity. So too, there were scholars as diverse as Eliezer Berkovits, who saw the Holocaust as raising issues that only God would resolve, Arthur A. Cohen, who saw it as the mysterium tremendum, and Irving Greenberg, who spoke of its revelatory power. Elie Wiesel, the chronicler of the Holocaust, spoke of Sinai and Auschwitz, the former where all of Israel encountered God and the latter where again all of Israel encountered the anti-God and anti-man and heard the anti-revelation that shatters and that leaves a void. Even the Messianists in late twentieth- and early twenty-first-century Judaism, whether in the form of Chabad or Gush Emunim, see the destruction of the Holocaust as so extraordinary as to constitute the anguish that precedes the redemption—hevlei mashi'ah.[6]

These and many other scholars have also argued over what Steven Katz has termed the "Olympics of Genocide," but this is clearly not what I have encountered in my own work on genocide and the *Shoah*. As a Muslim, I would argue that through a religious lens, the *Shoah* has been the only event that set out to eradicate Jews and, with it, Judaism. The Final Solution resulted in the hastening of killing more Jews even though the killing was not only of Jews but also gypsies, Jehovah's Witnesses, the disabled, homosexuals, and others that would not be considered acceptable under the Nuremberg Laws.

In my "Religion and Holocaust" class, we focus on the dimensions of faith before, during, and after the *Shoah*. I have my students read very challenging texts, from the Orthodox responses to secular and atheist responses of survivors, theologians, and commentators. This question of faith is an enormous, almost daunting, question for all people of faith, Jewish or not. How could God let the inferno of Hell burn in the midst of faithful and God-fearing people? What was the role of God? How could God punish his own people? Was Hitler an instrument of God? Did God break his

---

6   Michael Berenbaum and Fred Skolnik, eds., *Encyclopaedia Judaica*, 2nd ed. (Detroit: Macmillan Reference USA, 2007), vol. 9, 388–402.

covenant with his people? Does God not have a say in the matter of human evil? And yet, a significant question is raised: whether *we* can even ask these questions as ones who did not suffer through the camps as survivors or the dead did. The power of such questioning also adds a unique and rare element to the *Shoah*. Having delved into books by Richard Rubenstein, Emil L. Fackenheim, Eliezer Berkovits, Saul Frielander, and Michael Berenbaum, I am rattled by these questions of faith, meaning, and the absurd. However, Jews and Jewish scholars also warn us of the fatal mistake of seeing the *Shoah* as the beginning or end of Jewish history. It marks an epoch, in Edmund Husserl's terms, or a parenthetical in Jewish history, but by no means is it the seminal event for Jews or even for the establishment of the state of Israel.

> It is not very meaningful to interpret the entire course of Jewish history exclusively on the basis of the death-camp experience of European Jewry. If the believer's faith in Israel's "encounters" with God in history is false, it must be so not on account of Auschwitz, but because the "encounters" just did not happen. On the other hand, if these manifestations of the divine presence did occur, then they are true events and will not become lies because of the Holocaust.[7]

The shift and transformation of post-*Shoah* theology was deep, but seen by non-Jews as a victimization, or the perception that Israel was established overnight because of the guilt of the British and United States. The many rumors that I encountered about Jews and the *Shoah* compelled me to face the antisemitism and delve into both the history and theology of the *Shoah*. The questions of faith that I reflect on with my students are also questions that Muslims must reflect on at this time of disarray in many Muslim countries.

As mentioned earlier, there are personal and intellectual experiences that led me in this direction: interviewing survivors, teaching about genocide, antisemitism within Muslim communities, and the spiritual guidance of the Qur'an. Through these, I became a witness of witnesses of the *Shoah*;

---

7 Eliezer Berkovits, "Faith after the Holocaust," in *A Holocaust Reader: Responses to the Nazi Extermination*, ed. Michael L. Morgan (New York: Oxford University Press, 2001), 100.

simultaneously, I witnessed directly antisemitism, *Shoah* denial, and its relativization.

What is witnessing? A witness is someone who experiences an event as an onlooker, bystander, or perpetrator. A witness can also be a victim and bear testimony as to what occurred. I am not a direct witness to the *Shoah*— I am a witness of the witnesses. But I have witnessed directly the denial and refusal to accept the *Shoah* as a unique genocide in the history of genocides. I began witnessing the accounts of the *Shoah* when I started to interview survivors whose stories grew and clung inside me like ivy that is without end and without beginning. Witnessing the suffering of the survivors has impacted me deeply; there were nights I lay in bed thinking of the humanity in their stories and the dehumanization of men, women, and children. I have become a witness. Truth should neither be concealed nor misrepresented, as the Qur'an, Torah, and Christian Scripture all confirm: "Do not withhold any testimony by concealing what you had witnessed. Anyone who withholds a testimony is sinful at heart."[8]

As Muslims, we are told that we should not argue with the followers of earlier revelation, other than in the most kindly manner, unless they are bent on evildoing (and are therefore inaccessible to friendly argument), and say, "We believe in what has been bestowed from upon high upon us, as well as that which has been bestowed upon you: for our God and your God is one and the same, and it is unto Him that we (all) surrender ourselves."[9]

With this verse in mind, and the prophet Mohammad's (PBUH) own proclamation of egalitarianism and social justice, as Muslims we must try to eradicate prejudice and hatred toward others. In a long history of violence among the Abrahamic traditions, we have created a lot of misunderstandings that stem from the historical limitations of geopolitical histories. For example, one of the ways that I have come to understand the complexity and nature of geopolitics is teaching through the historical and mythological lenses in the area of genocide studies. Significantly, I find that many of the long-standing myths about one another's religion or culture are carried forth as propaganda into future moments and years of genocide.

---

8   Assad, *Message of the Qur'an*, 2:238.
9   Ibid., Surah 112.

This has been a learning experience for me, as so many of us are unaware of so many inhumane acts that have led to large-scale displacement and death, the creation of the Jewish Diaspora, and generational hatred between groups. Historical imprints remain in the minds of later generations, and it is up to our generation to try to combat hatred and cultivate distaste for war, murder, and mistrust. We have been reminded that massacres lead to more misunderstanding, to put it mildly. As a Pakistani with parents who migrated from India with their own parents during the partition of Pakistan and India, I am aware of the awful memories that my grandparents and parents had of Hindus; such animosity set these two countries at war, and fostered mistrust, prejudice, and, eventually, nuclear brinksmanship.

Faiz Ahmed Faiz (1911–1984), an Indian Muslim poet who lived in Pakistan, was arrested for suspected involvement in a conspiracy to overthrow the Pakistani government in a coup d'état. He wrote many poems and novels. One of the poems that comes to mind, "No Sign of Blood," was written in 1965 after he was released from prison, and after the partition of India and Pakistan. This poem is special to me because it could have been written about so many epochs of injustice and tyranny.

> Nowhere, nowhere is there any trace of blood.
> Neither on the hands of the assassin,
> Nor under his fingernails, not a spot on his sleeve, no stain on the walls.
> No red on the tip of his dagger,
> No dye on the point of his bayonet.
> There is no sign of blood anywhere.
> This invisible blood was not given in the service of kings
> For a reward of bounty, nor a religious sacrifice
> To obtain absolution.
> It was not spilled on any battlefield for the sake of honor,
> Celebrated later in script on some banner.
> The orphaned blood of murdered parents screamed out for justice;
> No one had time or patience to listen to its cries.
> There was no plaintiff, no witness;
> Therefore no indictment.
> It was the blood of those, whose homes are made of dust,

Blood that in the end became the nourishment for dust.[10]

Faiz's deeply powerful words, that "there was no plaintiff, no witness, therefore no indictment," echo so many stories of genocide in which all were killed, no one left alive to bear witness and no one brought to justice. This poem and many others that were written during the bloody partition of India and Pakistan echo other similar stories. I incorporate literature into my teaching as a means by which the personal story becomes emblazoned in students' minds more fully.

My parents' experience of the India and Pakistan partition is for me a historical fact as a first-generation Pakistani—these memories of killing and hatred and stories of murder stayed with me as I explored the *Shoah*. How could Indian and Pakistani Muslims negate the *Shoah* while having lived through their own pain and suffering? This question implores me to follow in the path of Elie Wiesel's dictum of "Never Again!"

Teaching Genocide

One of the books that I often assign in my classes is *S: A Novel about the Balkans* (2001) by Slavenka Drakulić, a book that takes one directly into the Serbian camps where thousands of Muslim women were raped during the war that raged in the Balkans between 1992 and 1995. The story is based on a woman's journey of dehumanization, survival, and birth. It's a story that describes the plight of so many women trapped in the evil machinations of genocide. Drakulić replaces the names of the characters with letters, just as the victims of Auschwitz-Birkenau had numbers tattooed on their wrists. By leaving the victims and perpetrators largely nameless, she allows the reader to imagine the narrative of victims of any nation and ethnicity in any camp or atrocity. As Drakulić writes:

S. watches how the girls from the "women's room" cling together now, when there is no need for it any more. They are used to each other. Once condemned to each other, they now sit together as friends. Perhaps it will always be that way; they will all be marked by

---

10 Faiz Ahmed Faiz, "No Sign of Blood," in *Against Forgetting: Twentieth Century Poetry of Witness*, ed. Carolyn Forche (London: Norton, 1993), 524–25.

their common experience and will, in a way, remain bound together. She can barely recognize some of them now that they are outside the room. She notices H. has covered her head with a kerchief, tied the way peasant women do. She is surprised; she has forgotten that H. is actually a peasant woman. J. offers her an apple. Where did she get that from? S. wonders, as if they were still back there, inside. All the same, she is grateful to J. for the friendly gesture.[11]

I see the parallels between her story and victims living through the *Shoah*, remembering Gisela Glaser's account of how she was humiliated and compromised at all levels in terms of hygiene and her femininity. Gisela, now a friend of mine, was in several camps, including Auschwitz, and her message is always about the humiliation and suffering of Jews, but she always stresses that we must give a universal message to all humanity. She wrote in 2004:

> The Holocaust is a critical event, not only in the twentieth century, but in the entire history of humanity. The lessons of the Holocaust are first of all historical—having to do with Jews—but then universal, having to do with the impulse to commit genocide.
>
> What happens to human beings when they are subjected to propaganda that consistently dehumanizes the so-called "enemy"? What happens when the highest authorities of a land call for the persecution of a minority? What happens when human rights are restricted? What happens when good people say and do nothing?[12]

Her question looms before us: "What happens to human beings when they are subjected to propaganda that consistently dehumanizes the so-called 'enemy'?" This question is significant when we find negative propaganda in the Muslim context against Jews. Even though Muslims were murdered in the Bosnian genocide, it was and is overlooked by many Muslims globally, and many testimonies are still crying out for translation. Like *Shoah* survivors, victims are struggling to speak out in unimaginable ways about how human

---

11 Slavenka Drajulić, *S: A Novel about the Balkans* (New York: Penguin, 2001), 126.
12 "Gisela Glaser," HGI Manhattan College, accessed July 7, 2014, http://www.hgimanhattan.com/gisela_glaser/.

beings could dehumanize their own people. In my class on "Religion and Genocide," I teach articles from a book called *In God's Name: Genocide and Religion in the Twentieth Century.* Edited by Omer Bartov and Phyllis Mack, it is book that looks at old myths about different faiths and how they are used as propaganda during genocide. For most Muslims, the disintegration of the Ottoman Empire was an end of an era; for others, it was the end of a dominant empire. For example, Serbian perceptions of Bosnian Muslims were still connected to a distant past. For example;

> Although historians have considered the battle of Kosovo (in which both the Serb Prince Lazar and the Sultan Murad were killed) as inconclusive, in Serbian consciousness it became a symbol for the eventual defeat of Serbia and its 500-year absorption into the Ottoman Empire. In the 19th century, certain strands of Kosovo legend were reconfigured and made more explicit. In art, poetry, drama, and other literature of the period, Lazar was portrayed at a "last supper" surrounded by knight-disciples, one of whom, Vuk Branković, was a traitor who was to give the battle plans to the Turks. The Turks were thus Christ-killers and Miloš Obilić, the Serbian knight who assassi-nated Sultan Murad in revenge for the death of Christ-Prince Lazar, became the object of intense veneration. The most famous Serbian Bishop of the twentieth century, Nikolaj Velimorović, wrote that Serbian religious nationalism was built on the "altar of Obilić."[13]

Serbian nationalism and genocide against the Bosnian Muslims was therefore connected to the many old, long-standing myths of deicide, mistrust, and hatred of the Turks. Such propaganda can lead to genocide, as it did for the Bosnian Muslims, but also the Jews. These comparisons are important among genocides, but one must be careful in examining how and why these tactics of propaganda can also be differentiated. Bosnian Muslims were the targets of the genocide because they were never seen as assimilated citizens; however, the Serbians did not venture into Turkey or Albania to annihilate *all* the Muslims. The Germans and, to a much lesser degree, the Vichy

---

13 Omer Bartov and Phyllis Mack, *In God's Name: Genocide and Religion in the Twentieth Century* (New York: Berghahn Books, 2001), 181–82.

government ventured all over the world to destroy all the Jews. Assimilation was a deep problem, but it was to Germans a universal one.

Furthermore, in a genocide class, it is essential to look at the perspective of the perpetrator, as Hannah Arendt does in her work on *Eichmann in Jerusalem: A Report on the Banality of Evil*. Drakulić has also collected the perspectives of war criminals in a small but gripping book entitled *They Would Never Hurt a Fly: War Criminals on Trial in the Hague* (2004). The purpose of such a book is to demonstrate how ordinary men could commit evil crimes, and how evil is not banal; these men, as Arendt's work shows, exemplify the "banality of evil"[14] and the ordinariness of the men and women involved in such heinous crimes. In other words, the men and women were ordinary, but the evil committed was not. In post-*Shoah* research, one can find a plethora of such books, including Christopher Browning's *Ordinary Men: Reserve Police Battalion 101 and the Final Solution in Poland* (1992), that reflect Drakulić's own mission as an author; they describe the complicity in genocide. Ordinary people committed heinous crimes such as murder, rape, and brutal suffering against others.

Drakulić describes an interview that Tim Sebastian conducted on BBC TV in September 2001 with Mira Marković (wife of Slobodan Milošević, president of Serbia from 1989 to 2000), not long after Milošević was extradited to the war crimes tribunal at The Hague. The interview is described as "excruciating" and intolerant, and underlines the fact that genocide is overlooked in times of war when those involved believe that they are protecting something. As Drakulić writes:

> She (Mira) is deeply offended by Sebastian's questions, and instead of answering she lectures him about nineteen countries plotting against Yugoslavia and her heroic husband who "fought for freedom and independence ... Our responsibility for that bloodshed is minor. The responsibility should be borne by those outside of Yugoslavia who financed this bloodshed."[15]

---

14   Hannah Arendt, *Eichmann in Jerusalem: A Report on the Banality of Evil* (New York: Penguin, 1963), 23.
15   Slavenka Drakulić, *They Would Never Hurt a Fly: War Criminals on Trial in the Hague* (New York: Viking, 2004), 141.

Statements such as Mira Marković's echo the horror of so many ongoing genocides that are treated like war crimes after genocide. According to the international tribunal, some of the Serbian soldiers indicted could only be proven guilty of a few deaths, crimes that fall outside the term "genocide."

> In Bosnia numerous war crimes had been committed before 1995 by participants on all sides of the conflict, all in the name of the nation. The offensive on the Srebrenica enclave was apparently in retaliation for an earlier attack of the Bosnian Muslim forces on the neighboring Serbian village of Kravice, in which many Serbian civilians were killed. Hence, perhaps, killing Muslims was justified in the eyes of the perpetrators, including those of Krstić himself. But what took place in Srebrenica was not just military operation—with "collateral damage"—but a deliberate act of ethnic cleansing. In a concerted effort to rid the Drina valley area of its entire Muslim population, more than seven thousand women, children, and elderly people were forcibly deported. This was done according to the instructions of the president of the Rebublika Srpska, Radovan Karadžić, to "create an unbearable situation of total insecurity with no hope of future survival or life for the inhabitants of Srebrenica and Zepa.[16]

Drakulić's description of the events that took place in Srebrenica as an act of ethnic cleansing and how the perpetrators were acting in revenge is an old cyclical genocidal problem. However, in the cases of the Bosnian and Jewish genocides, evidence that met the burden of proof in court was very hard to obtain—except for the case of General Krstić, who was confronted with the evidence of his own orders and recording that essentially indicted him finally. The denial of the Serbian generals and president Milošević is another common trait in genocide denial under the cover of war or sheer ignorance of the killings. For example, Milošević was not indicted for thousands of deaths because he was not the direct executioner; had he lived through his trial, who knows of what he would have been accused? As Drakulić states, as she watched him on trial at The Hague:

---

16 Ibid., 97–98.

When I saw him for the last time in the courtroom, it was evident that he was becoming increasingly agitated. He was furious. He moved back and forth in his seat. He took his jacket off. He pulled faces. He tried to speak but was silenced by the judge. He stopped speaking English and would speak only Serbian; perhaps he had grown too frustrated to keep taking the time to show off. At the beginning he had made me feel like a child visiting a zoo. I was watching a once dangerous wild animal now in captivity, and I felt thrilled but also a little uneasy, awestruck but apprehensive, incredulous at being so close to the beast, almost close enough to touch it. Maybe Milošević did not realize yet, but this was exactly what his situation had come to: that of beast in a cage. This man who himself had not lifted a finger in violence but whose decade-long murderous nationalist politics threw Yugoslavia into a whirlpool of death and chaos is responsible for the deaths of more than two hundred thousand people.[17]

What is responsibility in the eyes of the world? As for the *Shoah*, "the Nuremberg Trials, held in Bavaria, Germany in 1945 to 1946, attempted to indict many German war criminals, but they could only bring 22 to trial because, according to Ben Ferencz, they could only hold 23 seats on the dock."[18] This was the beginning of both post-war justice and testifying to the atrocities of the Jewish Holocaust. The crimes committed in Nazi Germany were so organized and documented that military personnel and even ambassadors could be tried for the establishment of concentration camps and collusion to exterminate all Jews. The trial did not consider the Holocaust, a term not yet defined and not yet used, but instead investigated Crimes against Peace and Crimes against Humanity.

Teaching about evil and how any one of us is capable of these crimes takes the classroom to another level; it challenges our morality, weakness, and how we view others. Students are shocked and dismayed by how

---

17 Ibid., 137–38.
18 Patricia Heberer and Jurgen Matthaus, *Atrocities On Trial: Historical Perspectives on the Politics of Prosecuting War Crimes* (Lincoln, NE: University of Nebraska Press, 2008).

genocide continues, even in their own generation. It is no longer an event in the historical black-and-white past, as it were, but can be seen in motion in color images in real time in the media. This engagement compelled me to take this journey and implement my work on Islam and Judaism in all my classes.

Why the *Shoah*?

One aspect of the *Shoah* that has been debated is whether it was indeed unprecedented, and whether the term "Holocaust," indicating a burnt offering to a deity, should be applied to it. As Jacqueline Rose writes:

> Commentators have also pointed out that to see the Holocaust in this way comes dangerously close to giving the worst catastrophe of Jewish history a type of divine sanction—implicit indeed in the term "Holocaust," which endows the disaster with the status of an act of God. "To name the Nazi genocide 'the Holocaust,'" writes Gillian Rose in "Athens and Jerusalem: A Tale of Three Cities," "is already to over unify it and to sacralise it, to see it as providential purpose—for in the Hebrew scriptures, a *holocaust* refers to a burnt sacrifice which is offered in its entirety to God without any part of it being consumed."[19]

Jacqueline Rose and many other scholars have debated the deeper meaning of the Jewish Holocaust, its sacred place in the long history of genocides, and its aftermath. Rose demonstrates that the word itself gives to this genocide a meaning that may lie in the realm of the sacred, which is why I prefer to use the term *Shoah*. I also call it *Shoah* because this denotes it specifically as the Jewish genocide of the twentieth century. In addition, the very term "*Shoah*" speaks to the horror of the event in a particular way.

> [T]he expression "fabrication of corpses" implies that it is no longer possible truly to speak of death, that what took place in

---

19 Jacqueline Rose, *The Last Resistance* (New York: Verso, 2007), 216.

the camps was not death, but rather something infinitely more appalling. In Auschwitz, people did not die; rather, corpses were produced. Corpses without death, non-humans whose decease is debased into a matter of serial production. And, according to a possible and widespread interpretation, precisely this degradation of death constitutes the specific offense of Auschwitz, the proper name of its horror.[20]

Agamben's statement brings us to question of whether the *Shoah* was "rather something infinitely more appalling" and I am often asked why the *Shoah* is unique. Why is it that the Armenian, Native American, Cambodian, Darfurian, Rwandan, Russian, and Gaza incursion (battle of al-Furqan, 2008) massacres cannot also be called holocausts. "Holocaust,"[21] a word generally used specifically to refer to the *Shoah*, can be used to describe other genocides that have been equally horrific and perhaps even larger in scale; however, I maintain that the *Shoah* is unprecedented in the way in which it carries forth a weight of silence within Muslim communities, and an enduring sense that Jews were part of the states, nations, and even political process that perpetrated their own murder. Jews as a people were also nationless in this period and had no unified state, nation, or political government. In the Germany of the 1930s, the word "Jew" came to denote a subhuman creature that needed to be eradicated by the Nazi machine or collaborating governments. This marks the *Shoah* as unique because Jews were hunted for extermination everywhere in the world where the Nazis could get to them. In Bosnia, hatred of Muslim Bosnians goes back to Ottoman times, but that hatred was not pursued globally. African and Asian Muslims have always been looked down on by Arab Muslims, but the Arabs in Sudan were not prepared to take their war to Egypt or Morocco. The Nazis sought to "purify" their world by eradicating Jews everywhere within it—and they sought to establish their world as far and wide as possible. Bauer writes:

---

20 Agamben, *Remnants of Auschwitz*, 31.
21 "Holocaust" is a word of Greek origin meaning "sacrifice by fire." See "Introduction to the Holocaust," *United States Holocaust Memorial Museum*, accessed June 10, 2013, http://www.ushmm.org/wlc/article.php?lang=en&ModuleId=10005143.

[T]here is no precedent, I suggest, to a universally conceived genocide. Thus, the Ottomans did not bother about the Armenians in Jerusalem, because that was not Turkish ethnic territory. Hutu Power wanted to "cleanse" Rwanda of Tutsis, but there were apparently no plans to kill all Tutsis everywhere (although after the Rwandan genocide there were Hutu attempts to kill Tutsi-related groups in [the] Eastern Congo).[22]

This, to me, establishes that the *Shoah* is unprecedented.

Admittedly, this does not sit well with everyone. David E. Stannard asserts: "In recent years, a number of people inside and outside academe have begun using the same techniques employed by Holocaust deniers to assert their own claim that the agony endured by Jews under the Nazis was— and remains—historically unique. That is, they have attempted to make their case for the incomparability of Jewish torment by denying or trying to minimize the suffering of all other victims of genocide."[23] This is a weak argument, since all the survivors that I have met, interviewed, read, and heard in public discuss other genocides and deliver the universal message of humanity. Jews do not need to find a unique place in the history of human horror; on the contrary, they have encouraged victims of other genocides to speak out precisely because of their own experience of the *Shoah*. One of the *Shoah* survivors I interviewed, Renee Firestone, is deeply invested in talking to survivors of the Cambodian genocide and their children. She decided that her life would be spent helping all victims to speak out against genocide. Her strength comes from her own victimization at Auschwitz-Birkenau—not as someone who believes that her experience is graver than others', but as someone who has felt compelled to act as an instrument of truth against injustice. As I developed my workshop on genocide in Darfur, I found that the most active group in helping these victims was Jewish World Watch, a group founded in Los Angeles, California by Rabbi Harold Schulweis and directed by Janet Kamenir-Reznik, who volunteered to come to my class and

---

22 Bauer, "Holocaust and Genocide Today."
23 David E. Stannard, "The Dangers of Calling the Holocaust Unique," *The Chronicle of Higher Education* (August 2, 1996), accessed August 2012, http://chronicle.com/article/The-Dangers-of-Calling-the/96089/.

gave a solid and informative presentation on the work that had been done and can be done in Darfur. As a Muslim dealing with reports of Muslim women being raped and killed, I was reminded that we as Muslims have yet to learn how to help those outside our community in similar circumstances. In the documentary *The Devil Came on Horseback*,[24] a male victim of the Darfur genocide, living in Chad as a refugee, thanks the United States for its attempts to help, then says: "Where are my Muslim brothers?" I was struck silent by this.

The Amorphous Face of Antisemitism

No matter what political events take place in a Muslim country, there is a tendency to critique how the event is reported and who is in control of the reporting. Conspiracy theories invariably abound, and the general public is skeptical regarding what is being reported—in some cases, rightly so. This skepticism seldom surfaces for negative reports pertaining to Jews. Antisemitism lurks in the back alleys of Cairo, on the Alborz slopes in Tehran, at the Al-Burj Al Arab in Dubai, on the freeways of Damman in Saudi Arabia, in the Cant train station in Karachi, in the camps in Ramallah— everywhere in the Muslim world.

What form does this antisemitism take, and why is it so prevalent in the Muslim world today? Bassam Tibi has made the argument that there is a new, emerging antisemitism in Muslim countries that has its roots in European antisemitism. In other words, he is observing a new Islamization of antisemitism that has flared up due to the Israeli/Palestinian conflict, Khomeini and Iran, US foreign policy, and many other political factors. As Tibi asserts:

> One of the core arguments of this [Tibi's] article is that the prevalent form of antisemitism throughout the Islamic world has been imported from Europe and given an Islamic shape. This variety of antisemitism more closely resembles the Nazism in which the Jew is seen as the source of all evil. There is a further implication that

---

24 *The Devil Came on Horseback*. Directed by Ricki Stern and Anne Sundberg (New York: Break Thru Films, 2007).

Jews are capable of manipulating others—including the US—in a conspiracy to rule the world. Historically, this kind of prejudice is European in origin and it resulted in the Holocaust annihilation. Previously, although Judeaphobia existed in traditional Islam, it was not antisemitism of this type. This murderous form of antisemitism was a European idea that became indigenized in an Islamization process.[25]

How did this process become "indigenized"? What do Muslims really believe about Jews? How did two religious communities become imbued with intolerant views of each other?

These are questions that need to be answered, with the understanding that in Muslim communities, Judaism and Zionism are seen as separate identities. Many Muslims I speak to have said, "I don't have a problem with Jews, but I have an issue with Zionists." However, when we witness extremists in certain parts of the Muslim world, the slogan is "Death to the Jews!" This becomes very convoluted when a Muslim has an issue with Zionism or Israel and yet sustains a belief in Jews and Judaism. For example, the Egyptian Dr. Mohammed Helmy was the first Arab recognized by Yad Vashem in Israel, as it was discovered that "when the Nazis began deporting Jews, Dr. Helmy hid 21-year-old Anna Boros, a family friend, at a cabin on the outskirts of the city and provided her relatives with medical care. After Boros' relatives admitted to Nazi interrogators that he was hiding her, he arranged for her to hide at an acquaintance's house before authorities could inspect the cabin. The four family members survived the war and immigrated to the US. Yad Vashem offered the relatives"[26] the honor of being recognized as Righteous Among the Nations, but the family refused. Many could speculate that it was because of the association with Israel, as "Mervat Hassan said the family didn't want an award from Israel, but she quickly added: 'I respect

---

25 Bassam Tibi, "Public Policy and the Combination of Anti-Americanism and Anti-Semitism in Contemporary Islamist Ideology," *The Current* (Cornell University) 12 (Winter 2008): 124.

26 Yori Yanover, "Relatives of Egyptian Righteous Gentile Refusing Yad Vashen Award," *The Jewish Press,* accessed October 23, 2016, http://www.jewishpress.com/news/breaking-news/relatives-of-egyptian-righteous-gentile-refusing-yad-vashem-award/2013/10/20/.

Judaism as a religion and I respect Jews. Islam recognizes Judaism as a heavenly religion.'"[27]

I recently discussed this issue with a Jewish friend, who also confessed that he held a long-standing disagreement with Zionism and is fearful of Jews who support Israel blindly. There are many layers to this dismissal of Zionism[28]; I will try in this work to spell out some of these complex ideological terms.[29] The purpose here is to create reconciliation and not hatred, to step beyond oneself to see another person's struggle. For example, I was asked a pointed question when applying for a job at an Islamic center in Southern California: If I were to choose a side in the Middle-Eastern conflict, would I choose the Palestinian or Israeli? I refrained from answering this question by saying that I was both pro-Palestinian and pro-Israeli. I declined to silence either group of human beings in their struggle for peace, land, and religious freedom. Why assume that all Muslims are going to align with the Palestinian cause and want to eradicate Israel? I asked.

What Is Zionism?

I remember the word "Zion" being sung in churches whose services I sometimes attended while I was growing up in Europe: "By the rivers of Babylon, there we sat down, yea, we wept, when we remembered Zion" (Psalms 137:1 KJV). I assumed that it was a biblical place that Christians referred to; then, I learned that Zion is what Jews call "Israel" today, and that Mount Zion in Jerusalem was conquered by David and Jerusalem was named the city of David. My parents owned a Boney M album, on one song of which the group sang this verse from the Psalms to disco music, so it was familiar in my years growing up. My first encounter with actual Zionism was when I befriended a Jewish Argentinean writer in Jerusalem. He educated me about what he believed was a form of "Zionism" in Argentina. During the 1990s,

---

27 Ibid.

28 Also see Jeffrey Herf's edited book, *Anti-Semitism and Anti-Zionism in Historical Perspective Convergence and Divergence* (New York: Taylor & Francis, 2008); the articles discuss how Muslim political leaders have seen Zionism as a political and imperial ideology.

29 Aylin Kocaman, "Zionism Means Something Different for Some Muslims," *The Jerusalem Post*, accessed July 7, 2014, http://www.jpost.com/Opinion/Op-Ed-Contributors/Zionism-means-something-different-for-some-Muslims.

there had been a large movement among Argentinian Jews to make *aliyah*—a word literally meaning "ascent," and the term used to indicate the return to the homeland of Israel of Jews from around the world; it is a fundamental tenet of Zionism. Argentina then having the sixth-largest population of Jews in the world, it was a haven for them, but also a place of deep antisemitism. The desire to make *aliyah* and enjoy a certain freedom not possible in a Catholic country remained strong with many Jews, including my writer friend. When he arrived in Israel, he was required, like other young Israelis, to serve in the military for the protection of the country, and he did. However, when he discovered what he felt was severe pressure placed on Palestinians, and their unjust killing, he deserted, and was still in hiding when I met him. He worked at a bar and wrote during the day to keep his sanity. One late night, as I was returning from a field trip with my class at Hebrew University, I knocked at his door, and there was no response. I was certain he was there, since he had invited me there to read some of his writings; the house was dark, and the Jerusalem moon lit a back room where I could see a glass of half-drunk wine and a burning cigarette. I started to bang on the door, and all of a sudden an arm extended to grab me and muffle my mouth. It was my friend, sweating and petrified of a military search.

This personal story and many others have convoluted the concept of Zionism, not just for me, but for many Jews who don't wish to live in Israel. Israel is not "home" for all Jews, and not all Jews believe in the actions of its government or compulsory military service. I believe that we in Muslim communities need to reimagine the diversity of Jews and to deconstruct the monolith of the Jew. But Israel is home to many Jews who feel comfortable there and serve in the military willingly even as they take issue with some governmental policies and with some of what they do in the military. There are Arab Jews, African Jews, European Jews, American Jews, and so on. Jews have a long history of victimization but also success in many parts of the world. Jews have held onto their cultural identity even in the face of persecution and humiliation; we can learn a lesson from them. As I think of how many vignettes in my life have been full of conversations with strangers and friends about Jewish conspiracies, Jewish power, Jewish colonizers, Jewish money mongers, Jewish diseases, Jewish 9/11 plots, or how Jews started World War II, I am appalled at these matter-of-fact nods in public and private. As a woman and a Muslim, I have imagined that my communities globally would find a space to acknowledge that Jews have the same humanity as everyone else.

Zionism, like antisemitism, has many different meanings and has been applied and manipulated in various ways. Zionism has been described by Walter Laqueur in *The History of Zionism*: "It is debatable whether there is a history of Zionism beyond 1948, and not only because many of its functions have been taken over by the State of Israel."[30] I think a discussion of the emergence of Zionism is significant to understanding the situation of Jews in Europe, but it is also important to look at how and why this idea of establishing a state for Jews, a safe haven and place to live, emerged. Jews have experienced antisemitism since the destruction of the Second Temple in 70 CE. The history of antisemitism is a long one: from the Greek period to the Roman Empire; to pogroms in al-Andalus, Cordoba, and Granada; to the first and second Crusades[31]; to medieval persecution in England, Holland, Germany, France, and Italy[32]; to the United States under Ulysses Grant[33]; to Russia under Czar Alexander II; to World Wars I and II; and the *Shoah*. Today, a new form of antisemitism has seeped into Arab culture in the form of revived tales of blood libel and from the infamous *Protocols of the Elders of Zion*.[34] The *Protocols of the Elders of Zion* has had an enormous influence on the world in regard to antisemitism; it accuses the Jews of wanting to take over the world, a claim still seen as a real threat and rather than a conspiracy theory. This new antisemitism is aimed particularly at Zionism and the state of Israel.

> The *Protocols* have become a Bible of anti-Zionis[m], adopted by enemies of the State of Israel to justify their attempts to destroy it. Thirty years ago the king of Saudi Arabia distributed copies of the *Protocol* to foreign guests ... Today, the *Protocols* continue to serve

30 Walter Laqueur, *History of Zionism: From the French Revolution to the Establishment of the State of Israel* (London: Tauris Parke Paperbacks, 2003), 42.

31 Bernard Lewis, *The Jews of Islam* (Princeton, NJ: Princeton University Press, 1984), 21–24.

32 Martin Gilbert, *Dearest Auntie Fori: The Story of the Jewish People* (New York: HarperCollins, 2002), 34–37.

33 Jonathan D. Sarna, *When General Grant Expelled the Jews* (New York: Random House, 2012), 27.

34 Steven L. Jacobs and Mark Weitzman, *Dismantling the Big Lie: The Protocols of the Elders of Zion* (Los Angeles: Simon Wiesenthal Center, 2003).

the same purpose, used by governments, organizations, and individuals to whip up hatred against Israel and Jews.[35]

I have listed a number of periods in history when Jews faced persecution, a long story of suffering leading up to the *Shoah*, which sought to exterminate all Jews. Zionism, essentially a turn-of-the century-movement, was a response to the many accusations, prohibitions, and incidents of scapegoating that Jews had long endured everywhere, but especially in Europe. What follows is the text of a letter that was written by Robert Weltsch in the *Central-Verein-Zeitung*, a German-Jewish newspaper, in 1933. Jews had not yet been ordered to wear yellow stars on their clothing to identify themselves as Jews, and Weltsch urged Jews to band together in the face of the sociopolitical climate in Germany. In 1933, Hitler ordered a huge boycott against the Jews; this letter demonstrates the fear and need for Jews to organize and create a strategy.

The first of April, 1933, will remain an important date in the history of German Jewry indeed, in the history of the entire Jewish people. The events of that day have aspects that are not only political and economic, but moral and spiritual as well. For however much the Jewish question is now debated, nobody except ourselves can express what is to be said on these events from the Jewish point of view, what is happening in the soul of the German Jew. Today the Jews cannot speak except as Jews. Anything else is utterly senseless … Gone is the fatal misapprehension of many Jews that Jewish interests can be pressed under some other cover. On April 1 the German Jews learned a lesson which penetrates far more deeply than even their embittered and now triumphant opponents could assume …

We live in a new period; the national revolution of the German people is a signal that is visible from afar, indicating that the world of our previous concepts has collapsed. That may be painful for many, but in this world only those will be able to survive who are able to look reality in the eye. We stand in the midst of tremendous

---

35 Ibid., 8.

changes in intellectual, political, social and economic life. It is for us to see how the Jews will react.

April 1, 1933, can become the day of Jewish awakening and Jewish rebirth. If the Jews will it. If the Jews are mature and have greatness in them. If the Jews are not as they are represented to be by their opponents.

The Jews, under attack, must learn to acknowledge themselves.

Even in these days of most profound disturbance, when the stormiest of emotions have visited our hearts in face of the unprecedented display of the universal slander of the entire Jewish population of a great and cultural country, we must first of all maintain composure. Even if we stand shattered by the events of these days, we must not lose heart and must examine the situation without any attempt to deceive ourselves. One would like to recommend in these days that the document that stood at the cradle of Zionism, Theodor Herzl's *Jewish State*, be distributed in hundreds of thousands of copies among Jews and non-Jews ...[36]

Theodor Herzl was the man who conceived the nature of "the Jewish question" as one that required a rapid international response to create a state for the Jews. Herzl was a Viennese lawyer, who, as correspondent for a Viennese newspaper in Paris, witnessed the Dreyfus Affair, and could see how Jews were being treated in a European empire that was rapidly disintegrating. Jews were being debarred from positions of moderate power, and their businesses were being annexed, with outcries from the French not to buy from them. Herzl wrote a pamphlet, entitled *The Jewish State*, that spearheaded the idea that Jews must have a state of their own. In Herzl's dealings with Joseph Chamberlain (British Colonial Secretary) and the Grand Vizier of Turkey (Sultan Abdul Hamid, the head of the Ottoman), the state that was offered as a potential Jewish homeland was initially Uganda, and then Argentina. The offer was declined because Herzl and his fellow Zionists felt that there was a need to return to the biblical "Zion," a

---

36   Leonard Baker, *Days of Sorrow and Pain: Leo Baeck and Berlin Jews* (New York: Oxford University Press, 1980), 362 [emphasis in original].

state where Jews could live and rebuild their religious spirit. Uganda was originally accepted by the Zionist Congress, but then the more traditional and more deeply Eastern Europeans, more religious and steeped in Jewish tradition, revolted and Zionism dropped the Uganda option. Weltsch's spirit and his recognition of how Jews were being treated was evidenced by Herzl and the community. The following excerpt shows the way in which Jews were being treated and accused.

They accuse us today of treason against the German people: The National-Socialist Press calls us the "enemy of the Nation," and leaves us defenseless.

It is not true that the Jews betrayed Germany. If they betrayed anyone, it was themselves, the Jews.

Because the Jew did not display his Judaism with pride, because he tried to avoid the Jewish issue, he must bear part of the blame for the degradation of the Jews.

The Jew is marked as a Jew. He gets the yellow badge.

A powerful symbol is to be found in the fact that the boycott leadership gave orders that a sign "with a yellow badge on a black background" was to be pasted on the boycotted shops. This regulation is intended as a brand, a sign of contempt. We will take it up and make of it a badge of honor.

There is great distress in German Jewry. We German Jews bore our share in the general distress in Germany. We contributed our contingent to the great army of people who were without work and without income, and seemed to be excluded from meaningful life. New distress has overtaken us. Jewish people are torn away from their work; the sense and basis of their lives has been destroyed.

Those who are lucky enough to have work and an income must help those who have lost everything. Anyone who is still able to give must sacrifice the maximum! The greatest possible demands must be made on everybody! Whoever evades this duty is an enemy of the community. Every sacrifice must be made, every sacrifice in aid for those who are now in need, but also every sacrifice in contribution to our communities, on whom innumerable persons now depend. Shame on those whose lack of willingness for sacrifice, whose criminal evasion of taxes forces our communities to dismiss officials or employees! We must not be the cause of making one of our own people lose his job or his bread![37]

Robert Weltsch's letter is a reminder that Jews in Germany were aware of their plight many years before the *Shoah*. I wanted to demonstrate that there was an already existing hatred and prejudice in Europe for many years. However, Weltsch encourages German Jews to be proud of their tradition rather than be ashamed. There are many who question why the Jews were not more wary and able to escape their fate, but they were unaware of the unspeakable fate that awaited them. Weltsch's letter provides a small yet important description of the plight of German Jews. Their circumstances in Europe were defined by their struggle and strength in history as a people who, even when integrated into mainstream culture, were often or only seen as second-class citizens. Weltsch's letter and struggle as a Jew in Europe describes the situation with German-Jews in particular who had lived in Europe for thousands of years. His letter also demonstrates this struggle and is a testament to non-Jews about the circumstances of Jews in Europe. Zionism as understood by most people is misconstrued as a phenomenon that only appeared around 1948; as mentioned earlier, the modern Zionist movement is of nineteenth-century origin. But the term "Zionism" as used now pejoratively by Muslims/Arabs against Jews speaks to a concept brewing since the advent of Judaism. For example:

> We would contend that the Arab discourse did not develop into one coherent narrative. Rather it is more appropriate to speak of a reservoir and a repertoire of references, arguments and images that are scattered and intertwined in the vast literature on the conflict, Zionism, Judaism, World War II, and the history of the Arab attitudes toward Nazi Germany and the Nationalist-Socialist Party … For example, Arab leftists and liberals distance themselves from Nazi and fascist ideologies and most of them do not share themes

---

37 Ibid., 33.

of Holocaust denial, but they do not shun using the Zionist-Nazi equation or the Zionist-Nazi cooperation theme.[38]

Pre-*Shoah* history and literature (an prime example of the latter being Robert Weltch's letter) paint a very negative image of Jews in Europe. The fate of these Jews was often unfavorable, but never had Jews imagined a colossal event such as the *Shoah* happening to their community. I asked all the survivors I interviewed if they could have conceived of the reality of the death camps; all of them responded that they knew that during World War II, in some cases, Jews were being shot in large numbers and buried in mass graves, but never had any of them conceived that the gas chambers, crematoria, and hangings of the camps existed. Renee Firestone, one of the survivors I interviewed, said that her family in Hungary had heard of mass shootings of Jews, but "never could you imagine what befell us in the camps." In fact, the *Shoah* was literally incredible, not believable, not comprehensible to many of its victims even as they were going through it.

How was it possible that some Jews apparently had no knowledge of death camps and concentration camps? The existence of concentration camps was known since 1933. The death camps would not be known until 1942. Chelmno came online in December 8, 1941 and was running in 1942. Belzec was opened in February and Sobibor in the spring. Treblinka opened July 22, 1942. So people could not have known of it before 1942. Of course, few people of any sort knew of the death camps, although historically we know that the Warsaw Ghetto Jews sent a person to find out what was happening in Treblinka and he reported back to them the reality of the camps. This is one of the reasons that the Ghetto Uprising occurred in April 1943 and that the January 1943 resistance movement began even before the April Ghetto Uprising. The Germans wanted the extermination to be kept secret, for obvious reasons; they worked to obliterate all traces of the killings as the war progressed and their assumption of victory began to crumble. Theodor Malzmueller, an SS guard at the Kulmhof (Chelmno) extermination camp, recalled the instructions he received upon his arrival there:

---

38   Meir Litvak and Esther Webman, *From Empathy to Denial: Arab Responses to the Holocaust* (New York: Columbia University Press, 2009), 13.

When we arrived we had to report to the camp commandment, SS-Haupsturmführer (captain) Bothmann. The SS-Haupsturme führer addressed us in his living quarters, in the presence of SS-Untersturmführer (second lieutenant) Albert Palte. He explained that we had been dedicated to Kulmhof extermination camp as guards and added that in this camp the plague boils of humanity, the Jews, were exterminated. We were to keep quiet about everything we saw or heard, otherwise we would have to reckon with our families' imprisonment and death penalty.[39]

This secrecy required a plan that had never before been carried out in the history of genocide. Although the lack of communication technology that makes secrecy an impossible thing today may have aided the Nazis in this respect, this sort of silence required tremendous coordination and will; even the murders and related rebellions of Armenians earlier in the twentieth century were known to some of the outside world, although they were justified under the guise of war. It was well known, in fact, that the Turks planned to rid themselves of the Christians in their midst—and the Christians among them were Armenians. "The outside world had known that the Armenians were at grave risk well before Mehmet Talaat (Ottoman leader) and the Young Turk leadership ordered their deportation. When Turkey entered World War I on the side of Germany against Britain, France, and Russia, Talaat made it clear that the empire would target its Christian subjects."[40] In remarks reported by the *New York Times* in January 1915, Talaat said "there was no room for Christians in Turkey and that their supporters should advise them to clear out."[41] Unfortunately, nothing was done for the Armenians, even *with* newspapers openly reporting the intolerance of Christians under the Turks. In the time leading up to the *Shoah*, many knew of intolerance toward Jews that was common all over the world, including within the United States, but no one could imagine

---

39 Lipstadt, *Denying the Holocaust*, 106.
40 Samantha Powers, *A Problem from Hell: America and the Age of Genocide* (New York: Basic Books, 2002), 1–2.
41 Samantha Powers, *A Problem from Hell*, 1.

the evil that was taking place against them in Europe, Tunisia, and Morocco—not even Jews themselves. Hitler said time and again what he would do. He wrote of it in *Mein Kampf* in 1925; he spoke of the annihilation of the Jews to the Reichstag on January 30, 1939, and repeated the prophecy from the same rostrum in 1942. He was not to be believed, as he was to remark in 1942.

There is some evidence that Jews worldwide and the international community knew what was happening to the Jews in Europe, but it was not believable to many and was consciously and subconsciously suppressed. There may have been many reasons for this but the disappearance of Jews, eyewitness accounts of both Jews and non-Jews, and the German secret that thousands of people shared was too much of an atrocity for people to swallow, or in Laqueur's words:

> The case of Belsen was unbelievable for more than one reason. Three years had passed since the world had first been informed about the existence of extermination camps. There had been much detailed information about the names of these camps, their location, the millions who had been killed there, even the names of the commanders had been published. But ... no one had "imagined what a camp would be like." And thus Belsen triggered off a wave of violent anger even though, ironically, it was not an extermination camp at all. ... In comparison with the death camps, Belsen was almost an idyllic place; there were no gas chambers in Belsen, no mass executions, death was merely by disease and starvation ... There had been a steady flow of information, but it had quite obviously not registered. Or had it been perhaps a case of some vague rumours which could not be given credence because there was no way to verify them?[42]

Furthermore, the famous trial of Adolf Eichmann provided further proof that the SS wanted to obliterate all traces of their crimes. Even though

---

42 Walter Laqueur, *The Terrible Secret: Suppression of the Truth about Hitler's "Final Solution"* (Boston: Little Brown and Company, 1980), 1–2.

numerous *Shoah* survivors attended Eichmann's trial, there was only one direct witness to him having killed a Jew; the murdered Jew was a boy named Abraham Gordon, who stole some berries on Eichmann's farm and was consequently beaten to death by Eichmann. This witness brought the trial to a close.

Eichmann was hanged in Israel on May 31, 1962. His body was cremated, and his ashes were taken out to sea so that they would not soil the land of Israel and his burial place did not become a shrine. His trial was unique, and represented some measure of justice for Nazi crimes. How, in the face of actual evidence and witnesses, can anyone claim the *Shoah* was exaggerated or was some sort of elaborate hoax designed to give Palestine to Israel?

The Uniqueness of the Denial of the *Shoah*

> The Holocaust did not occur until the mid-twentieth century, but conditions necessary, though not sufficient, to produce it were forming centuries before. Decisive in that process was Christian anti-Judaism and its demonization of the Jew … The reason for that defamation was the Christian belief that Jews were, as Ruben-stein puts it, "the God-bearing and the God-murdering people *par excellence*." Jesus, the incarnation of God according to Christian tradition, was one of the Jewish people, but Christian telling of the story depicted the Jews as collectively responsible for his crucifixion and thus for rejecting God through deicide, the most heinous crime of all.[43]

The murder, what the Nazis termed extermination, of Jews was done quickly by Nazi Germany. Soon, 6 million Jews, 1.5 million of whom were children under the age of fifteen, two-thirds of European Jews—and about one-third of the Jews worldwide—were dead. Dead because of the long-standing hatred that stemmed from the belief that Jews had crucified Christ, thus Jews were deemed guilty of deicide. "Building on a long history that went

---

43   John K. Roth, "Reflections on Post-Holocaust Ethics," in *Problems Unique to the Holocaust*, ed. Henry James Cargas (Lexington, KY: University Press of Kentucky, 1999), 171–72.

beyond religious to racist antisemitism, the assaults reached their zenith when Nazi Germany became a genocidal state."[44]

These facts are unknown to many Muslims and non-Muslims, but the danger that one can see is that Muslims, although not the perpetrators of European crimes against Jews, have developed a pattern of antisemitism. "The amorphous face of antisemitism" is a phrase I came up with after being in different situations all over the world in which, invariably, the Jews would become a topic of conversation. Whether we were discussing economic failure in Dubai or bombings in Afghanistan, Jews lurked in the corners of the room or the garden like ghostly scapegoats. There was no logic or reason to this, but the Jews were instantly invoked, regardless. One of the enduring conspiracy theories was that Jews attacked New York City on September 11, 2001, and that all the Jews in the twin towers of the World Trade Center were safely evacuated—a ridiculous story, demonstrably untrue, but still a popular theory in some quarters today.[45] Many prominent Arab and Muslim papers will still proclaim that "Jews were warned to stay home" on that day.[46]

---

44 Ibid., 172.

45 On Jews and 9/11, see Jeremy Stahl, "Where Did 9/11 Conspiracies Come From?," *Slate*, accessed May 2, 2016, http://www.slate.com/articles/news_and_politics/trutherism/2011/09/where_did_911_conspiracies_come_from.html.

46 The claim that Jewish employees were warned not to come to work at the World Trade Center on September 11 was quickly accepted by the Arab media as incontrovertible fact, according to MEMRI.

Syrian ambassador to Tehran, Turkey, Muhammad Saqr, said at a conference held at the Iranian Foreign Ministry: "Syria has documented proof of the Zionist regime"s involvement in the September 11 terror attacks on the US" and that "4,000 Jews employed at the WTC did not show up for work before the attack clearly attests to Zionist involvement in these attacks."

The Iranian daily *Kayhan* also referred to this "fact": "It is known that 4,000 Jews worked at the WTC in New York and that these people did not come to work that day."

In an editorial, the Saudi Arabian government daily *"Ukkaz* said "six Israelis suspected of involvement in New York and Washington were arrested in the US, to be later released. This confirms our strong suspicions about the involvement of Israel"s Mossad in the ugly crime."

The Egyptian opposition weekly *Al-"Usbu"* published that as a scoop, building it up somewhat and giving it the title, "True Perpetrators of the September 11 Attacks Arrested—Zionists with Maps of the WTC, the Pentagon, and the White House and Large Quantities of Anthrax."

Ambassador Saqr viewed Israeli Prime Minister Ariel Sharon"s unexpected postponement of his visit to the US as "additional proof linking the Zionists with this tragedy."

Syrian columnist Mu"az Al-Khatib gave another example in *Al-Hayat:* "Barak's presence in the BBC"s head office minutes after the explosion, at a meeting set in advance, to speak for 30 minutes of the danger of terrorism and chastise the "rogue states," particularly the Arab" was, he said, further proof of Israel's involvement.

These newspaper claims appeared not only in Arab/Muslim papers, but also in the media of other groups that espouse that Jews had a hand in the 9/11 attacks.[47] The term "antisemitism" emerged in nineteenth-century Europe to refer to feelings of hatred or prejudice toward those of Semitic origins. The term "Semite" was coined by European philologists in the eighteenth century, who categorized languages into "families" descended from one "mother" tongue, to which they were all related. These philologists claimed that languages including Arabic, Hebrew, Aramaic, and Amharic were "Semitic" languages. This is why some Arabs claim that to be antisemitic is also to be anti-Arab or anti-Muslim."[48] In numerous conversations, I have been criticized for using the term "antisemitic" to refer uniquely to Jews; I have tried in various ways to explain that Jews were specifically denoted as such by Europeans as a way of singling them out from other Semitic peoples and their languages. "Antisemitic" was a term adopted specifically for and applied exclusively to Jews, and not Arabs. Joseph Massad points out:

> The defensive claim made by some that Arabs cannot be "anti-Semitic" because they are "Semites" is equally erroneous and facile. First, I should state that I do not believe that anyone is a "Semite" any more than I believe anyone is an "Aryan," and I do not believe that Arabs or Jews should proudly declare that they are "Semites" because European racists classified them as such. But if the history of European Christian anti-Semitism is mostly a history targeting Jews as objects of discrimination and exclusion, the history of European Orientalism and colonialism is the one that targeted Arabs and Muslims, among many others. This does not mean that Arabs are not considered Semites by European racialist and philological classifications; they indeed are. Nor does this mean

---

Some speculated on how Israel carried out the attack. Orkhan Muhammad Ali wrote, in *Saut Al-Haqq Wa-Al-Hurriyya*, the mouthpiece for the Islamic Movement in Israel, that "the planes had not been hijacked—rather, they had been directed by remote control using a system developed by a Jewish-owned company."

47 Marc Levin, "Protocols of Zion," *Thinkfilm Productions*, accessed May 12, 2016, http://worldfilm. about.com/od/documentaryfilms/fr/protocolsofzion.htm.

48 Joseph Massad, "Semites and Anti-Semites, That Is the Question," *Al-Ahram,* accessed December 10, 2016. http://www.campus-watch.org/article/id/1455.

that much of the hatred of Arabs today is not derived from a prior anti-Semitism that targeted Jews. Indeed it is.[49]

Antisemitism is far more complicated than we imagine, and I am not happy with any position that posits that all Jews are Zionists and that all Muslims are antisemites. This defeats the purpose of trying to understand the history and meanings of the two terms. We need to unpack these terms and listen to one another when speaking of the *Shoah*, as well as of racism against Arabs and Muslims today.

I have already discussed the many dangers of declaring any one genocide superior to another mass murder, such as Armenia, Bosnia, Sudan, or Cambodia. However, one needs to assess and consider each genocide on its own and remember, above all, that each represents the murder of human beings—something that should require no qualification and should find no justification. As I write this book, I am facing a very difficult question: what will Muslims understand from this book? Will Muslims even read this book? Will they ever allow the fact of the *Shoah* to enter their history books? As I interviewed *Shoah* survivors, whom I will discuss in detail in the next chapter, I was reminded that I was facing, one by one, people who went through a severe dehumanization process. Speaking to survivors who were directly at Auschwitz-Birkenau, and about events that led up to their families being gassed, shot, or killed in other ways, left me in deep pain at the thought of *Shoah* denial. How can anyone deny the documentation by the Germans, French, and, in some cases, the Russians, of these events? In Michael Shermer and Alex Grobman's book, *Denying History: Who Says the Holocaust Never Happened and Why Do They Say It?* (2002), the authors discuss how deniers come to false historical speculation about the *Shoah*, and to "this fundamental flaw in their reasoning ... [that the] Holocaust is not a single event that a single fact can prove or disprove."[50] Their research focuses on *Shoah* deniers who live in Europe or in the United States, mainly those aligned with the Institute for Historical Review (IHR), which is a leading *Shoah*-denial group. Shermer and Grobman follow the deniers' arguments and show how

---

49 Ibid.
50 Michael Shermer and Alex Grobman, *Denying History: Who Says the Holocaust Never Happened and Why Do They Say It?* (Berkeley: University of California Press, 2002), 33.

denial is based on small cracks in knowledge. They also relate well-established evidence proving that the *Shoah* happened—written documents, eyewitness testimonies, photographs, and other evidence.

People disappeared every day and no one dared to notice or react for fear of their own lives, except for a handful of people who courageously helped save many lives, especially of Jewish children. My own awareness of the *Shoah*, years after it happened, came relatively late in life: I was in college when I was a teaching assistant for a professor with a class on post-*Shoah* studies. I was deeply disturbed and scarred by the class and the testimonies that we read about the actions of the Nazis and the silence of bystanders. The hatred of Jews has a long history; Jews herded into European ghettos as the *Shoah* approached knew they were encircled by a fortress of hatred, especially in Italy, France, and Germany.

As I write that the *Shoah* to me is unprecedented, I write as a Muslim with compassion for and some understanding of what Jews have suffered and are suffering. I also know that many Jews have spoken out against atrocities committed by others, and by the Israeli Defense Force (IDF); righteous Jews, against the background of their own historical suffering and experiences of antisemitism, will not stand silently by while others are victimized. In return, I, too, believe that there were millions of (estimated) deaths during the *Shoah*, of which 6 million were Jews. And among those dead were not only Jews but Roma, some of whom were Muslims, as well as Christians, communists, homosexuals, Soviet POWs, and many who risked their lives trying to help people from these groups. There are heroic stories as well as many atrocious ones among survivors of Hitler's Final Solution; as Muslims, we should applaud the memory of the many Jews and Muslims who helped one another, and those who risked their lives under the very principles of Islam (I discuss this in the last chapter). The denial and relativizaton of the *Shoah* must stop, and we must educate one another about it so that it will not happen again. This is the message of my survivor friends, but also of so many victims, not just Jewish but also Muslim, of World War II.

As a Muslim, I had much trepidation and many questions for myself as I began interviewing *Shoah* survivors. How could I interview survivors? What perspectives and biases would I bring to the process? How would *Shoah* survivors relate to a Muslim woman? And, most important, why did I feel compelled to interview survivors at all?

Chapter Four

The Document

In post-*Shoah* (post-Holocaust) studies and conversations, there has been a deep vein of concern about the idea of "witnessing." I use this term advisedly, but before I let the reader delve into my understanding of my own witnessing of survivors' testimony, I wish to say clearly that I am neither a direct victim of the *Shoah* nor am I a descendant of a victim. Instead, I am a witness to false rumors and to the denial of the suffering of a people. I am also a witness to the testimony of *Shoah* victims, which I seek to relate in writing to the fullest of my abilities. I began this book with reference to Maurice Blanchot, and he lurks in the corners of every page, telling us that it is impossible to tell the story of such an event, and especially difficult for a witness who is so far removed from the *Shoah*—a Muslim woman.

> How can anyone deny the Holocaust when the Germans, the Germans documented everything? How can people be so blind? (interview with Renee Firestone)

When I decided to write this book, I was not sure what direction it would take, how I was going to give testimony to the *Shoah* as a Muslim, or how I could document the event in a way that spoke to readers. The events of the *Shoah*, I believe, are best documented not on paper or in photographs, but in the testimony and voices of the victims; this testimony is what I call "The Document." Deep within me is the echo of the popular lie that the *Shoah* was fabricated, records were falsified, and numbers were exaggerated, that it was a Jewish conspiracy to win them a homeland in Israel. These lies ultimately led me to my firsthand documentation of *Shoah* survivors' testimony of the horror that befell them and their families. As I sat face-to-face with them, asking questions, listening to their stories, and looking into their teary eyes, I would ask myself, *what compels anyone to lessen the reality of another person? How can a survivor of something horrible tell a story of humiliation to others and be accused of exaggerating?* It was shocking to remind myself during these interviews that the men and women who were speaking to me had actually been in the camps, had seen what they spoke about. When her sister was crying for her parents, survivor Renee Firestone remembered asking one of the guards at Auschwitz, "Where are our parents?" He had laughed and pointed to the ashes in the sky, floating up from a crematorium chimney, and said, "There go your parents. . . ."

When I asked Firestone what she thought about people who deny the *Shoah* and then asked her about evidence, she smiled at me warmly and said, "How can anyone deny the Holocaust when the Germans, the Germans documented everything and they themselves have admitted to the atrocities [and made] reparations?" I was going to say, "Yes, this is known all over the world, but people continue to deny it anyway"—but I stopped myself, realizing that Firestone herself was my own document, my evidence and record, that could speak both to the reality of having lived through the *Shoah* and to the aftermath.

In 2007, I was invited to a conference entitled "Judaism through Muslim Eyes and Islam through Jewish Eyes." It was held in Munich, and hosted by the University of Munich and the University of California at Berkeley. After the conference, my husband, daughter, and I decided to visit Dachau. I had never visited a concentration camp site, and since I was in Munich, I felt this was an important opportunity to pay my respects to the many victims of the Dachau camp. I was also curious to see a Nazi camp as a Muslim, even after having seen many images of these camps; I wanted the raw experience that I had imagined one might feel visiting such a place. When I returned to my home in Los Angeles after my visit, I wrote an article about my powerful feelings that was published in the *Jewish Journal* in October 2007. In it, I wrote the following:

But why did I want to visit Dachau? For whose memory? Perhaps I wanted to be a witness, a Muslim witness, who could testify against the outrage of Holocaust denial in the Islamic world and point out the deep danger in ignoring history and the memory of narrative ... I wanted to go to Dachau because I wanted to pay my respects to the many Jews, Christians, and Gypsies who had perished and been abused there; I went as an act of simple respect for the dead.

Dachau was a Nazi German concentration camp built on the grounds of an abandoned munitions factory near the medieval town of Dachau, which is located about 10 miles northwest of Munich, in southern Germany. As one walks toward the camp, there is an iron gate nested in between bushes and tall oak trees with the slogan: "Arbeit Macht Frei" ("Work Will Set You Free"). When the Nazis opened Dachau in March 1933, Heinrich Himmler, Munich chief of police, described it as the Nazi's first camp for political prisoners. One can still visit the barracks where the many prisoners and guards were housed: the long, gray buildings with low ceilings today contain exhibitions of old propaganda, art, and SS paraphernalia. It is not hard to envision the harsh reality the prisoners had to face, or the lives of the guards themselves.

Witnessing is, as so many post-*Shoah* writers have spoken of it, a form of speaking. And Dachau is a place where silence can be broken and where the atrocities can be declared openly. I became a witness to the ghosts and survivors of Dachau. But more notably, I felt that even by witnessing just one camp—or one death—it were as if I had witnessed a million camps and a million deaths.[1]

My own document had begun then and there amid the ashes, memory, and horror of Dachau. One of the survivors I interviewed told me on the phone that Dachau was one of the "nicer camps," and Birkenau was hell. I laughed,

---

1 Mehnaz Afridi, "Elmau & Dachau: A Muslim's Testimony," *Jewish Journal* (2007), accessed March 15, 2015, http://www.jewishjournal.com/articles/page2/elmau_dachau_a_muslims_testimony_20071005/.

even as I realized, as I put the phone down, how bitterly unfunny the humor was. That one camp might be better than another never crossed my mind; I had never been imprisoned, and I knew and recognized that this was too strange for me.

I spoke with the survivors either at their homes or at the Museum of Tolerance in Los Angeles. I witnessed their testimony and carry with me the weight of their generosity and the time they took to share their experience.

I had some hesitation about contacting survivors. Why should they let me interview them? I also felt somehow that survivors must be fragile people, thus I was not confident in approaching them. Through the director of the Museum of Tolerance, Liebe Geft, I became acquainted with Elana Samuels, the coordinator for *Shoah* survivor talks. Elana and I spoke about my project; I could tell that she was moved and that she could hear behind my loose book proposal the voice of compassion and truth. She said to me in her very direct but kind voice that I was "an angel sent from God, I can see it in your face" at which I blushed and was quite taken aback; as Muslims, we believe in angels, but human faces are never said to be angelic. This encounter was the most important one for this project; without Elana, I would neither have had the honor of interviewing the survivors nor, I think, of gaining their trust. Elana has been tremendously generous with her time to help a Muslim woman; I will be indebted to her forever.

My knowledge of how to interview someone was almost nil. I had no idea how this part of the project would flow— then, I thought of filming the interviews to give the reader visual material to accompany this journey of testimony. I was fortunate again to have a friend, Art Kellner, do the filming as a favor, and he has been invaluable to this process. Elana, Art, and my husband anchored me in my project and made things less daunting.

I selected interview subjects by location, age, gender, and, of course, willingness to talk. Most *Shoah* survivors are now elderly and ailing, so most of my interview subjects were contacted first by Elana, after which I got in touch with them to ask for an interview. The reader should know that, aside from the criteria mentioned here, interview subjects were picked randomly. There is no sequence to the interviews, which were simply planned around my then infant daughter's schedule. I also kept my questions to a minimum, and asked each survivor several of the same questions, including what they thought about Muslims; what, if any, contact they had ever had with Muslims; whether they thought the *Shoah* was a unique event; and what they thought of Israel/Palestine today. I also asked them what their message to Muslims would be.

I have transcribed all of the interviews here. They are written as spoken; English was, for these people, a second language. There were many moments of stress and sadness during the interviews; this is reflected in the language at times.

Interview One: Robert Clary

Robert Clary (born Robert Max Widerman; March 1, 1926) is a French-born American actor, published author, and lecturer, famous for his role in the sitcom *Hogan's Heroes* as Corporal LeBeau. As a Jew, he was deported to the Nazi concentration camp Buchenwald with 12 other members of his immediate family. Clary thought that he was the only survivor. When he returned to Paris after the war, he found out that some of his siblings had not been killed and had survived.

Per Robert's website, "In 1980, Robert felt the need to talk about his experience during the war; he began speaking publicly through the Simon Wiesenthal Center's nationally acclaimed outreach program. 'For 36 years, I kept these experiences during the war locked up inside myself. But those who are attempting to deny the Holocaust, my suffering, and the suffering of millions of others have forced me to speak out.'"[2]

He invited me to his home in Beverly Hills to interview him. I was very nervous and prepared the following questions for him after reading his autobiography, *From the Holocaust to Hogan's Heroes*, and watching a documentary on him and his visit to Buchenwald. My anxiety stemmed from a lack of experience as the interviewer, but more important, I was to meet, face to face, a survivor. I was not certain about what to expect or how to act, and at times my gaps of silence indicated the horror of the testimony and my own feelings as a witness. The nagging, overwhelming question that encompassed my mind was: how was it possible for any survivor to live a

---

2 Retrieved October 23, 2016 http://robertclary.com/bio.html

normal life after the trauma of the *Shoah*? How does one heal the wounds, the loss, and the trust in humanity? How can ordinariness be normal? These are some of the similar questions that my mother asked after my father passed away in 1991. Looking out of their high-rise building in Abu Dhabi, United Arab Emirates, she looked down at the cars and asked me with tears pleadingly: "How can people just go around living ordinary lives when my husband is dead?" I was speechless and held her in my arms for the rest of the night. The loss of my father and many loved ones is the deepest suffering that I have experienced, but to see a loved one murdered and dehumanized in front of one's eyes is a suffering that can be avoided and is unjust. I will never understand fully what this type of suffering is. . . .

For every interview, after doing some research on the survivors, I would come up with a set of seven or eight questions. At times, I was able to ask all the prepared questions, or divert from them and find a whole new story that I wanted to know more about. I wrote up the following for Robert Clary, although some questions came up in the course of the interview.

As I entered Robert's home, he was warm and happy to meet me, my husband, and Art, my documentarian. I brought with me some flowers, which he immediately put in a vase. He was delighted with the flowers; for me, it was a small gesture of gratitude for his time and generosity. He asked me to come in the kitchen, showed me his autobiography, and sat with me to get to know me. I noticed the paintings on his walls and remarked on them; he got up and took my husband and me on a tour of his paintings, which are marvelous—artwork in various media, including still life, people from the past, his family, and landscapes. In 1941, Clary's sister managed to put him in art school; now, he paints every day. As he walked me around, he told me that he had agreed to my interview only because he thought my project was worthy, and that he had stopped interviewing. I was very humbled by his comment and told him that I would not take much of his time. His home was bright, clean, and comfortable, in a posh neighborhood. He was warm but nervous, understandably, letting a complete stranger into his home. Clary is a funny man—he has a sense of humor that makes one feel light and comfortable. He is a short man with a thick French accent, who became successful and beloved in the United States as an actor. His clothes were neatly pressed and his tone was jumpy at times, but he expressed his own overall feeling about how tired he was of the world and its extremists. He had kept his silence for 36 years, then purged at our interview.

Clary is a positive man who decided that he wanted to look forward and live his life freely; he did, however, watch a documentary by Kitty Hart-Moxon, *The Return to Auschwitz,* which broke his silence. When he explained that he had been in the United States working in show business on *Hogan's Heroes,* never telling his story, it dawned on me that Robert was clearly trying to live his dream of being a performer, which he describes in the camps. He had a talent as a child, and, as he told me, he used it at Auschwitz and pursued his talent in the United States when he was liberated. As I sat and listened to Clary, I saw in his eyes a wit but also a sad twinkle that entranced me. At one point in the interview, I reacted with silence, and he asked me "Did I say anything wrong?" What caused my silence was how I was directly witnessing this man's life now and in the past in his home. He was a Jew and I a Muslim, facing one another, speechless. This was my first experience face to face, one on one with a *Shoah* survivor. In the past, I had visited museums where I had heard survivors speak publicly, but here was a man willing to share his story, his happiness, and his suffering with a Muslim woman. Robert began his interview by saying "This is the first and last one." He had not ever spoken with a Muslim, but as he said to me: "I've done too much of this, there are tapes, my book, and I am only doing this because I admire what you are doing." When Robert said this to me, I felt honored and admired the fact that he wanted to speak to a Muslim and give his energy to a complete stranger. Robert had invited a friend, Ari, who was in show business with him in the past. I understood why he would have wanted someone with him in his home as strangers walked through. Ari is a gentle man who had lived in Israel for several years. He said to me: "Aren't you afraid that Muslims will kill you when you testify to the *Shoah*?" I smiled at him, and said: "Muslims or others may want to silence me, but it's my own interpretation of Islam that compels me to speak out. ...."

Robert's interview was compelling and, again, he was funny, but at times a bit uncomfortable when we got to the topic of religion and belief. He clearly is not a believer nor does he understand, as he put it, "rules and laws of living by a prescribed God," and I agreed with him, but knew that his perception of religion was strictly encoded rather than spiritual, which

I deeply respect. I have to admit that disagreeing with him or wanting to explain to him how I was religious without encrypted laws came to my mind, but I refrained. This interview was not about me, but him. I tried to keep this in mind, but as I continued with Robert and subsequent interviewees, there were many moments when either I or the survivors disagreed with one another. This was not my intent nor did I expect this in an interview, but as I deeply reflect on these interviews, I think this was the first time that anyone had asked them about Islam, Muslims, Israel, and Palestine. It was also, for all of them, the first time that they had heard of concentration camps in places like Morocco and Algeria. I will share the transcription of the interview with Robert, which was filmed and recorded. It was conducted in January, 2008.

Describe your life briefly. Who are you? What do you do? What do you enjoy?

I am absolutely bored. [*chuckles*] My life these days … I'm going to be 84 very soon, I'm preoccupied with what I want to do. If I don't want to do something, I don't do it. I have good friends and I have wonderful children and grandchildren. I go to the gym, I paint and I watch TV, but not the things I used to watch years and years ago like comedy series or dramas, but I watch game shows so that I can be entertained … I used to say "don't you know that answer?" because I talk to the television constantly.

Tell me a little about your painting. I've been marveling at them this afternoon.

I've always had the facility since I was a little child, and it was 1941, when Jews could not be in show business anymore in France, and one of my sisters sent me to an art school to learn about posters, and that was great. When I came back from the camps, I always doodled and did things, and I took myself seriously in 1971. I started to paint. A very close friend of mine who is in show business, her name is Kate Ballot, when she saw the first painting said to me: "Don't stop!" I did listen to her. And that's what I do, and I try to do every day, even if my neck or my hands hurt, I still do it.

You mention 1941. What actually happened in 1941 in terms of sending ... ?

... I was born in Paris, France. I come from Polish parents who immigrated in 1923 to France, and I'm glad [and] grateful that they did that even though my father went to South America— Argentina—and could not make a living and he came back to France and he schlepped all his family to Paris. Only two were born in Paris, my sister [who] is one and a half years older than I am, and I was born in Paris. We had a great *great* childhood, not rich, not poor. My father worked constantly and I was the last child out of two marriages. My father was a religious man without being a fanatic. I don't like fanatics. We'll talk about that, people who don't see anything but their way of thinking, and they have no control or they don't want anybody else to be because they are not like that, I don't care for, that is including the Hasidic Jews, Muslims, anybody who is a fanatic, or Christians. I just don't like it.

So, what year did your family move to Paris?

My father moved in 1923, my sister was born in 1924, I was born in 1926. We stayed in France until we were deported in 1942 and, unfortunately, when the Germans occupied Paris, it was complete chaos. Suddenly the Jews were not allowed to do anything. They could not be in show business, they could not ride subways, and they could not go to schools anymore. It was just ... you had to wear a yellow star, you could not be in the streets after 8 p.m., there were curfews, otherwise you were arrested, and there was a curfew, and then they started to do round-ups. People who were not born in France, those were the first ones arrested.

So before the occupation?

Life was great.

Was there any feeling of ... antisemitism?

No, I'll tell you why, because I lived in an apartment building that was built by the Jewish Rothschilds. Right in the center of

Paris there are two islands, *l'Île de la Cité* and *l'Île San Nuit,* and she built this apartment for Jewish families that had lots of children that could not afford to pay rent, and it was absolutely remarkable, people would take care of us when we came back from school. Therefore, the whole building was with Jews, I really ... I used to go to a school in the Jewish ghetto until I was 12 years old, so I really didn't know anything about antisemitism and I really didn't care. I had a very nice childhood with lots of wonderful children. My father was a religious person but not fanatic, never forced [us] to do anything. The only thing he wanted from us was you do your Bar Mitvah, and then if you want to continue to be like me, fine if you don't. He said all this in Yiddish, he never spoke French. My mother had to speak French because she had to do laundry, and go to the market, not well, but she spoke French.

I wanted to ask you a little bit about your mother.

My mother, like all Jewish mothers, and I bet they all are like this, was fantastic ... my mother was remarkable. This is a woman who married my father, who had 5 children before with his first wife, who had died. She did not have a good life with her family, and she was 15 years younger than my father and she had 8 children with my father, and she raised his children and her children with love and affection. Nothing was too hard for her. She was the first to get up, see that we were fed, and last to go to bed, make sure we were happy. She was not educated and did not know how to read French but somehow ... [she] loved movies, oh she loved to go to movies, she loved it!

You talk about your mother spoiling you. ...

With great affection ... I talked about my parents even though when I was a child I was selfish, and at times I look at them and say, those are my parents? But great affection when I think about them ...

And she used to spoil you with ice cream?

Ahh ... she used to spoil me. I was the smallest and the last one. My father had so many daughters and when I was born he was

56 years old, and he probably did not have sex anymore with my mother; she said "Thank God."

You talk about your mother. Where was she from?

My mother was from Poland, a little town outside of Warsaw. So was my father, and they both eventually moved to Warsaw.

Ok, both together or before they met?

The trouble is, we really don't know—we children have a bad thing that we don't ask questions. We should know more about our family and they never told us, we really don't know, and if they did tell us we did not want to hear it. We were so involved with our own lives, who cares you know when you met your husband, we wanted to be with our peers. That's the sad part and I think it continues, I think that hasn't changed really.

So, Robert, I want to move to that day in September 1942, and I want you to briefly describe what happened on that very day in September.

We knew about roundups already, it was not something that was strange to us. But that night they came to arrest only this apartment house, September 23, 1942. You were given 10 minutes to grab your belongings and come downstairs, the buses are waiting for you.

So tell me about these roundups that you knew about before September ... What were these roundups about?

July 1942, they arrested most Polish people and, except for my sister Madeline and I, we were only the French people; nobody else was French except one brother who was in military service, who automatically became French. My sister Ellen, [who was] 18 or 19, was Polish at that time and they arrested her. I have another sister in Arkansas right now who was younger then Ellen, she used to work at a Jewish doctor's office and he knew that on July 16, 1942, they were going to arrest Polish Jews, so he told her to stay in his apartment: "You're not going home." When they came to arrest my sister Nikki and Ellen, my mother said I don't know where Nikki and Ellen were. "Here I am," Ellen said . . . what amazed me, sometimes I go through these things and it was just what can happen in life that you can really guide your own life. She asked the policeman, "Can I go downstairs and buy a newspaper?" And all she had to do was to go downstairs and never come back, but she came back and got arrested. She was sent to Drancy to a camp outside of Paris, and then sent to Auschwitz, I would say three weeks before we were arrested, and she died at Auschwitz.

Did you know anything about her being in Drancy or ... ?

I knew she was in Drancy, yes. First of all, if someone says to you that we knew about extermination camps, they lie. We did not know about concentration camps. They lie that we knew about extermination camps, this was kept a huge secret. Eventually, later on in life when you were in camps you would know about these things, but anybody that was arrested thought they were going to extermination [labor] camps, the ones that are coming back, are not telling the truth. I always say that when I talk, I say: if we knew that we were being sent to extermination camps, we would have done something about it. As long as we are going to die we might as well fight for it, and we would have done something in the beginning when we were arrested and not waited until they sent us to the gas chambers.

So, again I want to go back to the roundup in Drancy. There was a big camp and small camp?

No, Drancy was just one camp.

When Jews were being arrested ... were people aware of roundups?

They were sent to Drancy for a while, they did not know what they were going to do, they did not deport them ... the deportations started even if you were arrested, like in 1941 they were sent to a small village in the middle of France, or they went to Drancy. They were not sent to concentration camps until July 1942, when they started to deport all the Jews to concentration camps. We did not know, because I wrote a letter when I was in the train for three days and my mother told me to write a letter, which I did and I threw it in a slot. And I wrote in that letter, "We hope to join some of our sisters in the camp in Alsace-Lorraine." We had no idea where we were going.

One of the things that comes up in my conversations with my community—I belong to the community of Muslims or talk to Arabs around the world—how is it possible that so many people could be arrested and the message was not being told to one another, people who were in these towns, for example, in Paris, the non-Jews were not doing anything?

Very few non-Jews helped Jews, most people are antisemitic since the world has been the world—why, I don't know, why do they hate Jews, they've always done, why do the Muslims … they don't want to recognize Israel? I don't know why—why don't you wake up! They are human beings like you are … There are great Muslims that are sophisticated and wonderful people, same like Jews, some are sophisticated and others are not, not nice people, but antisemitism has always been terrible, not just in France but all over, that's why Hitler did what he did—he knew what he was doing when he said: "the Jews, they made this country worse in 1933 and we have to get rid of them," and everybody said: "Heil Hitler yes!" And in France, most people … were thrilled to see us leave, let's get rid of those Jewish bastards! That's all over, even though Holland was a little less antisemitic than most countries in Europe, but a lot of Jews were deported from Holland and died, the only country was Denmark.[3] You're going to wear the yellow star of David—the king said, I will wear one as well, he did not deport them, but he sent them back to Sweden. The only country.

---

3   Jews in Denmark were not required to wear a Jewish star, but they were persecuted and some did escape. This is a commonly held myth, not a historical fact. Please see "Denmark in the Holocaust," *Encyclopedia at USHMM*, accessed July 8, 2014, http://www.ushmm.org/information-tion/exhibitions/online-features/special-focus/rescue-of-the-jews-of-denmark.

I want us to move backward and forward in terms of memory and I know it took you a long time to talk about the Holocaust ... to talk about ...

I'll tell you why, I was very innocent, even though I knew where I was, I never really realized how terrible the situation was, as long as I was in camp. I was 16 years old, I was healthy, I could sing. He is small and cute, he sings, he is so sweet, he sings Jewish songs, let's give him a piece of extra bread—that was my life, even though I worked really hard—it was just that they are not going to do to me, they are not going to kill me. When I came back from the camp, I realized most of my family died. That God is not really something you should be proud of, that's my thinking. When I talk to kids who are religious, if you want to be that (religious) and can be a nice person when you're religious, fine, if you're going to be a hypocrite and believe there is a God there then don't come to me. I don't believe that there is something supreme. Try to be nice to other people and then that is your God. When I came back from the camp I was 19, and I was already in show business before that, and I said I'm alive. I still ha[d] some brothers and sisters and I told my brother that I wanted to be in show business. He wanted me to be a tailor. Are you crazy? "No," I told him, "I want to be in show business." I loved it and that's what I did—I did not want to talk about it. I told my sisters and brothers I don't want to talk about it, I spent three years in camp, I'm going to enjoy my life and I don't want to talk about it. I want to be selfish and do something I really want to do ... and try to live a happy life. Until I saw a documentary by Kitty Felix Hart—Kitty, who was at Auschwitz with her mother and survived and made a documentary in London, and with her son, who is a lawyer. And I watched this documentary with my wife, and at the end, she said one thing at the end that resonated with me: "[the reason] I'm doing this documentary is because 30 or 40 years from now most of us who are writers will be dead and anyone can say anything they want." Anyway, they're denying that it did happen and that's why I started doing it and I turned to my wife. I thought that it is enough water under the bridge and tried to open up. People were happy and they gave me all the access, and they were thrilled because by then I was already on *Hogan's Heroes*, that I was kind of not that a great star, but known, and they took advantage of this. They said that they would like me to go and talk to schools and I said fine, and I made up my mind that I had to do something. I could not be quiet anymore—I felt that I could not be silent because people were denying the Holocaust. It always bothered me that cemeteries were being desecrated, and I have attached on my arm (he shows me the numbers), I suffered for 31 months and you can't tell me that it didn't happen, and that's when I made up my mind to do it (talk in the open), and I did it and I devoted a lot of my life to going to high schools, junior high, colleges, universities, synagogues, and churches.

The reason I ask you this is that in my own research I've read Primo Levi and Richard Rubenstein discussing post-Holocaust life, and a French writer, Maurice Blanchot, who talks about writing about silence. In the 1970s and 80s, when witnesses gushed out and spoke up, what happened?

Few people wanted to talk about this. They were like many other survivors who didn't want to raise their children and bother them about their experiences. Somehow I admired Kitty Felix Hart and Simon Wiesenthal, who set an example. I was very selfish and wanted to focus on my business.

Okay, thank you—good. Robert, you know I am studying post-Holocaust studies and having the opportunity of going to Israel on my own in 1995 and being mentored by Jews and befriending Jews and spending time in Jewish communities and talking at temples, I would like to know how you understand Holocaust denial?

What bothers me is why you have to defend somebody, why can't it be just simple? Why can't we human beings just say we are a human being as much as I am here? I respect you as much as you want to be respected and one of the questions I want to bring up not just about Muslims and Arabs and for me personally is that during the Holocaust and during antisemitism, which has been there for thousands of years—we were hiding the human face of people.

Does the German have a human face, what do you mean?

Most of them were very happy to see us dead, I am not saying all of them were, but the second the war ended, I was there at the end of the war and there was a man who took over. He was an SS man, I don't know what his name was, but he was the only one whom I heard him say to me in the camp: "Don't lose faith, one of these days you may have a better laugh," and this was the only nice thing that I can remember the Nazis said. The SS people were cruel and they were terrible, but we were just vermin and that's all. We only existed because they needed people to work in the factory, otherwise all of us would have gone to the gas chambers—none of us would have been alive and been liberated.

How did you gain humanity and how did you let me, "Mona" [he could not pronounce my name, Mehnaz, so I used my nickname], in your house, for example?

I put a curtain in front of me that was the past, and I wanted to be in the future and I wanted to be recognized as a show business man and that was my goal; it was a selfish goal, but that's what it was. I learned a great deal from people on the same level because if you're all on the same level, some people are fantastic and most of them are not.

I have another question. I've read Robert Satloff's book and it's a book about talking to Muslims about the Holocaust and making it reality for the Muslim community. One of the things that he mentions in the book is the camps that existed in Morocco and also in Tunisia. Did you know anything about any of this?

I didn't know anything about this but it doesn't surprise me that it did happen. No, I did not know anything about it. I ask because I am always wondering what people think of places like

Morocco and Asia. As long as they are not bothered I think they don't care. If their family is not bothered, if they are not the victims of it, they don't care. It's part of the selfishness of human beings, because the Vichy government ... I think announced they were going to create these camps—yes.

One of those things is that many people helped Jews to escape but also became perpetrators under their governments. One of the things I'm trying to find out through people who were in the Holocaust is whether they heard anything about Muslims and Arabs having a hand in the Holocaust.

I can't really talk about all survivors of the Holocaust. I really was not close to Muslims before the war or after the war, I really was not, but to me a human being is a human being. I don't care what color you are or what you do in life as long as you're a decent person, that's enough for me as long as you don't want to kill me because I'm different from you. Today, Muslims and Arabs are going all over Europe, but the bad part of this is because when the Jews went to France they went to the Jewish ghetto because they do not speak the language, and that's probably what Muslims are doing when they go out of Europe. I hope they will teach the children not to be like that and they will assimilate and be kind to other people.

That's a struggle that Muslims are having, it is assimilation and how to incorporate religion into their life, and these questions are religious. Religion is good if it makes you a nice person and it is not good if you're a beneficent hypocrite but if you use religion as a crutch, then that's not good!

That was a big silence, did I say something terrible? We can talk about that later?

Looking back, do think that the *Shoah* could have been stopped if human beings were better informed?

No, people thought that Hitler was doing something terrible in Germany. Also a lot of Germans were killed by the bombs and he let the Germans to be killed.

Tell me your memory of Hitler.

I have no memory of Hitler. As a matter of fact, when I was a child I had one radio at home but my uncle and my father were listening to his speeches—and they understood most of what he was saying and they were screaming. I was 14 and as I listened to it, I did not know about Hitler, I did not know what he was doing, and I learned the hard way later. But not when I was a child, it was not my life so there was no conversation in the house either morning or evening, it was not part of my current situation. The issue was whether we could eat now, not what Hitler was doing.

Robert, in my book I argue that the Holocaust is truly unique or unprecedented; what do you think?

This is the first time that they just send people to gas chambers by the thousands. That it's the first time, that's why it is unique, but unfortunately they keep on repeating that there's always something in this world that's impossible. How to learn that this world is a very fragile piece of earth. You must remember the Armenian genocide as a matter [of] fact, yes, I was [a] reckless child and knew a friend who was raised as Armenian and he knew what I was talking about when I mentioned the Holocaust. He said, what about us Armenians? I said I know that, it's up to you to do something about it, and I guess he did. Okay, let's talk about this— how is the Jewish Holocaust truly unique is one of the arguments by many, and it's not unique because the overlooked massacres of Native Americans, Bosnians, but the reason I think it's unique [is] because it was genocide. At that time it was nothing like this could happen before, I guess the Armenian massacre, but they did not send them directly to the gas chambers to get rid of all the Christian population. That's what makes it unique, yes. For example, [there was] no real Armenian solution, it was more a genocide against Armenians within one singular country, a local genocide in which 2 million people died. The Jewish Holocaust—it was unprecedented because the murder of Jews went beyond the boundaries of Germany. Racism against the Jews was fed through generations.

Was the State of Israel created because of what happened to Jews during the Holocaust?

In Palestine there were always a lot of Jews—it is quite possible, but I can't really talk about it thoroughly. Yes, the State of Israel, because Jews lived everywhere else and this is, they believed, was their country, and this is where they wanted to live for the rest of their life—that's probably why it was created. I am not quite sure … so the argument on the other side is what about all the Palestinians? That's the problem, and here we go again, and I am very proud to be Jewish, but why do we not like each other, why can't we live together? As an impossible situation, I don't see how it's going to get better with the Palestinians.

One of the focuses and the main focus of my book as a Muslim woman is to give a testament to the Holocaust and to make people aware, especially Muslims and non-Muslims, that the Holocaust actually happened, it happened exactly how it's been reported …

I agree, but let's go back to the Muslim religion, to the fanatics as of the twenty-first century—come on now, why do you have a woman as a second-rate class citizen? The attacks are from but the fanatics—they use religion as a weapon at their women. How dare they would have you think they are, and that's the way they raise their children, and to me it's fanatics that are a problem.

I can't understand it, I don't understand it either as a Muslim because Islamic teachings are different and the call to do something different than what we are seeing. There's an inner conflict right now, but I would want to ask you as a Muslim woman, as I'm giving testimony to your witnessing of the Holocaust because I feel that this lesson has to be learned not just for Christians in the United States and Europe, but in Muslim countries and Islamic societies.

I want to use a French expression "*chapeau*" [*he made a gesture as if he were taking his hat off*]. I am taking my hat off for you because it is wonderful and remarkable for me what you are doing as a Muslim. I feel that we cannot bear injustices to anybody by your religious Muslims—yes, I believe you believe that some of the Muslims serve as good guys. But to make you a better person? I don't think that persons who make me a better person, that there is something there that is guiding me, so you go through life with rules that the Muslims are giving you. I'm not judging you know, I don't go with the rules because a lot of people do that, including the Jewish religion, is one of the problems we have in terms of the rules. If you read your Bible to take on a lot of our verses that have been directed against the Jews, but even the Jewish Bible! If you're a smart person then you can't believe everything that is written in the Bible, that God has written those lines.

Yes—one of the issues that we Muslims are struggling with is that people are literalist and they follow them literally. My question to you: if a Muslim or Arab is listening to you, what do you want to say to them?

I say get an education, learn about life, don't bring your sphere only, and don't only see yourself but [see] others. If you do that and you get educated—we would have a better chance in this world.

We ended our conversation here and stopped recording. I sat with Robert and he went on to ask me why I was doing this and why I needed to justify anything to my people. As I sat in his home and began to feel warmth as well as a certain resistance to religion and God, I failed to explain to him that my religion, Islam, was not all about rules, but was about justice. A justice that has fermented within me as a child, the sort of justice that recalls the story in the *Hadith*, which discusses two Muslim men, one who is a drinker and gambler and the other who is pious. They are both Muslims, but one follows the pillars of Islam while the other chooses to live his life of weak habits. However, when they both die, the man who followed the rules was sent to hell and the one who practiced bad habits was sent to heaven. So, people asked prophet Mohammad (PBUH), how could this be? How can it be that God could judge the pious so unworthy? The response from the prophet was that the pious man had no heart and sense of justice, while the other was full of love and justice. This story has stayed with me since I was a child, as the path of Islam, and the rancor of laws and regulations without commitment, have left me in a place where Islam feels freer and perhaps lighter.

Interview Two: Renee Firestone

I met Renee Firestone a few times. The first time, I saw her speak at the Museum of Tolerance in Los Angeles. The second time, we met in the Hertz Theater, where I interviewed her at the museum. The third time was when I picked her up to bring her to my home for a brunch after I had finished my interviews with all of the survivors. Renee is a gentle woman who lives with her daughter and son-in-law in a small, modest apartment. She asked me to enter her house and meet them, and I was very happy to greet all of them. The walls of her apartment were covered with photos of Bill Clinton and Elie Wiesel and accolades of her work as a survivor. She is an amazing woman who kept up the memory and motto of "never shall I forget" through education. Renee's blue eyes pierce me as I write this, and her smile that grew as she spoke of the most traumatic moments of her experiences in a calming manner haunts me. Her softness and melodic Hungarian-American accent that lilted at times when she described her sister's death reminded me of her as a young girl of 16. A beautiful, blonde, blue-eyed girl who was stopped by Dr. Josef Menegle as she proceeded to go to the camp with her sister, stopped and asked if she was indeed Jewish, had responded proudly: "Yes." Her account of the incident with Dr. Mengele confirmed how the Nazis were so convinced that Jews looked a certain way, that could not be blue-eyed and blonde. Face to face with Dr. Menegle, who instructed Dr. Hans Münch to conduct experiments on her sister, I imagined the pain and the regret that she may have felt. So many thoughts came to my mind as I sat with her and she spoke to me as a familiar stranger in the darkness of the theater, then later in the lightness of my home.

Renee Firestone describes herself as "a Holocaust survivor who travels the country telling audiences about her experiences in Auschwitz. She was the founding lecturer for the Simon Wiesenthal Center's Education Outreach

Program and is a presenter in the Tools for Tolerance Program. She appeared in the Academy Award-winning documentary *The Last Days*, narrating the story of her Holocaust experiences."[4]

Renee Firestone, born in Hungary in 1927, was in Auschwitz when she was 16 years old. Renee and I agreed to meet at the Museum of Tolerance for an interview; I told her that I would meet her in the main lobby. As I thought about meeting her, I wondered if she would recognize me. I knew what she looked like from the many documentaries I had seen of her and her life. As I waited in the lobby while Art set up the camera in the Hertz Theater, my mind started to wander in many directions, thinking of her life and her bathing suit, the bathing suit that she took with her when she and her family were rounded up by the Nazis in Hungary. Why her bathing suit? Why would anyone take a bathing suit, of all possessions, I wondered—then, I thought of my own memories as a child swimming with friends and family, and the joy of water and the freedom of swimming in water, where life seemed endless and mysterious. Perhaps as a young girl, she was thinking of swimming and did not know what was to come in the future. ... As I pondered the question of the bathing suit, Renee walked in wearing all gray with a slight smile that papered her face even as she spoke about the most difficult times of her life. Her smile curled through the pain and anguish of death and suffering. She shook my hand and I gave her a hug and thanked her for coming to see me and give her time; she replied that she was happy to meet me. She added that she was interested in my project and wanted to know more. I told her that I was simply giving the *Shoah* a Muslim voice and giving testimony. The impetus of my work was to give respect to millions of lives, and create a bridge of understanding between Jew and Muslim. She smiled again, and her blue eyes peered into mine with comfort and ease. We sat across from each other chatting about my interview with Robert Clary, who is a friend of hers. She seemed disappointed that he was no longer involved with speaking out, and asked me how the interview had gone. I told her how lovely and gracious he had been. She smiled again. Renee has a presence of a gentle woman, with a voice that is soft and melodic, which carries with it a melody of sadness and regret. At times, she showed strength in her voice when I asked her questions about the

---

4 "Bob Barboza & Renee Firestone in Los Angeles," accessed October 23, 2016 https://www.youtube.com/watch?v=uZ7MXsa6Mqg

ignorance in the world regarding the *Shoah*. She told me her story, and I listened to a woman's testimony for the first time as a woman. What struck me most was her description of her sister and her getting clearance, which meant that each prisoner/victim was doused with antiseptic, unclothed, and their heads were shaven. After they had been doused in antiseptic, they were made to stand outside in a line completely naked. She described this moment of horror to me as one of the most shameful moments of her life. As a Muslim woman, I was deeply engaged and could completely understand the horror that befell women who were forced to stand naked before men who screamed orders at them and sometimes had them standing in complete silence. Shame for one's naked body was a concept that she and I were both taught at home. She went on to state how, even in her household, the sisters were always asked to be modest when her father or brother were present, a common sign of respect in my own household. The following is the transcript for my interview with Renee, conducted June, 2007.

I just wanted to talk about you right now. What is your life like? How would you choose to describe yourself? What do you enjoy?

You should know that I am 86 years old, and I have been working at the Museum of Tolerance for 36 years and professionally I'm a retired fashion designer. I just finished my memoir and it is being edited right now. I came to this country after the Holocaust of course and I have been very fortunate, I had a wonderful life here. I have been successful in almost everything I've encountered. In the early years, when I was still in the fashion business, I worked a lot with the homeless because I found that I could not even imagine that in the United States there are homeless people. When I found out that it exists, I got involved. I also worked with drug addicts. I don't know if you know, but I worked with an organization that helps drug addicts for almost 10 years. While I was still in business, I came to work to the Simon Wiesenthal Center when it first came to Los Angeles in 1977, and from then my life started to change. I all of a sudden realized that we did not want to remember the Holocaust, did not want to speak about the Holocaust, and all of a sudden my consciousness was completely involved in starting to promote and speak out.

And this was in 1977?

Yes, '77. I was at the same time teaching at UCLA at a fashion class, and slowly I left my teaching business and later on I gave up my fashion business and got totally involved in Holocaust business. [*Laughing*]

What do you mean when you say "people were no longer remembering the Holocaust"?

First of all, when we came to the United States, people did not want to hear about the Holocaust. We were trying to figure out why. But I can understand; because the Jewish people felt guilty they did nothing, they really did nothing to save us in Europe.

You mean the Jews in America?

Yes. And then non-Jews after the war was over and they did not want to speak about the war and their sons and daughters were back. We, the survivors, needed to tell the story and we could not. We did not, just brought it up in a look and never spoke about it publicly, only amongst each other. That also was interesting. We never talked about the Holocaust itself, but we would say things like at a party, "Do you remember when we did not have a piece of bread?" We would be satisfied and we would look at all the tables full of food. We never talked about how my mother was murdered or my sister was murdered in the Holocaust. So when I finally started to work at the Museum of Tolerance, I started to remember things and started to talk about it. It's now full of people at this institution when it's not raining, the buses are all lined up with schoolchildren and we are very successful in creating awareness.

That is important. One of the things I wanted to ask you, Renee, a lot of literature and articles were written in the 1980s about the Holocaust because of the Holocaust denial all over in Europe and the United States. What was one of the compelling factors for a lot of survivors to speak in the 70s or 80s?

Not really, that became just part of the situation. We already knew we had to talk about the situation. In 1993, when *Schindler's*

List came out, that was actually the first time that the general public somehow started to acknowledge it, not even talk about it, but just acknowledge it. In that same year, Steven Spielberg opened the *Shoah* Foundation and we started to interview survivors. I must tell you how interesting that was, because Steven insisted we do not approach survivors but we advertise that we are going to interview these people, but they have to come to us. Well, many survivors at that time absolutely did not want to be interviewed. Some of their children used to call us and say: "I would love my parents to be interviewed but what can we do?" But today now when we stopped interviewing, now the survivors are coming to us and [ask if] we still do the interview. They wanted to leave it to their children and maybe now they are realizing about the deniers and they feel that the story should be told.

I want to go back to the time of the Holocaust in 1944, when you were taken to the camp with your family, and I believe you have a brother?

I have a brother, he died last year [2006]. My brother was not in camp, he was a partisan. After liberation, we settled in Prague because we found my father in Terezin—he died four months after liberation. And then we decided we wanted to leave Europe. I married a man who had already had a call (visa) number to come to the United States. But my brother did not, and he went to France and he was approached by the *Hagganah* (Jewish paramilitary organization)—they approached him and he went to Palestine to fight for the State of Israel, and he remained in Israel for 15 years, and then we brought his family here to the United States.

Let's go back to 1944 and let's just talk about what the image of the Jew was like.

Let me tell you first that I was raised in Czechoslovakia, which was a democratic country. I knew no antisemitism personally. I hadn't ever encountered anybody who would call me a Jew or something of that sort. I never encountered personal antisemitism. In 1939, when Hitler destroyed Czechoslovakia, our region was given to the Hungarians, so overnight we became Hungarians and at that point we realized what antisemitism was, because Hungary too in 1939 had similar laws as the Nuremberg Laws in Germany. So we were being stripped of our rights but still at home, in our own homes, my father's business was taken away from him, but we had a beautiful home there. My parents were not religious and I had a little sister who was four and a half years younger than me, and we had no idea at that time that concentration camps exist[ed]. In 1944, they were already in existence, because Birkenau [Auschwitz II] was built in 1942, but we had no idea what we were fearing. We knew that they were shooting Jews and [there were] massive graves, and so we thought if anything our president would give us up to Hitler, that that would be what would happen to us, that we would be taken to Poland and be shot.

Wasn't that terrifying enough?

Very—it was very terrifying. But in '44, the Russians were already pushing Hitler out of the Soviet Union and we already heard rumors that England and France were fighting on the western front. So we believed that Hungary and us were going to be the only ones to survive at home. This would never happen to us because our president always refused to give us up to Hitler. Jews were in forced labor camps in Hungary, and Horthy—our president—told Hitler that he needed his Jews to work for him and he referred to these forced labor camps. But later we found out that he was playing a game, because he figured out that if Hitler would win the war and wanted the Jews to be killed anyway because they were the closest Allies, Hitler and Hungary—why should he spend training and military escorts to send the Jews to ball, and he could just kill them, and he had already killed plenty of Jews in Hungary, but he figured that maybe if you could save some of the Jews he could convince the Allies that he was the only country in Europe that saved the Jews. This negotiation was going on in 1944 when Hitler's armies reached our borders, and that was the downfall. He invited our president to Berlin, where he kept him hostage while the German army just marched in, and at that point we knew we were doomed. But then again, we thought we would be taken to Poland to be shot dead. We did know about the extermination camps that existed in Poland.

I'm writing a book as a Muslim to give testimony to the Holocaust as a fact and a reality and I'm and discussing antisemitism, what that means and its history. However, one of the things that shocks me over and over again, although I'm not a survivor and I'm not Jewish, but as a human being, is that the gas chambers are still seen as a fabrication, somehow the chambers have been fabricated or the numbers and data have been fabricated. As difficult as it is to ask you this—can you perhaps shed light from your perspective?

Well . . . you know only a totally ignorant human being would say that it did not happen. The Germans acknowledged it, the Germans have records of everything. I've found in the archives of Germans the records of my sister, of how she was taken to a clinic and was experimented on. I spoke to the doctor who experimented on her and he tells me how they killed the victims afterward. I witnessed the fact that when the crematoriums were so full that they could not destroy people fast enough, they dug pits and they burned the bodies in the pits. There are witnesses . . . eyewitnesses that are still alive. But the fact is that the Germans acknowledge everything, they recorded everything. How much truth do people want when the perpetrators said "yes, we did it." Who is the person who would say "no, this is not true"? What an idiot would say this when the perpetrators said "yes, we did it." The records of my sister and how she was taken to a clinic and how she was murdered. I spoke to them afterward and it is the fact. They couldn't kill fast enough and have room to store the bodies so they dug up the pits everywhere. The technology companies have even paid for reparations.

I was invited to meet a group, they call themselves One by One (http://one-by-one.org/), I don't know if you've heard of them. I went to Berlin and spent, interestingly enough, time in a beautiful castle. We met about 15 people. For a period of one week, we stayed together every night and we sat in a circle and we talked. These are not [just] victims' children or Holocaust survivors and children of Holocaust survivors—they are the perpetrators' children too. Not just tell their stories, and we tell our stories, and then for you maybe this would be interesting to get in touch with them and sit in on one of these conversations. They are not denying it is a fact. How can somebody say it never happened?

Let's keep on this thought for a second ... while I have been writing this book, in one of my chapters I discussed Bosnia, and one of the novels discusses the rape camps where 500,000 women were raped. It's a novel, but it's fiction that is based on fact. She gives the women a number instead of a name because they don't have an identity and the way they were treated is similar to the way survivors of the Holocaust are seen, nameless. ... One of the things I'm trying to say in this book is that all genocides are unique, but I do argue that the Jewish Holocaust is unprecedented in many ways. Could you shed light on that please?

In many ways, the Holocaust is the first where there was technology involved, the culture, the religion, and nation was involved. That in itself is very unique. The genocides in Rwanda and Cambodia, we know that one group of people attacked another group of people with guns, machetes, barbarian murderers—but [in] the Holocaust, there were great minds who figured out how to do it so that there was no evidence. That's what they were hoping. They gassed the people, then they cremated [them] and the ashes were dispersed. That's what they were hoping for. That is the difference. The way it was perpetrated is too different than any other genocide where one group of people attacked another group of people. And also, the other groups of people may have had a way of defending themselves if there was a chance—we had no idea, there was no chance, we had absolutely no idea that we were going to be dropped at camps and be murdered.

One of the things that I read recently is Robert Satloff's book *Among the Righteous*, that he hopes through his writing of the book that perhaps Muslims and Arabs would recognize the Holocaust. One of the things he mentions is prisoner camps in Morocco and in Tunisia. One of the arguments I make is that the Final Solution is truly the Final Solution, where Jews are picked from every single part of the world, from Asia to Europe to Africa. Did you hear of any of these camps in the Arab or Muslim world?

Well, we knew that some of the Arab states when Hitler reached Africa, but also I heard, just recently saw a film, where they saved the Jews. I'm trying to remember the film. It was an amazing film.

Two more questions. How did you regroup in your life after being in Auschwitz? What was it in you as a human being that kept you going?

As far as the Holocaust goes, I'm not sure I've ever really recouped. Many Holocaust survivors did it and I don't think they want to talk about it—they don't talk about it and not even with their children, and I think I'm still upset with the Holocaust and I think I'm still upset because I see what is going on in the world. The upset I have is not so much about what happened to me but why is it happening still?

So what would you say to people, or especially to Muslims or Christians? People who are in conflict perpetuating the notion that we are different but we are other and we are less than one another?

That's what I do here and all kinds of people come here, and I'm sure Muslims come, I'm sure that Christians and atheists [come] and I'm sure Muslims come here to listen to survivors speak. That's what we talk about—we talk about how ridiculous it is for human beings to kill each other, especially when I don't understand the person, I think I know somebody who is evil and so I hate them because he's so evil. People just don't know one another and kill because they are told that this other person is evil or different.

But people you know … don't know we have no idea who they [are] and how we can hate to the point that you are willing to murder them? I work with this *Shoah* Foundation now, and at the present time we have just trained a lot of children from Cambodia who are going to interview survivors of Cambodia and it will be an archive like ours was. We also spoke to people from Rwanda, and they were going to interview their survivors. So we will know the differences of how these genocides are conducted. What started it and we really don't know what starts it.

There is a young girl. Now a young woman, maybe she was 14 years old when the genocide was going on, she wrote a book like Anne Frank's book and she came here many times; she spoke, you know about the freedom writers, right? She wrote with their freedom writers and I work with the freedom writers. Perhaps you should contact her. She was saved by some French and they found out about her book and they saved her and her family and brought her two friends.[5]

One of the things I mentioned in the book is: what can we take away in the name of religion? Stories of genocide are horrible and to deny one is like denying them all. We know that the Armenian genocide has been denied for almost a hundred years. Even today, the government of Turkey is hard pressed to admit the crimes of 1918 against the Armenians. The present government had nothing to do with it, but why are they still denying it?

Look at us and look at us, how did the United States treat the Native Americans? It keeps going on. …

My last comment, although I could talk to you forever—you are a complete pleasure. I just wanted to ask; how did you feel after liberation?

Oh God, everybody wants me to say "oh, it's wonderful," but when I was liberated my sister did not make it and I was almost sure that my mother did not make it. I was hoping that my father

---

5 Freedom Writers Foundation, accessed July 13, 2014, http://www.freedomwritersfoundation. org/our-story. This website explains the stories that Renee refers to and her own involvement with the group.

survived and that somehow, I was hoping, my brother survived. How am I going to find them? Here I am in a cotton dress on my body. If I leave the camp, where am I going to get my next meal? It was harder to find anyone and terrifying. Again, we were liberated by the Russians. Not like the Americans, they just told us go home. Here I was thinking that we were liberated by other Jewish Soviet officers, but when he liberated us he started to cry, saying that he was also a Jew but he never told the Russian army that he was Jewish because in Russia you cannot be a Jew, it's not good to be a Jew. Here I am, he tells me I am liberated, go home, I am free. I was thinking, what does it mean to be free? I'm returning into that same world that put me in here, good to be free there? Are they going to let me stay now? Where am I going? How might it be free? How might that ever forgive the world what happened? So as I say most people think liberation was a great thing, [but] it was horrible.

I don't have the right to forgive. God is the only [one] who can forgive. I have to remember and be aware all the time of what can happen. So you know I try to do my job like you are doing yours. And I see it is wonderful that you're doing this and I hope there will be many more like you.

This is something I said to Robert on Tuesday—he asked me if I was Muslim and if I believed in rules but I don't think Islam is about only rules … it's not really. I am doing this because of Islamic principles of justice. If you kill one person you murder humanity, to save one person you save all of humanity—we have the exact same belief as the Jews.

How is it that Osama bin Laden or these extremists are out to kill Jews?

I know the Qur'an is very similar to the Jewish Bible. We are cousins; that's another thing. We are really the same tribe, that's another thing I don't understand.

One of the things I wanted to talk about, but since we are not politicians, is about Israel and Palestine and what's happened there. Why is it that in Muslim countries or in the Arab world, there is no education about the Holocaust or other genocides? If you believe that Jews are controlling everything and America, what are you learning as a child? Not only that but they are giving weapons to children that are five years old. That's terrible.

Do you think the Holocaust is an excuse for the Jews to have Israel as a country and that the US and British felt guilty and this is what they did?

It was not only US and British, but also Russia also agreed, and all the other countries and the United States.

I want to ask you a question now—have you been threatened?

Yes. ... I have in both my community and outside of my community, and I spent a lot of time at synagogues showing the similarities between Islam and Judaism, talking about Moses, values, peace, and justice. Attempting to look at issues from the Jewish and Muslim perspective, we share some lovely stories and some tension. I find that people who are completely anti-religious don't understand the depth of these stories and are deeply skeptical.

I'm amazed at your bravery because I also speak to neo-Nazis and skinheads and know how it is to walk into a room with everything against you.

Unfortunately for me, even my family does not want me to bring up these questions. My mother is open, but the rest of the family is not. Perhaps they are scared for me . . . I'm from Pakistan and there's a lot of turmoil in my country. For example, there were some bombs in the city of Karachi when I left Pakistan the last time I visited—and you wouldn't believe what one of my family members said; he said that "the Jews are the ones that are creating the violence in Pakistan." My mother said to him, "Why didn't you talk to Mehnaz about it?" He said: "Because she is an American, she will never understand." I imagine I would have gotten upset with him and so he did not say anything to me.

This antisemitism is something that I am personally and emotionally aware of, this within my family. Brainwashing is the best tool for these people. This is what the Germans did, but you know this is very frightening for me, since we have a community of extremists in the Muslim community, even Jews. We have those fanatics. I'm terrified of fanatics. A friend of Robert Clary's asked me if I was scared to speak out against antisemitism. I said no, I'm not scared because I'm speaking the truth.

And I feel you have to do what you have to do.

I can't keep silent anymore, I have to speak out.

Yes, you're right, and we are very grateful to people like you who speak out.

Inshallah it will happen, there will be more awareness.

Interview Three: Elisabeth Mann

I called Elisabeth Mann in 2009 to ask her if I could interview her, and she said that she would be happy to talk to me but wanted to meet with me at first alone at the Museum of Tolerance. I was happy to meet with her and talk with her before I taped and transcribed her interview. I waited for her on the ground floor of the museum, experiencing a bit of nervousness and anxiety about the meeting. I was never sure why I felt this way, but I think I was uncertain of myself and why I was even involved in such a project. What was I, a Muslim, doing in this space? As I interviewed survivors, there was something that changed within me about my own understanding of the *Shoah*; it was not historical, but emotional. It is my belief that when one has a personal story or experience to share with another, it bears heavily on one's soul. I spent many sleepless nights thinking about the victims and the many scenes of terror that the survivors recounted as they sobbed, and I with them. Human, all too human; I kept my mind in balance by my deep belief in God and that there was hope for the survivors as they spoke with me and lived their own lives in the United States. How does one live after the suffering and torture of the *Shoah*? To know that your family was sent to the gas chambers, siblings killed and experimented on, and families torn apart. This haunted me night and day as I interviewed survivors and still maintain my relationships with them.

"Elisabeth Mann was born in Hungary. At the age of 18, she, along with her family, was sent to Auschwitz and spent 12 months there and in five other concentration camps. Her entire family was murdered by the Nazis. Elisabeth immigrated to the United States with her husband in 1955. She now resides in Los Angeles and is part of the Simon Wiesenthal Center's outreach program, where she lectures at the Museum of Tolerance to students of all ages about her experiences as a Holocaust survivor."[6] The following is the transcript for my interview with Elisabeth, conducted July, 2007.

Elisabeth, just tell me a bit about what you do with your time every day.

What I do is actually too hard to describe, because you can take it as if I don't do anything or you can understand it as I do too many things, because I do. Because I do take care of myself alone, and speak at the Temples or the Simon Wiesenthal Center, I also go to high schools, and universities to speak. I visit old people and try to help them; that's funny because I am also old, but they are old and sick and I try to help them with shopping for their groceries and that takes up all the time for me, and also taking care of my own existence.

That's quite a lot.

Yes, it is quite a lot, that's what I mean. But if you measure it with money, I don't earn any money so that's not a job actually.

Yes, but it is your life. So tell me about your painting—you paint, don't you?

Yes, I paint. I paint and joined a group of people and we paint for 3 hours. We paint whatever we want.

That's interesting, where you do that?

That is at the senior citizen center.

---

6 "Son of Nazi/SS Faces Holocaust Survivor from Auschwitz," accessed October 23, 2016, https://www.youtube.com/watch?v=7razS3QPDDg

Do you have a collection of art? What is your art about?

Yes I have. I've painted all kinds of things, like landscapes of the Holocaust, different kinds of paintings, and I enjoy it, but such is the difficulty because my hand shakes, and that's why I can't write, but that's what I do and I read a lot.

I'd love to see your artwork. Elisabeth, I watched a small documentary of you on the Internet of someone interviewing you ...

So you know more about me, more than I do ...

Perhaps ... but that is not ever possible. Your life is so interesting and rich. In this documentary, there's a part where I saw a painting that you painted of a rabbi when you were on the train—tell me about that.

I don't know if it was a rabbi, but it was an old man who had a beard and was on the train with me going from my city to Auschwitz. He was sitting in the cattle car with a gray shawl over his head and praying through the whole ride, and he had such a horrible expression of pain on his face that after liberation I painted his face because I could never forget that horrible pain and what he must have felt, and that is in my living room on the wall hanging.

Yes, I remember that from your clip of your work in your house. [I had the opportunity of seeing this piece when I went to pick up Elisabeth for a brunch at my home in July 2010].

[Elisabeth was neither happy about her work being on the Internet, *nor* was she pleased that her video and images were public domain].

Elisabeth, can you go back a little to the time that you left your city in Hungary, and I know you and I have spoken before this interview. When I left you that evening when we spoke last, I felt very emotional for a few days because I think since we had been alone, there was something very intimate about our conversation.

The one experience I kept thinking about is the train ride from your town to Auschwitz. Could you talk a little bit more about that?

Usually I tell you the truth and tell you about the train ride because the rest of the concentration camp experience was somehow the same for everybody, it was just life, but nothing was so horrible for me than the train ride from my city. Definitely there was the horror after they take you from your home and put you in a situation like this ... if you want me to tell you I will. I don't know where to start.

How about when you were in the city?

Previously ... happened tremendous shocks to our family because my brother was in the Russian front as a Jewish soldier, fighting for Hungary and Germany because they were allies. We had very bad news about my brother, and my second sister was captured by the Germans when they occupied Hungary [on] March 19, 1944. Three days after their occupation started in Hungary, she was taken off the train in Budapest and disappeared—my parents did not know what happened to her, so my mother became very ill and we were all tremendously worried about her, and then everything fell apart. Everything started to happen, every day new laws came into effect into our city from the Germans. We had to have curfews; we could not even leave the house just for two hours in the beginning to go out for your errands. And when we did, I was the one to go to the closest store with my ration coupon and then the shopkeeper would see my yellow star, which was a brand-new law that we had to wear, and he would refuse to give me anything because I was a Jew, so I did not get any food or any milk or bread or anything, and anybody could beat me up and rob me and there was no protection. Every single day, two SS men came to the house[s] where Jews lived and knocked on the doors, beating them half dead to make them confess where the fortune of the Jews was. We had no fortune, but that did not stop them. When they came to my house I was the one who opened the door and they [told] me that they have come for my father, but

I told him that he was already taken away, and they would come back again and again and I would repeat [that] they already took them away. Finally they left. I shut the door and stepped into the hall and I collapsed because two yards away from the front door I was hiding my father. My father could not go to the backyard after that because if one of our neighbors would have seen him they would've called the German authorities right away and they would have taken him away.

Why would the neighbors tell on him?

Because they are wonderful Hungarians [*sarcastically*] and have no backbone. When the Germans came, they were dancing and playing music; when the Russians came, they were playing and dancing and playing the music. In my opinion they have no character, they are nothing. I don't say every single soul of them, but I am sure there are some Hungarians that are decent, but generally the whole country they did not say one single word against what was happening. They were coming to the house and taking stuff from us and they were serving the Germans, and so what else can you say? The best friends and neighbors that we trusted, that we thought we were good friends, proved it . . . you know.

Weren't you surprised? Was that shocking?

That was very shocking. It's still painful for me. Unbelievable that my father never wanted to believe it because it was another tragedy for my father, who fought in the First World War for Hungary and Germany, because it was the same king he went to war [for] when the Germans started the war. My father was decorated with medals, he was so sure that he was Hungarian, and he was fighting for years and [in] the war in 1941 my brother was drafted into the Army and also fought for Hungary, and was sent to the Russian front. So, how would you believe that this country would abandon you, put you out to the so-called enemy, even if they didn't think they were enemies? So then the occupation started; everything was ordered by Hitler, my sister was captured, my mother became ill, and then every day two SS men were coming and taking everything from Jewish homes, whatever was movable—carpets, pictures, or whatever they wanted to have. So you had one way to see how Hungary stood up for you, but they did not. Then came the law that all the Jews have to go to the ghetto. I don't know if you know what a ghetto is …

Yes, I have visited two former ghettos in Italy, one in Venice and one in Rome.

It doesn't matter if you have no idea what it means to live in the ghetto because a home owned by a Jew was named: the ghetto. Especially in my city because there were very few Jews compared to the rest of the population. These homes consisted of one bedroom, one kitchen, and the one closet that was used as a refrigerator and then the backyard. That was what all the houses were like. Maybe some were bigger. Fifty people were ordered into these houses, 50 Jews in every house. The second you were sent to these ghettos you are locked in. In the windows in the small houses were dark and so you could not look out in the streets. People were so many in these houses, like sardines, there was not enough space …

How long were you in the ghetto?

I don't remember, but you could not go out to buy groceries and there was no water in the faucet. There was only one toilet for 50 people. In there were small babies and children and sick people out of the hospital because they were Jewish and the ghetto and so on, it's indescribable, and it started to get really hot and warm. Every single day two SS men came into the ghetto, I don't know what they wanted to see, with guns and pistol and looking at us and telling us horrible stories. Then when they left, many people committed suicide … and the people who died were in the backyard and a strong hot sun, and that's how we lived there, but we were still together. Before we left our home, they told us we could take everything we wanted to from our house to the ghetto, whatever we could carry in our two hands. How much can you carry in your two hands, and what shall you carry? Your baby or your mother's hand or blankets or what? And that was far from each other when we had to walk. They came in every day and I still remember that we had 10 minutes to pack everything—whatever we wanted to take with us, because we were going to be relocated, we will be somewhere where we will have plenty of space and we will be together with our family—we did not understand what they were saying.

They said that there would be plenty of space?

Yes, they were talking about Auschwitz and the gas chamber, but we had no idea what they were talking about. We had not heard of Auschwitz. So everybody grabs what they could in 10 minutes, and blankets for their babies, and walked to the railroad station. As we walked through the city, people were standing and watching as the good Hungarians and some people were asking for water because it was hot and nobody gave us a drop of water. When we came to the railroad station, we were beaten very badly to hurry up to the cattle car. There were no benches, there were no blankets, there were no windows in this cattle car, just four sides. [In] one little corner was a small opening, there was a little wire and you could cover it with your two hands. That was horrible, but we finally made it inside the cattle car, sat on our folded legs because of the lack of space, touching each other's arms. We had no sanitary facilities, we had no water, and no food. They shut the door. All the babies were screaming and crying, scared in the darkness. All the sick people were begging us for water and medication and we had nothing to offer and that's the way we were travelling. After two days, all the babies died. They never stopped crying. All the children died, all the sick people died, all the rest of the people were sick. Some of them became crazy, banged the side of the wall at the cattle cars, stopped the car. I wanted to get off and I didn't want to go anywhere. The whole cattle car was in such a chaos that every one of them was sick, the heat, the stench, and the noise was deafening. I looked around at the people's heads and I thought to myself: My God, hell cannot be so bad [as] that cattle car ride. And that's the way we traveled for four and a half days.

And the cattle car finally stopped. I was so happy when I did not hear the wheel hitting the tracks that sounded like drums through the whole trip, but my happiness flew away the second the door opened up and I looked out and it was pitch dark flames, torture everywhere, and two SS men were standing by the cattle car looking at us. I felt like a butcher's knife was cutting into me. On each side of the SS men there was standing a German shepherd dog with two tremendous, big bulging eyes, hanging out from his mouth a giant tongue between sharp teeth, whose body looked like a big balloon blown up tremendously and shaking—it was terrifying. Later on I learned that these dogs are trained to jump on you and beat you [to] a pulp. At that moment I felt the terror in them. On the other SS man's side was standing two young men wearing blue and white striped uniforms. They were at the (so-called) zone to come on [a] special unit. As I later found out, they were Jewish guards chosen by the SS men for that horrible job, but they had to do it. To take care of us, take us through hell, and they were forbidden to answer any questions. Everybody in the train started to scream and cry and ask them where are we? And what will happen to us? And they were repeating again, again, and again: Jump! I don't know if you ever sat on your legs for four and a half days. We could not move and even today I cannot remember how I got off the train and how did my father manage to do that, but we two held onto my mother and my little brother. I was holding my mother's and little brother's hand so desperately and my father was holding them on the other side, making a very tight ring out of us four so that the people coming out of the train should not push us apart. Everybody was screaming for each other and everybody tried to stay together.

I looked around, it was pitch dark and [there were] torturous flames and SS men, German shepherds wherever I looked, and then the loudspeaker came on and told us to separate. The men should form one group and the women and children form a second one. Unfortunately, my little brother turned to me and asked me "where do I belong? To the men or to the women?" *You see* he had a dilemma because in the Jewish religion when you turn 13 years old, if you are a boy you have to study the Bible in previous years, but on your thirteenth birthday you have to go to the temple and before God you have to make an oath that from that moment on you are responsible for everything, for what you are doing, because you count as a man.

And that is the Bar Mitzvah, right?

And my little brother just five months earlier became Bar Mitzvah, became 13 years old, and he did not know where he belongs. And because he was so sick during the four and a half days travel, I told him to go with my mother because mothers are the people who take care of sick children. You see, I did not know. That was my advice. *I killed my brother* because all the mothers and all the children were taken to the gas chambers right away. [*Crying*] . . . I did not know that. . .

How would you know, Elisabeth?

[*Still crying*]

I could never forgive myself.

Would you like to take a break?

[*She goes on. . .*]

With my mother and my little brother I looked onto my father. My father, who is six feet and two inches tall, very strong man, he always knew what to do in any situation before, but now he was standing there so miserable and the tears were running all over his face. You see I never saw my father like that before, so I didn't even think a second where I was . . . I didn't even know where I was and I started to run to him. I wanted to tell him something, I don't know what . . . maybe I just wanted to hug him. An SS man stepped forward and started to beat me and screamed at me. "Stop!" You see, I did not know that I had arrived in Auschwitz-Birkenau, to the deadliest concentration camp ever built on this earth for only one reason, to kill people. I did not know that a Jew was not allowed to talk to a German. So I started to talk to him and beg him, "Please let me go to my father just for a minute, half a minute, a second, please!" He never ever stopped the beating. I felt the blood running all over my face and back and he was furious and screaming at me: "Go back where you belong! You will be together with your father tomorrow midmorning." I don't know what happened to me, I could not move, I was just standing there and receiving all the beating. I don't know how long I was standing there. Finally, I realized I had no choice and when I did go back where my mother and little brother stood before, they were nowhere—they disappeared. [*Crying*]

Then I felt a tremendous push behind my back. I did not even hear the loudspeaker telling us previously to us that single women should step out and form a third group when I was busy with my father. This third group was going forward and I was pushed by it and there was standing a young SS man as we were getting in line. His name was Dr. Joseph Mengele. When I came face to face with him, he was smiling, he was just moving people left and right. He was saying left, where people were taken directly to the gas chamber, and right, you are saved as long as you are young and strong and could work for their German Reich. When you are no good for work anymore they sent you to the gas chambers or shot [you] to death at the spot. Or you just stop dead from work and exhaustion and hunger. From the atrocities. We did not know anything about it. When we came to the right side, they told us to take off all of our clothes that were sent to the German people ... then we were pushed into a tremendous drum that was a shower. And then they threw us some clothes. I got a man's shirt and it was very cold, it was 11 o'clock at night. I tried to cover myself. That was the only clothing I ever got, no button on the shirt. I was so ashamed, so humiliated [that] I was naked. I looked around at every one of them and they were bald. I did not realize I looked the same way. As we were waiting for everybody to come out from the bath a tremendous fire caught our eyes, shaped like a Christmas tree, and little babies' faces looked back at us from the flames, little arms and legs hanging out like Christmas decorations, and then the girls started to scream around me, "Look, they are burning us alive." And that was the first time that I realized that horrible stench in the air was the burning of the human flesh. Finally, the SS men came and jumped over the burning bodies and the girls started to scream: where are her parents? He was laughing and said: "Look up, what do you see?" And we saw big heavy smoke hovering in the sky, and he said, "There are your parents and there is where you are going. The only way out from here for you is through the chimney."

Elisabeth, I want to change gears a bit at this point … one of the things I'm finding when I do my research on the Holocaust is that some people are denying the Holocaust; they are putting in question the numbers of people who died, but especially denying the existence of the gas chamber and claiming that somehow the gas chamber was never employed during the Holocaust. How can people say that?

Idiots! They must be idiots because there is so much proof, there are facts, you know, about how there were gas chambers! And people are alive like I am! Some of us that are still alive are ones who lived through the Holocaust, and I'm convinced that God just let us live just to be a witness to tell to the world what happened to us. These people are rotten, mean, and bloodsuckers, that's what I can tell you. No word can describe them, and before my eyes they are not even human beings.

This is interesting to me, especially in light of the Holocaust, because if you look at other genocides, like Cambodia, Bosnia, Rwanda, and what happened recently in Darfur in 2010, why is it that people are denying specifically the Jewish Holocaust? What you think is happening in terms of this?

Listen, if I knew the answer, this would solve the problem, because why, I have no clue, because the Jews have suffered thousands and thousands of years innocently. And one of the Popes after 2000 years finally came out and told the world that it was not the Jews who killed Christ but the Romans, but 2000 years in many different countries, many different cities, even Hungarian Jews were killed and burned alive because they said that we were Christ killers. So how can you say we need proof, that is what I cannot understand.

My book is about giving testimony as a Muslim to the Jewish Holocaust, and I also discuss how the Holocaust is unprecedented compared to other genocides. But one thing I keep coming across is that the Jewish Holocaust somehow gave Jews the right to create a state called Israel, it gave Jews more power and image of victimization, gave Jews more access to things of power. The Holocaust happened but it was not the fault of the world, but the responsibility of Germans. What do you think? Whose fault is it?

Why is it that we are struggling with Jews as victims even today, after the establishment of the State of Israel? I have no idea, but I'll tell you something, I'm picky about some things. Maybe you can try and understand that I came out of the concentration camp, but I never felt I wanted revenge on Germans, Hungarians, or the Poles, or anyone. I believe in every kind of people and nation. There are many good people. I don't generalize *you know* because during the war, even some German people were good and not all were killers. I cannot understand *you know* there might be somebody that can understand better than I can do … but I cannot understand what God's motive might have been? Why did he choose the chosen people to suffer and then let them survive? You know 6 billion people live on earth and Jews are not even one fourth of that percent of the whole world, and they are always accused that they want to be the leaders of the world. That is ridiculous and abnormal! And one thing I want to tell you, something completely out of the picture, that Hungary was always an antisemitic country. I do [not] know if you know anything about Captain Alfred Dreyfus (the lone Jewish officer on the French General staff who was falsely accused of passing secrets to Germany)? After that, Dreyfus was sent to Devil's Island. … I don't know why I brought it up, but it was an example I wanted to share with you. Always the Jews were tried and nobody wanted to defend them except one French writer by the end [Emile Zola, *J'accuse*]. Oh my God, I got so excited. Each time I get very angry and very excited when we talk about this! I find it very cruel that the world wants to accuse the Jews for everything, but the Jews are the one people who will always come back and forgive and help the other people.

How would you talk to people like Muslims in my community, or Arabs or even non-Muslims today that are very upset with the State of Israel and what the Israel Defense Forces (IDF) policies are doing and resettling Palestinian people? And some people are comparing what Israel is doing to Palestinians to genocide. For example, the Palestinians are not given any land, water, or access to economy and travel. How do you respond to this? Israel is a land for the secular, but it's mostly for Jews at the same time. How do people understand that today? This is the only country that Jews have had a right to?

You know, this is so hard to put into words so that you should not get hurt, because that is not my intention to hurt you. Israel was called Palestine but it was always Jewish land. There were always Jewish people living there, they were suppressed you know by the history and by all the people and powers who came and went. They were the only ones who always tried to help the people … I think, I think it was Lebanon or whichever country that had a gate which was called "Good Hope" that Jews lived by, and the Lebanese people had all kinds of sicknesses and these people came to the gate and the Jewish doctors treated them. Even though the head of the country was suppressing the Jewish people, I want to point out that the Jews are always willing to help and help people. You know when Israel finally came into existence, I don't have to tell you, people came out of concentration camps, lost their whole families and they had nowhere to go . . . okay, no family … no home … nothing, gone home to Palestine. Because in Hungary, at least when I was young, we saw that in Hungary, they had written on fences and walls, "Go to Palestine!" This was before Hitler.

But when the Jews wanted to go to Palestine they were stopped by others, and even the British captured their boats, and these people had nothing and had lost their family and homes ... they just wanted to come to Palestine to live. They never could because 100 million Arabs attacked them the second the country was declared to be Israel. And they had to fight ever since, and even then, even then, fighting on the border, they've built a country on the sand. Just think about that. Many Arabs want to come back to the country from where they left and want to be there because they have decent living and the Jews gave them every chance, every right, but there is still putting four-year-old children and 24-year-old women to blow up the Jews. You explain to me why? And Israel was willing to give back to the country and even when they paid with their own young man's blood they did give back, but that is not enough. [The] Syrian President openly says that they want to push Israel into the Mediterranean. Why? Why? Instead of reaching out and being in peace, that's what I wanted to know. Why ... why do they say that?

I think, Elisabeth, this is one of the goals of my book, is to talk about these positions . . .

I'm sorry, I don't want to misguide you; I want you to understand my side of the story.

That's okay. I want you to talk to me about your side of the story.

I want you to understand that Israel takes it harder and wants to be stronger than the Palestinians because they want to protect themselves every step for self-protection. I would not go to Auschwitz, I would not go to the train, and I would not have gone through what I've been through. I would fight, and that's what you would do. That's why I bring this up and that's the reaction.

Since we're talking about Israel and Palestine, do you know many Muslims, have you talked to many Muslims?

No. I wish I had. As a matter, if you're Muslim you are human being. I love people. When I speak I never think this is a Catholic or Protestant. I just see a human being, and that's the way I was raised actually. My mother never made any difference, but their friends did. And returning to asking me a question and how come we were punished and killed so much, I have no answer.

I now know what I wanted to tell you. Hungary thinks they have big giant heroes, they think they are courageous, they are everything, and they are not that! I just tell you they have never ever had a Nobel Prize in this country (Hungary), but the first Nobel Prize they got a few years ago—a Jew who was put into the concentration camp [as an] inmate got this. They sent a 15-year-old boy to the concentration camp and he survived and came back to Hungary and wrote a book, and he got the Nobel Prize for Hungary (Imre Kertész, 2002). Now that's the irony of the Jewish people that shows you. I'm sorry that I've gone away from what you asked.

Not at all, this is fantastic. I have one more question, just a general broad question: If there are a lot of Muslims watching us and reading my book . . . I consider you my friend, not just a survivor. But I want you to be part of the voice of this book and project. That's why you are with me and helping me. What is your main message to Muslims and Arabs about the Holocaust that you want to give to people? Someday you might go to a mosque with me and talk to people; what message would you give?

What I would like to say to the Muslim and Arab people about the Holocaust is that I don't know if anyone completely understands what happened there. What happened was true up to 100 percent. But why it happened, and the whole world was watching and did not do anything, I do not understand. One thing I understand is that we should all like each other, talk to each other, and try to understand each other. Because I believe you tell me what you think and I tell you what I think and by the end we shake hands and still like each other. That's what I would like to say about the Holocaust.

That's perfect. But at the same time, Elisabeth, you are a Jew and I am a Muslim, you're from Hungary and American, I'm from Pakistan and American. How would we ever meet?

That's my message. ...

So we have to go out and meet with another?

Let us understand each other when you tell me that is red and I think that is green. Let me come to explain why it's green for me and why it's red for you. Then we will understand each other. You know what the two color mixes—red and green together and that makes a human being. You have the right to think and believe that you have the responsibility to accept the other one, that's my opinion. I don't know, maybe I'm old and maybe you don't understand me at all!

I do understand, I think ... maybe I'm too young and you don't think I understand at all! [*laughing*]

It's hard to explain that I sincerely believe that maybe 1000 years it will take, but people will be liking each other in the whole globe if they allowed themselves to like each other . . . *you know* if I don't say I hate you, but I say let's talk and maybe I like you. You don't have to be in love with everybody. You have that responsibility in my opinion to give a chance to each other. Now you really got crazy with me ...

Crazy with you, why?

Because I said things that you don't understand?

But Elisabeth, I must ask these questions that people, and I want people to hear what your perspective is about the Holocaust, Israel, and about being a Jew, a Hungarian Jew. These are important things that many people want to understand. The world is not listening all the time, and if I can bring this to a global audience this will be very special. You don't need to talk to more Jews. I don't need to talk to more Muslims. I need to talk to

more Jews and Christians and people who are different. This will create the dialogue. Even if you and I do not agree, we can try and understand each other. For me as a Muslim, when I say to Jews I accept the State of Israel, it's a big thing for people because still in the Arab world they have not accepted the state.

I think the biggest thing is that people are not informed.

Just, for example, today I learned that an Iranian person is writing a book about the history of the Holocaust. For example, the prior president of Iran has said that the Holocaust never really happened, has also held a conference on the denial of the Holocaust. Many people are not taught Holocaust studies in schools, especially in places like Iran and Pakistan. I was different, I was interested in Judaism and I have the capacity to have Jewish friends and admire Judaism, and that's why I am on this path. I was very fortunate to have access to all this knowledge.

Mehnaz, I'm not sure how much [you] understood about what I said. I'm serious. I got too excited and have said more than I should have said. My point is again and again I wish—people would say let's sit down and talk to each other before they would condemn each other. What do I think?

[*Both laughing*]

I am not attacking you, I am just telling you that I may have surprised you that I got so excited. . . .

No, I'm not surprised. I think it's very good . . . this is wonderful.

I just want to make sure you got my point.

Yes, I got your point. I think you were clear, and I love the excitement! We will keep talking about this, this is not the end of my friendship with you and maybe you will have dinner with us?

Whenever, I would be honored to have dinner with you!

Elisabeth and I saw one another a couple more times, and we maintained our friendship for a couple of years. I have lost touch with her since I moved from Los Angeles. I think about her often, and as I read and hear her interview I can hear her Hungarian accent and see her smile, as she and I would at times mishear, misunderstand, and even challenge one another. I had two other interviews with survivors that I did not transcribe due to permission rights, but they are mentioned in my book as people who did give me their time, home, and personal nuances. I was honored as a complete stranger, a Muslim, to enter the depths of their experiences and to be able to listen, laugh, cry, and touch one another in such a way. My interviews were challenging at times because I was still, even as open as I can be, "protective" of Islam and nuanced about Israel.

Chapter Five

Is Islam Antisemitic?
No

What is the nature of antisemitism among Muslims? How and when did it enter the forefront of Muslim nations and politics? What is Zionism and how is it seen by Jews? Is Zionism misunderstood by Muslims? These are a few questions on which I hope to shed some light. Islamic extremists target Jews—why? What is underlying this ideology and how is this connected to Zionism? These questions are the basis for a lot of other questions and misunderstandings that stem from both Jews and Muslims. However, the ideological point of many extremists is to align Jews with crusaders or even, as I mentioned before, the colonialists. As Tibi points out:

> Two themes in Islamist ideology underlie its version of antisem-
> itism. The first is the Islamist idea of "Islam under siege," and
> the second is the idea of a competition over the political order of
> the world. Islamists propagate the idea of a besieged Islam facing a
> *mu'amarah* (conspiracy) devised by *al-yahud wa al-salibiyun* (Jews
> and crusaders), and they tamper with historical facts to present the
> Jews as the instigators of the Crusades, when in fact the Jews were
> victims of the invaders as much as Muslims were.[1]

In Germany and France, where there were almost no Muslims during the Crusades, Jews were victims. Bassam Tibi, one of the scholars of Islam,

---

1 Bassam Tibi, *Islamism and Islam* (New Haven: Yale University Press, 2012), 58.

discusses how one can see Islamism as an issue in the global context in today's world. He makes a distinction in his work between Islamism and Islam and supports the school of enlightened Muslim thought in media and education. He goes on to say:

> The second theme relates to the Islamist ideology of creating a new political order throughout the world. Islamists see themselves as competing against the Jews, who they believe are equally poised to shape the world order around Jewish beliefs. These two strains of thought unite to create the vision of "cosmic, satanic evil that underlies Islamist anti-Semitism."[2]

Tibi's assertion is that Islamists or extremists believe that Jews want to control and shape the world order, and this strain of thought justifies the internal conflict within the extremist view. Extremists have been influenced by the old European antisemitism that was virulently disseminated in a major part of the Muslim Arab-African regions between 1933 and 1945. Antisemitism is not an Islamic creation; rather, its roots, in terms of religion, can be traced to Christianity.

Antisemitism has been a long-standing problem—it even preceded the accusation that Jews were Christ killers, progressing to charges of blood libel—that Jews slaughter innocent Christian children to make their Passover matzohs (unleavened bread), the claim that Jews were controllers of the world, and finally, the persecution of Jews and the *Shoah*. The negative perception of Jews has transferred to many parts of the Muslim world, especially Islamists,[3] who engage in deceitful ideologies of Jewish-driven agendas. Jews historically were persecuted by Christians since the accusation of Christ killers was conceived at the time of the crucifixion of Christ. It is believed that the rabbis at this time persecuted Christ, and the story of blood libels begins with the discovery of a child's body. Christians believed that

---

2 Ibid., 59.

3 I refer to "Islamism" as Muslims who are political and religious in their view of the world. Islamists are those that will take Islamic tradition into the political arena using Islam as their tradition, but with no regard to humanism. For a lengthier discussion, see Tibi, *Islamism and Islam*, and for debates on this term, see Richard Martin and Abbas Barzegar, *Islamism: Contested Perspectives on Political Islam* (Stanford: Stanford University Press, 2010).

Jesus was crucified with the help of Jews, and this accusation stood within the church. The blood libel, a myth propagated by Christians, was popular in accusing the Jews of sacrificing a Christian child. This myth of the blood libel has also been transported to the Muslim world, beginning in 1840 with the Damascas Affair.

> Most commonly it is a boy, though occasionally it could be more than one child, or a girl. The body might be discovered in a sewer drainage ditch, perhaps in the woods. The setting is generally a medieval town. The child is a Christian and he is young. He could be two years old or twelve. He might have been missing for days, or just overnight. But the body's discovery is only the beginning. What happens afterward hinges on religious hostility and the misunderstandings it has often fed between Christian and Jewish communities. The Jews are accused of murdering the boy for obscure ritual purposes, and what begins as dark rumor might end in anti-Jewish violence, or perhaps a judicial inquiry involving the possibility of torture and execution. The many endings of this story, and the precise details of its escalation, vary over the course of the European Middle Ages, but its beginning becomes stereotyped in a script that plays out many times, extending beyond the medieval period to be revived as needed through the nineteenth and twentieth centuries. Once taken up for propaganda purposes by Hitler's Nazi regime, the notorious claim that Jews murder children has even now been reanimated in antisemitic discourse in the Muslim world.[4]

The myth may make some theological sense in Christianity, where the sacrifice of the innocent Jesus atoned for the sins of humanity and where the sacrifice is reenacted in the mass; where, through the Christian belief in transubstantiation, the wine that is consecrated and consumed becomes the "blood of Christ" and the wafer the "body of Christ." Yet there is no comparable murder at the core doctrine in Islam, no such doctrine is found

---

4 Hannah Johnson, *Blood Libel: The Ritual Murder Accusation at the Limit of Jewish History* (Ann Arbor, MI: University of Michigan Press, 2012), 1.

in Islam, and thus a migration into the Islamic world, which had always come through Christianity, is theologically alien. However, a case of the blood libel occurred in 1840 in Damascus, but this was not a religious doctrine or Islamic prescription, and was reported by a Christian who accused thirteen Jews in the murder of a Christian monk similar to the blood libel.[5]

In many of my classes, when I teach Judaism or the *Shoah*, my Catholic students have questions about the crucifixion of Jesus of Nazareth and the culpability of Jews in killing him. They ask me: Why and how was he killed? Why do Jews not accept Christ as a Savior? These myths are still being taught in some parochial schools in the Northeast of the United States. Many students still have the old stereotypes of Jews being in control of the government, rich Jews, stingy Jews, and the myth that the population of Jews has somehow grown miraculously to be about 1 billion, versus their actual number of 15 million. I am still faced with questions by my students after taking them for Shabbat service: "Why didn't they look like Jews?" These stereotypes are not restricted to Catholics by any means, but the audacious fact that this type of thinking is still being taught in some churches and schools is disconcerting. Similarly, Muslim schools and countries omit the history of the Jews, Israel, and the *Shoah*. The omissions in schools of Jewish history increase the vulnerability of Jews and Israel to vilification.

Teaching the history of antisemitism from Europe to the Muslim world is a daunting task that brings up questions of not only Christian scripture but Muslim scripture. As I attempt to deconstruct the stereotypes of Jews, I simultaneously find that the negative images of Muslims are also exaggerated. As I discuss the negative images of Jews in Europe, I also discuss the persistence of these images today, especially in Muslim communities. The misunderstanding of Judaism and Islam is a complex and historical issue. Having to teach about negative and false images of Jews and Muslims is equally interesting and complex. I must make parallels and distinctions that are difficult for students to decipher. I make comparisons of the images of

---

5 For more discussion on this, see the following books and references: Jonathan Frankel, *The Damascus Affair: "Ritual Murder," Politics, and the Jews in 1840* (Cambridge: Cambridge University Press, 1997); Mohammad A. Baymeh, *Intellectuals and Civil Society in the Middle East: Liberalism, Modernity and Political Discourse* (London: I. B. Tauris Co. Ltd., 2012), 77.

Jews and Muslims, and demonstrate the differences of the two groups in Europe and the United States. Antisemitism and anti-Muslim sentiment are on the rise between the two groups; Jews and Muslims are fairly antagonistic to one another as global conflicts continue. Relativizing the *Shoah* as I have discussed or denying it with the hatred of Zionism and Israel is a common conversation. On November 22, 2013, in Miami, Florida, I sat with five respectful and professional Muslim men who are considered leaders in the Muslim-American communities in Miami, a city with a large Jewish population. I was there to have a conversation about Muslim perceptions of Jews and how we can change our view taking into consideration principles of Islam. I was asked the same questions about Jews: "Don't you think they control political events? Aren't they all rich?" Some of them had never asked those questions openly and I was there as a Muslim to respond. This intimate conversation is one of several I have had about the perception of Jews in Muslim communities, whether they are Turkish, Indian, Pakistani, Saudi, Iraqi, or others. We discussed the *Shoah*, and I was instantly confronted with questions about other genocides in comparison. This discussion was immensely important in many ways: first, it allowed male Muslim leaders to listen to a Muslim woman speak about Jews; second, it offered a reference point in the religion when they go out in the community; and finally, they were open to pursuing the deepening of Jewish–Muslim relations. One of the many issues that were brought up was the concern about the Qur'anic scriptures that discuss Jews or Christians in a negative light. The Qur'an has many such verses that can be negative and ambiguous for the non-Muslim and especially Muslims. "Is the Qur'an antisemitic?" I am asked frequently in Jewish community centers and synagogues. My response is clearly: no. Such a response requires that we understand the Qur'an and the representations of Jews in the Islamic tradition.

The verses that are in question in the Qur'an are those that have various meanings in the context that they were revealed to prophet Mohammad (PBUH), revelations that had meaning in a holistic context rather than isolating the verses from that context to cause the reader to see them as a negative impulse within Islam. For example, the crucial verse (5:51): "O ye who believe! Take not the Jews and the Christians for your friends: They are but friend to each other. And he amongst you that turns to them is of them.

Verily Allah guideth not a people unjust." This verse can be distressing and complex, but given that God has declared that Jews and Christians are recipients of divine revelation and guidance, it is far-fetched to see Jews or Christians as the opposite of friends. In the Qur'an, Muslims are told that the earlier revelations (Jewish and Christian) were from God and that these revelations are sacred and the historical underpinnings of the Islamic revelation. Furthermore, the term *awliya*, here translated into "friend," means "those that have authority" rather than friend. In other words, one who can be a friend but not one who has authority on your own belief in Islam.

> The verse in question suggests that while Jews and Christians have been given divine guidance, some of them have erred. How is one to distinguish between those Jews and Christians who are righteous and those who are errant? Muslims have their own scripture to guide them. Therefore for Muslims to take as authorities in matters of morality those Jews and Christians who are errant in their understanding of their scripture is to lead these Muslims toward tyranny. At this point, they are in danger of losing God's guidance, for, as is quoted in Qur'an 6:144, "Allah guideth not people who do wrong."[6]

The danger of interpreting sacred text literally is where the problems arise. It is not that one changes the content of revelation. In Islam, one must take the full or overall meanings. I have been accused of sounding defensive when I have attempted to explain certain terms and contextualize certain verses in the Qur'an. The revelation that came to Muslims from the prophet Mohammad (PBUH) was a complicated one that had to grapple with other prophets, cultures, and revelations that were deemed as plausible, sacred, and truthful as the Qur'an. If Muslims would hear or read this message in the Qur'an, it would be an easier task to redefine Islam and pluralism. Each religious tradition of the great monotheistic faiths has sacred texts that disparage the other, but also those that embrace the other as a fellow creature or the benevolent God; the task involved in religious pluralism is emphasizing the latter and

---

6 Zayn Kassam, "Whom May I Kill?," in *Encountering the Stranger: A Jewish, Christian, Muslim Trialogue*, ed. Leonard Grob and John K. Roth (Seattle, WA: University of Washington Press, 2012), 27–28.

reinterpreting the former. However, Islamists/extremists have created a new agenda for Muslims that beg for explanations and reinterpretations.

For example, another common question and verse from the *Hadith* (tradition of the Prophet) that is brought up numerous times is the following;

> The Last Hour would not come unless the Muslims will fight against the Jews. The Jews would hide themselves behind a stone or a tree and a stone or a tree would say: "Muslim, or the servant of Allah, there is a Jew behind me; come and kill him"; but the tree Gharqad would not say, for it is the tree of the Jews.[7]

The next one states:

> So that Jews will hide behind trees and the tree will say "Muslim! The servant of Allah! Come, look there is a Jew behind me, he hid here, behind me, come and punish him." Only the tree Gharqad will not say, for it is the tree of the Jews.[8]

When I am giving talks on Islam, these lines are flung at me as evidence of how many Muslims could indeed believe that Jews are the enemy. MEMRI (The Middle East Media Research Institute) TV[9] has been in the forefront of recording such violent verses and edits against Jews on Arab, Asian, and African Muslim TV around the world. Embarrassing to Muslims, it is a fact that needs to be reckoned with in terms of the message of Islam to these many communities. The *Hadith* accounts just presented have been used too frequently by Islamist groups to reiterate a political agenda, such as: "this *Hadith* prescribes the 'killing of the Jew' as a 'religious obligation' and thus includes the most extreme implication for making antisemitism a religious obligation. When applied to Israel, it implies eradication."[10]

---

7 Imam Muslim, *Sahih Muslim, Kitab al-Fitan wa Ashrat as-Sa'ah*, Book 41, 6985, trans. Abdul Hamid Siddiqui, accessed June 2, 2016, http://www.theonlyquran.com/hadith/Sahih-Muslim/?volume=41.

8 *Kitab al-Fitan*, hadith 2239.

9 Middle East Media Research Institute TV Monitor Project, accessed May 3, 2016, http://www.memritv.org/. Also, see my own speech at Capitol Hill, sponsored by the Tom Lantos Foundation and MEMRI, at http://www.youtube.com/watch?v=2et3NJtN2Zs.

10 Tibi, *Islamism and Islam*, 77.

It is a challenge to teach scripture that at certain points discusses mistrusting and/or killing Jews. Interpretation of such verses by extremists have challenged my own thinking about sacred text and how to receive revelation as a Muslim. For me, the approach cannot be literal, but has to be contextual and encompass the many positive meanings that the religion upholds to procure an understanding from a humanitarian point of view. It is significant to take a deeper look at how we interpret religion for our daily lives in matters of ethics and social life versus a political order. "What is the difference between Islamism and Islam? The essential answer is that Islamism is about political order, not faith. Nonetheless, Islamism is not *mere* politics but religionized politics."[11] And all religionized politics pose a danger, for in politics there must always be the possibility of compromise, whereas faith is most often non-negotiable, absolute.

For millennia, some interpretations of the New Testament were highly antisemitic, focusing on the role of Jews in the murder of Jesus. The Vatican Council II has reinterpreted and changed these views to include Jews and Muslims favorably in their use of the language and beliefs in *Nostra Aetate*.[12] However, one still finds antisemitic leanings within Christian communities. For example, I was talking with Gisela Glaser, survivor of Auschwitz, who recounted a story about her Polish caretaker when she was bedridden. She had a stroke and needed assistance, so her daughter hired a Polish nurse, thinking it might comfort her to speak in her native language in 2010. When Gisela came down from her bed, she was confronted by this nurse, who told her: "You should all have been killed, you murdered my Christ." The remnants of such antisemitism stem from a long belief in Jews being a cult and a group who killed Christ.

The New Testament and the writings of the Church Fathers often refer to Jews and Judaism contemptuously. Jews were depicted as an accursed people, children of the Devil collectively condemned

---

11 Ibid., 1.
12 "Declaration of the Church to Non-Christian Religions Nostra Aetate Proclaimed by His Holiness Pope Paul VI on October 28, 1965," The Holy See, Daily Bulletin of the Holy See Press Office, accessed November 15, 2013, http://www.vatican.va/archive/hist_councils/ii_vatican_council/documents/vat-ii_decl_19651028_nostra-aetate_en.html.

by God to suffer for rejecting and killing Christ. This degrading image of the Jew was propagated over the centuries in numerous books, sermons, works of art, and folklore, and vestiges endure into the twenty-first century. Two thousand years of Christian anti-Judaism, which taught that Judaism was without value and that Jews were wicked, hardened Christians' hearts against Jews. Why should Christians feel compassion for a people cursed by God and fated to be victims for their unpardonable sin of rejecting Jesus? This mind-set, deeply embedded in the Christian outlook, helps to explain why so many people were receptive to anti-Jewish propaganda, were willing to participate in genocide, or were indifferent to Jewish suffering.[13]

This same type of propaganda has been used in the Arab/Muslim world to unite different Muslim groups with diverse and often conflicting agendas. There is an Islamized antisemitism and a nationalist secular Arab antisemitism. These two emerged from different places and times, but are now fused by extremists as a mutual weapon of hatred toward Jews. Raul Hilberg, Walter Laqueur, Bernard Lewis, Bassam Tibi, and many Arab, Muslim, and Jewish thinkers have shed light on antisemitism and anti-Muslim sentiment. Antisemitism was coined by Europeans specifically to describe Jews, just as the term "orientalism" came to refer to Arabs through a European colonial framework. The neologism "Islamophobia" has been used in both political and scholarly works to describe fear and hatred of Muslims. As I discuss antisemitism and anti-Muslim sentiment, or as referred to as Islamophobia in my work, classes, and lectures, I am always faced with criticism for using the term "antisemitism" to refer to Jews and not Arabs. I am not in any way saying that Arabs are not Semitic peoples, but for the purposes of my own work, I will refer to (Jewish) antisemitism and (Muslim) anti-Muslim sentiment. I find the term Islamophobia to be a psychological term that describes a phobia and makes it less erudite.

These two terms can be both frustrating and confusing. Antisemitism, for much of its history a largely European Christian prejudice, has seeped

13 Frederick M. Schweitzer, *Anti-Semitism: Myth and Hate from Antiquity to the Present* (Gordonsville, VA: Palgrave Macmillan, 2005), 25.

into and infused the Arab/Muslim imagination. Anti-Muslim sentiment, or what is called Islamophobia (a relatively a new term stemming from Orientalism), is now current in Jewish and Christian communities. The new antisemitism between Jews and Muslims post-1948 (founding of the state of Israel) has exacerbated modern tensions between Jews and Muslims. And even though antisemitism may be said to have a much longer documented history than what we currently call Islamophobia, much of the antisemitism now common in the Arab world is itself recent: "The pan-Arab nationalists learned antisemitism in many ways from the Nazis ... Nazis were ... active in spreading antisemitic propaganda in the Middle East, when Nazi Germany occupied France ... the Vichy regime opened such French colonies as Syria to Nazi penetration, giving a great boost to the propaganda of Nazi doctrines into the Arab world."[14]

We have further complicated the language of prejudice by adding terms like "Muslim extremism/terrorism" and "Jewish Zionists." These are part of a very polemical and polarized language that engages the extremes in both communities. These polarizations and partitions create a problem and strengthen the mistrust between Jew and Muslim, while the histories of Jews and Muslims living together, working together, and learning from one another before the founding of Israel has been forgotten. It is almost as if we have lost some hundreds of years of interaction, exchange, and contact.

The most notable experience that we have lost in regard to Jewish history is where and how Jews lived culturally and religiously in many parts of the world before the *Shoah* and establishment of the state of Israel. Who are the Jews? Where and how did they live? These questions have been repressed within the Muslim community, and it is important to decipher the diversity in the community of Jews just as it is significant to understand Muslims and their histories without the stereotype of the extremist. Jews who lived in Arab countries and flourished among Muslims—sharing food, language, music, and some religious rituals—are long gone and forgotten today.

As the twentieth century is about to begin there are more than 11 million Jews in the world, of whom nearly 7 million live in Eastern Europe, 2 million live in Central and Western Europe, and 1.5

---

14 Tibi, *Islamism and Islam*, 61.

million live in North America. Asian, North African, and Middle Eastern Jewry total less than one million.[15]

These facts are quite unknown and incomprehensible to Muslims, since their population was spread out around the world and was much larger in the twentieth century as well as today. Jews comprised then and continue to comprise now the smallest populations as an Abrahamic faith worldwide.

What do Jews and Muslims have in common, and what can they discover from one another in terms of their past, present, and future? How do Jews and Muslims share analogous struggles in Europe and North America? These questions have haunted me for several years, and I have had the opportunity to discuss some of these questions at synagogues, illustrating the countless resemblances that Jews and Muslims share. As so many *Shoah* survivors have reiterated that no one should forget the atrocity of the *Shoah*, I take from their lessons and explore the historical identity of Jews as an example for Muslims.

Today, Muslims struggle to assimilate into European and North American society. Some of the negative reactions to Muslims living in western societies have been highlighted by the banning of minarets in Switzerland, the banning of the *niqab* (a garment that covers the body as well as the face) in France, the controversy over the Cordoba House in New York City,[16] and the resistance to building mosques across the United States and Europe. Many seemingly anti-Muslim laws are based on democratic and secular laws that seek to encourage Muslims to assimilate, asking Muslims to shed some of their core cultural symbols. Other laws are based on intolerance of Muslims' visibility as a religious group that symbolizes extremism in the eyes of many westerners. In the media, Islam is often relegated to "Islamo-fascism," akin to Nazism, based on the extremist ideology of some Muslims who seek to live out Islamic ways through the imposition of *Sharia* law within western democracies. Muslims in Europe are the largest minority. They have been

---

15 Shavit, *My Promised Land*, 51.
16 The Cordoba House, or Park 51, controversy was over the building of an Islamic center in New York City near the 9/11 site. This was and has been referred to as the Ground Zero Mosque, creating friction between Muslim-Americans and other Americans. See Margot Adler, "Islamic Center Near Ground Zero Sparks Anger," *NPR*, accessed July 15, 2010, http://www.npr.org/templates/story/story.php?storyId=128544392.

living in Europe from as early as the 1950s, when they were invited into several countries as guest laborers. Sander Gilman, in *Multiculturalism and the Jews*, discusses the many intersections between Jews and Muslims, but also the differences:

> Now I know that there are also vast differences between Jews in the 18th and 19th centuries and Muslims today. There are simply many more Muslims today in Western Europe than there were Jews in the earlier period. The Jews historically never formed more than 1 percent of the population of any Western European nation. Muslim populations form a considerable minority today. While there is no Western European city with a Muslim majority, many recent news stories predict that Marseilles or Rotterdam will be the first European city ... [to] have one. In France today there are 600,000 Jews while there are between 5 and 6 million Muslims, who make up about 10 percent of the population. In Germany, with a tiny Jewish population of slightly over 100,000, almost 4 percent of the population is Muslim (totaling more than 3 million people). In Britain about 2.5 percent of the total population (1.48 million people) is Muslim. Demographics (and birthrate) aside, there are salient differences in the experiences of the Jews and Muslims in the past and today. The Jews had no national "homeland"—indeed were so defined as nomads or a pariah people (Max Weber and Hannah Arendt). They lived only in the *Golus*, the Diaspora and seemed thus inherently different from any other people in Western Europe (except perhaps the Roma). Most Muslims in the West come out of a national tradition often formed by colonialism in which their homelands had long histories disturbed but not destroyed by colonial rule. And last but not least, the Israel-Palestinian conflict over the past century (well before the creation of the state of Israel), the establishment of a Jewish homeland as well as the Holocaust seems to place the two groups—at least in the consciousness of the West—into two antagonistic camps.

The state of Muslims today in Europe has been a longstanding issue of assimilation, and how many Muslims emigrated from poor

Asian, African countries to make a life in Europe. In the 1950s Britain, Germany and France had a dire need for labor and allowed an influx of Muslim immigrants to enter their borders.[17]

Even though Jews and Muslims have both, at different times, struggled to assimilate into European culture, the two groups are poised to be antagonistic due to historical and social differences. How do Jews and Muslims living in the West talk to one another? How will the relationship of Jews and Muslims in Europe and the United States evolve?

As I reflect on this, the first fear I have is of Muslim extremists, who have in a sense taken their ideologies to a point of no return, while their actions have compromised Muslims who would like to preserve their diverse heritage and live alongside other cultures and religions in other nations. Extremists who espouse hatred toward Jews through broadcasts at Muslim centers, on TV, and at mosques frighten me. I watch in horror as the Jew becomes yet again a scapegoat and the "other" who must be hated in order to bring Muslims together under one umbrella. It is hatred of Jews that Muslims need to sustain the extremist fight against the West.

The relationship between Jews and Muslims has disintegrated due to political upheaval in Israel and the Middle East and the disturbing ploy of seeing Jews as "other" within the Muslim world. For example, the book *The Protocols of the Elders of Zion*, an influential hoax outlining a Jewish conspiracy to control the world, has seen a boost in popularity and, more important, a boost in credibility in recent times. In virtually every language in which the *Protocols* have been published, a book refuting the *Protocols* has also been published, except for Arabic.

The *Protocols* have become a Bible of anti-Zionism, adopted by enemies of the state of Israel to justify their attempts to destroy it. Thirty years ago, the King of Saudi Arabia distributed copies of the *Protocols* to foreign guests. Eight years ago they were cited as authoritative by leaders of HAMAS and other Muslim extremists,

---

17   Sander Gilman, *Multiculturalism and the Jews* (New York: Routledge, 2006), 8.

who claimed: "Their [i.e., Zionists'] scheme has been laid out in the *Protocols*."[18]

However, there is also propaganda on the other side aimed at stirring up anti-Muslim sentiment not in just one area of the world, but everywhere. Recently, I came across a group called the Quilliam Foundation, based in the United Kingdom and headed by Majid Nawaz, a British-Pakistani activist who was the leader of Islamist Hizb ut-Tahrir (UT) and spent four years in Egyptian prison for being an Islamist. "In his writings, he contends that Islamism is about not theology but a political ideology. Islamists politicize Islam in 'their desire for an Islamic state.'"[19] The Quilliam Foundation is a think tank against terrorism and *Jihadi* thinking that eschews hatred and ignorance in the Muslim world. The organization tries to differentiate between extremism and terrorism. They state on their website:

> For five years now Quilliam has been warning of the dangers of Islamist extremism and the symbiotic relationship it has with far-right extremism, in which each party's actions serve to provoke and fuel the actions of the other. To mitigate this cycle of hatred and intolerance, the UK requires a comprehensive and consistent strategy, which does not focus on merely reacting to terrorist incidents but is able to keep the rising threat of extremism at bay across the country.[20]

Muslims and Jews have faced similar issues and challenges that focus on their faith and are relayed through images in the media and theologically rooted rivalry. Perhaps this perception is perpetuated by geopolitics, but also the juxtaposition of images of Jews and of Muslims engaging in extremist activities within their larger communities. Israel can only be one excuse for Muslims. So how can Jews and Muslims communicate in a world that operates under the common misperceptions and acknowledges that there are serious issues that Muslims have to confront in order to hold a dialogue?

---

18 Jacobs and Weitzman, *Dismantling the Big Lie: The Protocols of the Elders of Zion*, 8.
19 Tibi, *Islamism and Islam*, 32.
20 The Quilliam Foundation, accessed November 18, 2013, http://www.quilliamfoundation.org/.

When I watch the news and see so many items about killing, bombing, torture, stoning, or beheading committed by Muslims or in the Muslim world, I am appalled, and confronted by my own faith in Islam. How can I be so strong in faith and see so many of my fellow Muslims take a path to destruction and, ultimately, self-destruction? There are times when, as an instructor in religious studies, I question what religion is. As I tell my students, religion is not something that walks to you through a door; it's not a thing in itself that reassures you, or compels you to believe, but it is you who chooses to be what you are ethically and morally. This consists not just of the rituals of fasting, prayer, and making Hajj, but is also a matter of ordinary life in which decisions are made regarding friends, family, work, and people of other faiths. It is the duty of every Muslim to conduct a self-critical inquiry into the depths of meaning of the Qur'an.

Jews and Muslims have lived together since the inception of Islam, whether under Christian or Muslim empires.[21] They have shared many experiences, and do to this day. Although many people believe in the myth that Jews and Muslims have been at war for years, the current conflict—having begun in 1948 with the founding of the state of Israel—is a relatively new one, with repercussions that affect Jewish–Muslim relations worldwide. For example, Gunther Jikeli did an analysis of the opinions of 117 young Muslim men living in Europe and their view on Jews. He found that their views were based on inaccurate historical information and that they did not have any concrete historical or religious foundation for their perception of Jews. The following is a very good example of the historical perspective on hostility between Jews and Muslims:

> Participants often referred to "Islamic History" or conflicts between Muhammad and his adherents, on one side, and Jewish tribes, on the other, to illustrate and justify enmity against Jews. Muslims' hostilities against Jews today were framed as revenge against Jews for things "they" did in the past or part of an ongoing historical struggle with the Jews. However, references to Islamic history were usually vague. The following French interviewee's argument is a

---

21 For a full and fair discussion of Jews living in Christian and Islamic empires, see Cohen, *Under Crescent and Cross: The Jews in the Middle Ages.*

good example. He was not sure what particular kind of mischief Jews made, but he was adamant that "the Jews" are to blame, that what they did is unforgivable, and that their actions resulted in eternal animosity between Muslims and Jews:

Sabri: We have a history with them[...], I don't know much about this kind of thing, but, a long time ago I think that they were the ones who betrayed the prophet [. . .]. After that, the Muslims, there's a story like that. Yeah, that's one thing. It's something that makes it worth going to war with them.

Interviewer: Even now?

Sabri: No, not war but to … well, we don't talk to them [...]. It's not a war between Arabs and Jews, and I don't know … it's about religion [...]. They did something that wasn't good, and it's unpardonable [...]. It's weird, you can't [. . .] everyone is obsessed about it [...]. They have to change it. It's the Jews who did something bad [...]. It's too late. It was at the beginning, [and] given the way they are. . . .

Sabri emphasized that the enmity was related to religion and mentioned an alleged betrayal of Muhammad by the "Jews," but he was uncertain about this event.[22]

Although Jikeli does his research in Europe, the themes are similar in many of the Muslim communities worldwide, including the United States: the betrayal of Mohammad, mistrust of Jews, Israeli–Palestinian conflict, Jews dispelling Muslims from their lands, Jews being materialistic, and many other themes. Examples of negative views that I have witnessed also come from educated Muslims, who believe in the control and power of Jews and the ability to align with the western powers against Muslims.

Furthermore, many scholars have done comparative work on Jews and Muslims from a theological and textual point of view, but there are very few who have read the contemporary situation in a comparative light. I see Muslims and Jews as being in similar predicaments of fear and prejudice, but with different histories and identities. What Muslims and Jews share are not only their religious roots and common notions of God, but, more important, the

---

22 Gunther Jikeli, *European Muslim Antisemitism: Why Young Urban Males Say They Don't Like Jews* (Bloomington, IN: Indiana University Press, 2015), 135–36.

struggle for identity in Western European and North American democratic society. I want to suggest that Jews and Muslims can share their challenges of living in the Diaspora today, and I want to explore how Muslims might combat some of the recent negative images of Islam, as Jews did with Judaism 200 years ago. One of the major differences between the images of Islam and Judaism is clear: antisemitism is something that has existed for centuries, and it is seeing a renewed currency worldwide, founded entirely in lies and myths; Islamophobia, on the other hand, is grounded in part in the many terrorist acts committed by Muslims against the West, against Israel, and against one another, including the most notorious of all: 9/11. Let me say clearly that Muslims who proclaim themselves as acting as agents of God in committing such acts have not only hijacked the name of Islam, but created a new form of Islam that is largely defensive and polemical. This is a distinct difference between the states of Islam and Judaism today.

I hope to bring the image of Jew and Muslim/Arab to a revealing reality that I think has not been discussed much in the media or by scholars. As a Muslim, when I read about Jews and their historical image, I am reminded of images of Islam and Muslims throughout history. When Muslims were in power, from the Mughal (1526–1857) to Saffavid (1501–1736) to Ottoman (1299–1923) Empire, many European writers and artists depicted the Muslim world as mysterious, sensual, and deviant. Jews and Muslims alike were often depicted and described as childlike and "dark." As Edward Said has pointed out, one has only to look at the paintings of Eugene Delacroix and Jean-Léon Gérôme to see the oriental image of Muslims. Said's *Orientalism*[23] defined this concept, and posited that Europeans not only described but prescribed the history of the Arabs/Muslims through their own observations and perspectives, depicting them as "other" through the European lens. Similarly, Ivan Davidson and Derek J. Penslar have pointed out in their book *Orientalism and the Jews*:

> The central fact around which all debate on orientalism and the Jews must be formed is that, historically, Jews have been seen in the western world variably and often concurrently as occidental and oriental.

---

23 Edward Said, *Orientalism* (New York: Vintage Books, 1978).

Even today, when the Jews are generally thought of as a western people, that perception is nuanced by the fact that, unlike any genuinely western state, Israel (home not only to Jews of European background but also to millions of oriental Jews and Arabs) is located in the East. More importantly, the Jews are identified, both by themselves and by the Western world, with the ancient Israelites who established themselves, and the monotheistic tradition, in that same oriental location. It is this latter identification with the biblical lands that allowed Jews to be seen during the centuries as an oriental people, a perception challenged only in the twentieth century as the result of Jewish-Arab strife in the Middle East.[24]

The Jew is typically seen as western, although millions of Jews are Arabs and Sephardic, with roots in Africa and the Magreb. The perception of the Jew changed after the *Shoah*, when they came to be seen as purely European, as refugees from Europe pouring into Israel. These images are mirrored by the Eurocentric gaze, but also convey a false sense of identity and its homogeneous aspect. For example, many Muslims/Arabs have been born in Europe and North America, yet are still perceived as "other" or "Arab"—can a Muslim be an American or a European? I am Pakistani-born, and a naturalized citizen of the United States. I am an American, like many other Muslims, having spent the majority of my life in Europe and the United States, and my life is "American," except, for example, when I choose to fast during Ramadan. This divisibility of identity becomes an excuse for rejecting the "other," the "Jew," and the "Arab" as un-European or un-American. Many Jews are also unaware of the persecution of Jewish-Arabs in Arab lands under the Vichy and Nazi regimes. Robert Satloff found this in his studies:

Arabs, however, do not have a monopoly on refusing to come to grips with the Holocaust's long reach across the Mediterranean. One of the strangest phenomena I came across in my research was the extent to which many Jews of Arab lands suffered persecution, too. Of course, the fate of those Jews never even approached the

---

24 Ivan Davidson and Derek J. Penslar, *Orientalism and the Jews* (Boston: Brandeis University Press, 2005), 1.

horror of the Jews of Europe. But that alone does not diminish what Jews in Arab lands had to confront. ... Oddly enough, though, Jews living in Arab lands today are themselves among the least likely to press for recognition of their communities' suffering six decades ago.[25]

My own personal experience of anti-Muslim sentiment began in Europe. As a child growing up in Western Europe during the 1970s and 1980s in places such as Zurich and Geneva before moving to the Middle East and then the United States, there were very few Muslims in my schools or in the areas in which we lived. We were seen as "foreign" or just as "Arab" by the Europeans around us, especially since we could not speak Swiss German or French. My mother had a difficult time navigating her daily schedule in grocery stores, running errands, and mapping out bus schedules. My brother and I were young children, attending yet another school and trying to make friends. I always befriended other foreigners, regardless of their religion. As a child, it seemed to me that Southeast Asians (Japanese, Koreans, and Chinese) had an upper hand in the Swiss schools, in which they were well assimilated, and they were invariably wealthier than the Muslims, Jews, and Hindus. In the British system, when I attended St. Mary Abbott's, a private Catholic school, mainly Catholic children were accepted, a few others, and myself. My experiences remain ingrained in my mind, and so began my journey into identity and my discovery of perspective. I was a Muslim who saw a Qur'anic tutor three times a week after school throughout my childhood, and yet lived in a western environment. Those years shaped a consciousness that made me feel my otherness and simultaneously opened my eyes to many different perspectives. These childhood memories also scarred me, as I would be teased by the Americans and Europeans on the private school van that transported us to school and back about being a "brown girl" who had a "smelly brown vagina"—I had no idea what these words meant, and was forced to ask my parents about them. I was not sure why my sexual organ had anything to do with the boys in the van—after all, we were children, not even close to puberty—but in the minds of these children, there was an image of brownness and dirt that compelled them to move away from any seat that I occupied

---

25 Satloff, *Among the Righteous*, 174.

and to laugh at me when I would wear traditional clothing on Eid-ul-Fitr (the celebration at the end of Ramadan). Wherever we lived, my parents would always take us to mosque; if there were no mosques, they would hold prayers at our home or at a Muslim center. These memories compelled me to move beyond the personal and relate stories of both Jews and Muslims in terms of political and social misunderstandings.

What is antisemitism? How can Muslims understand this history of antisemitism as Jews' reality for centuries, and, more important, how can we relate to this experience? I have chosen to look to Egypt as a nexus for both Jews and Arabs/Muslims who have connected to this vast cradle of civilization. It is a place where Jews once lived, but now, except for a minute, dwindling, aging community, do not. However, I want to be cautious in several ways: I want to be aware that, because history shifts, there are moments that—as Edmund Husserl says—are like epochs that shift migration and power. I also want to be clear that most of my terms, such as "Arab," "Muslim," and "Jew," are applied very generally for the purposes of this book. There are Arab Jews and Arab Christians, Muslim Europeans and Muslim Americans, Muslim Asians and Muslim Africans, and so on—I am deeply conscious of this in my use of terms.

Egyptian Arab Jews: Exile

In the 1930s, Egypt was a target for fascist and Nazi ideas because of the numbers of Jewish immigrants pouring into the Middle East and the end of the Ottoman Empire. This combination made the Egyptians more vulnerable and fostered a growing resentment towards Jews. These ideas were promoted by the fascist and Nazi parties but also by Palestinian Arab political exiles. Why? The Ottomans had fallen and the pan-Arab movement was just beginning. This movement held a hope for a rising economy, power, and restoration of the glory of a lost empire. The struggle of Arabs—and now, most Muslims—was around the Palestinian Question. To support the Palestinians, one had to be against the British, who were seen as the fatal flaw and colonizers of the Middle East. The anti-Jewish sentiment poured into the streets and, by the late 1930s, one could witness anti-Jewish demonstrations in Cairo from the intellectuals. These demonstrations and protests were the beginning of a fear between Jews and Arabs well before the creation of the state of Israel. This also created a tension and mistrust between Jews, Arabs, and the British. It is a tension that we can still witness in the many protests in the Middle East today that choose to burn an American or Israeli flag rather than a British one. In other words, the current tension has been directed toward the United States.[26]

However, very few Muslims know that approximately 800,000 Jews fled Arab countries from 1948 to the 1970s. This fact has gone unnoticed as a result of the creation of the State of Israel in 1948. This is an important aspect of Jewish–Muslim history that demonstrates the intimacy of their cultures through language and culture. I begin my discussion in Egypt to show the various encounters between Jewish Arabs and Egyptians through literature, and the ordinary life of Muslims and Jews in Egypt when they both thrived there. In this way, one might indeed see the many intersections of antisemitism not only within contemporary Arab communities but a history of such after 1948. Today, some Jews are more fearful of Muslims and some Muslims are more mistrusting of Jews than, perhaps, ever before in history. One need only look at the cartoons that circulate in the Muslim/Arab world, depicting Israelis and the IDF as Nazis, and Palestinians as victims of the *Shoah*, or those in Jewish communities depicting Muslims as terrorists and blind believers of a terrorist faith that compels them to kill.

Leila Ahmed, an Egyptian woman educated in the West, in her memoir *A Border Passage: From Cairo to America—A Woman's Journey* describes the period in which Egyptians changed their manner of seeing themselves as just Egyptian after 1948, but rather in opposition to Jews.

> Our new identity proclaimed openly our opposition to Israel and Zionism—and proclaimed implicitly our opposition to the "Zionists" in our midst, Egyptian Jews. For although explicitly Zionism was distinguished from Jewishness, an undercurrent meaning "Jewish" was also contained in the word. The word "Arab,"

---

26 Michael M. Laskier, "Egyptian Jewry under the Nasser Regime: 1956–70," accessed October 29, 2016, http://www.hsje.org/Egypt/Egypt%20Today/egyptian_jewry_under_the_nasser_.htm#. WBT05fkrLIV. For a thorough discussion on Egypt and Jews, see Michael M. Laskier, *Egyptian Jewry under the Nasser Regime: 1956–1970.* New York: Taylor & Francis, 1995.

emerging at this moment to define our identity, silently carried within it its polar opposite—Zionist/Jew—without which hidden, silent connotation it actually had no meaning. For the whole purpose of its emergence now was precisely to tell us of our new alignments and re-alignments in relation to both terms, Arab and Jew.[27]

I begin with this quotation from Ahmed to illustrate that the terms "Arab" and "Zionist" fall into superficial categories that have served the interests of political loyalties to nationalism, statehood, and polarization. However, these categories can be reconsidered through literature and tradition to carve out the first step in creating dialogue outside the particularity of nationalism. Whether Jewish, Muslim, Arab, Israeli, Zionist, or anti-Zionist, these terms have only blurred the Jewish–Muslim relationship. One can even look at the history of the images of the Jew and Muslim to see the larger influence and play of politics and propaganda.

> … the common British image of the Jews in the eighteenth century was a caricature of the Maltese Jew in his oriental turban, dark and deviant, almost oriental. By the nineteenth century, it was that of Lord Rothschild in formal wear, receiving the Prince of Wales at his daughter's wedding in a London synagogue. Religious identity (of Jew or Muslim) replaced national or ethnic identity it was Arab as Muslim and Jew as European—by then few (except antisemites) remembered that the Rothschilds were a Frankfurt family that had escaped the Yiddish-speaking ghetto. The Jews seemed to be assimilated and everywhere but they were all alike; Muslims seem to be everywhere and were becoming alike.[28]

Perhaps it is naïve of me to present marginal views on how both Jews and Arabs can rethink antisemitism; however, marginality is more common than we are led to imagine in a world filled with propaganda and political agendas. Muslims are marginal in the context of the world today, living as minorities in western cultures in which Jews since World War II have dominated the

---

27 Leila Ahmed, *From Cairo to America—A Woman's Journey* (New York: Penguin, 1999), 245.

28 Gilman, *Multiculturalism and the Jews*, 23.

geopolitical and economic agendas. Jews became increasingly assimilated and Muslims occupied the "outsider" paradigm. However, Jews were also exiled from Arab lands as Israel became stronger, and it became difficult for Jews to live in Arab countries.

As Edmond Jabès wrote in 1963 after his exile from Cairo, he swore that writing would be one way to speak of the silence:

> Do I know, at this hour when men lift their eyes up to the sky, when knowledge claims a richer, more beautiful part of the imagination (all secrets of the universe are buds of fire soon to open), do I know, in my exile, what has driven me back through tears and time, back to the wells of the desert where my ancestors had ventured? There is nothing at the threshold of the open page, it seems, but this wound of race born of the book, whose order and disorder are roads of suffering. Nothing but this pain, whose past and whose permanence is also that of writing.[29]

I believe that literature is a powerful tool and a means to exchange and transform dialogue through personal testimony and experience. As a Muslim woman who reads and teaches Jewish literature and history, I find this to be the most productive and intimate way of living within two different traditions, political views, and languages, and to share similar ideas about nation, longing, and home, not to mention God. What I came to was an obvious discovery that contemporary Jewish and Arabic Egyptian literature stopped discussing Jewish–Muslim relations and turned to antisemitic and anti-Muslim agendas post-1948 in light of Israel/Palestine and the involvement of Egypt. This does not by any means indicate that antisemitism began in 1948, but simply that propaganda took over the voices of Egypt at that time.

> The attack on the Suez Canal by British, French, and Israeli forces in 1956 was understandably followed by strict measures against British and French nationals as well as anyone accused of Zionism. Many suspected Zionists were arrested, detained in internment camps, and deported.

---

29   Jabès, *The Book of Questions*, 25.

There were a significant number of Jews who left Egypt in 1948 after Israel's declaration of independence and the aftermath of the first Arab-Israeli war. ... The antisemitism that began to appear was seen by them to be instigated by extremist groups such as the Muslim Brotherhood and was not seen as government policy.[30]

Egyptian Jews were threatened and slowly left their homeland. Today there are only two synagogues that are open for service and "... the last Jewish revival in Egypt was created with the opening of the Suez Canal in 1869 and ended with the attack on the Suez Canal in 1956."[31]

What is Antisemitism? It was and is still being seen in media, literature, and humor, as well as in cartoons that allow for propaganda and a certain freedom. The Jew was seen by Arabs as eastern, but this image changed drastically. The Jew was seen as one who brought the word of God to Muslims through Abraham (Ibrahim), but this is no longer the case. The Jew is now seen as the European Jew, who lusts for money, is cheap, untrustworthy, and liable to kill Arabs whenever giving the chance. The Jew is also seen and imagined in Western clothes and the Star of David (Muslims believe in King David), which is seen as a sign of fascist and genocidal ideology. These images changed Muslims' perceptions drastically, turning them antisemitic against the European-image Jew.

So how do writers read this antisemitism? Voices such as David Grossman and Ari Shavit dismantle the perception of Jews as solely people who think through their own lens of Zionism, and they suggest that a lot of the misunderstandings between Jews and Muslims rely on propaganda and historical difference. As Shavit writes:

In this sense the Zionism that emerges in 1897 is a stroke of genius. Its founders, led by Dr. Herzl, are both prophetic and heroic. All in all, the nineteenth century was the golden age of Western Europe's Jewry. Yet the Herzl Zionists see what is coming. True they do not know that the twentieth century will conjure up such places as

---

30 Liliane S. Dammond, *The Lost World of the Egyptian Jews: Firt-person Accounts from Egypt's Jewish Community in the Twentieth Century* (New York: Universe, Inc., 2007), 11.
31 Ibid., 12.

Auschwitz and Treblinka. But in their own way they act in the 1890s in order to preempt the 1940s. They realize they are faced with a radical problem: the coming extinction of the Jews. And they realize that a radical problem calls for a radical solution: the transformation of the Jews, a transformation that can take place only in Palestine, the Jews' ancient homeland.[32]

Shavit explicitly points out the very premise of Zionism and continues to retell the story of his great-grandfather, a religious British Victorian Jew who travels to Jaffa for a new life. His story is important because Zionism is seen as a threat in the majority of the Muslim world; it is seen as a kind of fascism attached to Israel and its occupation of the Palestinian people. However, the root of Zionism is elsewhere, displaced in fear and the premonition of the many European Jews who wanted to live in their own homeland. As we review the stories of European Jews who traversed the seas pre-*Shoah*, we also see a migration of Jews from Arab lands. When I am confronted with questions about Jews and Judaism by Muslims, Zionism is where the conversation stops and freezes. "We have no issues with Jews and Judaism but we can't stand Zionists!" David Grossman, who lost his son in the Israeli military by the Hizbollah during the war in Lebanon, sheds light on who his son was and what his son showed him.

> Uri was such an Israeli child; even his name was very Israeli and Hebrew. He was the essence of Israeli-ness as I would want it to be. An Israeli-ness that has almost been forgotten, that is something of a curiosity. And he was a person so full of values. That word has been so eroded and has become ridiculed in recent years. In our crazy, cruel and cynical world, it's not "cool" to have values, or to be a humanist, or to be truly sensitive to the suffering of the other, even if that other is your enemy on the battlefield.
>
> However, I learned from Uri that it is both possible and necessary to be all that. We have to guard ourselves, by defending ourselves both physically and morally. We have to guard ourselves

---

32 Shavit, *My Promised Land*, 63.

from might and simplistic thinking, from the corruption that is in cynicism, from the pollution of the heart and the ill-treatment of humans, which are the biggest curse of those living in a disastrous region like ours. Uri simply had the courage to be himself, always and in all situations—to find his exact voice in every thing he said and did. That's what guarded him from the pollution and corruption and the diminishing of the soul.[33]

The goal is to read beyond clichés, yet we are surrounded by them. How can we read one another's narratives as useful, productive, and different and still comprehend the juncture at which Jews and Arabs (Muslims) sit today as these groups experience antisemitism and a loss of identity in different ways?

Bernard Lewis, in his essay "Semites and Antisemites," notes that prejudice and hatred have long existed, in many different forms, and we should not be surprised at the very recent antisemitism arising in the Arab/Muslim world:

The growth of European-style antisemitism in the Arab world derived in the main from this feeling of humiliation and the need therefore to ascribe to the Jews a role very different from their traditional role in Arab folklore and much closer to that of the antisemitic prototypes. By now the familiar themes of European antisemitism—the blood libel, the protocols of Zion, the international Jewish conspiracy, and the rest—have become standard fare in much of the Arab world, in the schoolroom, the pulpit, the media, and even on the Internet. It is bitterly ironic that these themes have been adopted by previously immune Muslims precisely at a time when in Europe they have become an embarrassment even to antisemites.[34]

Jews have been known to live in Arab lands and the Middle East from the time of Abraham (Abraham lived in what is Iraq today). Stories in the Tanakh

---

33 David Grossman, "Uri, My Dear Son," *The Observer* (August 19, 2006), accessed January 4, 2014, http://www.theguardian.com/world/2006/aug/20/syria.comment.

34 Bernard Lewis, "The New Anti-Semitism: First Religion, Then Race, Then What?" *American Scholar* (2004), accessed July 2, 2006, http://theamericanscholar.org/the-new-anti-semitism/#.Usl_7U2A3IU.

describe the desert, Egypt, vast symbolism of Arab lands, and the feeling that somehow "home" rests in these environs. So, Jews lived in Arab lands and succeeded more under the Arabs versus the Christians. I discuss this nostalgia as well, but I think it is important to understand that Jews were seen as ethnically the same or even related through the patriarch Abraham. However, in the more recent times, the Jews suffered through unfortunate circumstances in Arab countries, especially in Cairo, where approximately "75,000 Jews lived in Egypt. About 100 remain today, mostly in Cairo. In June 1948, a bomb exploded in Cairo's Karaite quarter, killing 22 Jews. In July 1948, Jewish shops and the Cairo synagogue were attacked, killing 19 Jews. Hundreds of Jews were arrested and had their property confiscated."[35]

This fact that Jews migrated from Arab countries is still mostly unrecognized and when it is, the exodus is seen as a migration to Israel and places where Jews wanted to live and be in. This migration is seen as voluntary or, in a sense, a mark of separation between the local Arabs and Jews. Jews saw the rise of antisemitic acts as threatening, and the idea of staying in a country that would offer second-class citizenship was unappealing, to say the very least. Many Jews left for Israel and the United States. However, it should be noted here that these Jews—many Sephardic or Arab Jews—were welcomed, but in a different manner. The culture that Arab Jews brought with them was very different from that of the European Jews, including language, dress, and religious culture. The Arab Jews were seen as different and, at times, seen to be not as civilized as the European Jews. Jewish and Arab scholars have written on this problem extensively; however, very few Arabs or Muslims have addressed this issue within the Jewish community because of the perception of all Jews being homogeneous.

There were also times when Jews vilified Arabs/Muslims. One of these events is known as the 1954 Lavon Affair, which created deeper mistrust between the communities and exposed some Jews as malicious and "conspiring" with Israeli agents within their own borders.

The 1954 Lavon Affair served as a pretext for further persecution of Egyptian Jews. The Lavon affair was also called the "bad affair." As described on the webpage "The Lavon Affair: Is History Repeating Itself?":

---

35 "Fact Sheet: Jewish Refugees from Arab Countries," Jewish Virtual Library, accessed October 23, 2016 http://www.jewishvirtuallibrary.org/jsource/talking/jew_refugees.html

In 1954, Israeli agents working in Egypt planted bombs in several buildings, including a United States diplomatic facility, and left evidence behind implicating Egyptian Muslims as the culprits. The ruse would have worked, had not one of the bombs detonated prematurely, allowing the Egyptians to capture and identify one of the bombers, which in turn led to the round up of an Israeli spy ring.

Some of the spies were from Israel, while others were recruited from the local Jewish population. Israel responded to the scandal with claims in the media that there was no spy ring, that it was all a hoax perpetrated by "anti-Semites."[36]

The Lavon Affair catapulted into an increasing number of antisemitic acts and arrests by 1956; the Jews were no longer seen as part of the Arab context but rather outside the familiar and, in turn, conspirators with the colonizers. This turn in Egyptian history may have marked the entrance of true old-style European Antisemitism. The Lavon Affair demonstrated to people in the Arab world how Jews would demonize Arabs through blaming them for antisemitic acts. These acts on both sides by Egyptian Arabs and Jews created deep tensions that resulted in war, mistrust, and prejudice that still exists acutely today. Even in my conversations with Jews and Muslims now, these memories of mistrust have contributed to the deep divide in contemporary relations between the communities. Some of these memories have been passed down through generations, becoming part of the fabric of both communities.

"In October 1956, when the Suez Crisis erupted, 1,000 Jews were arrested and 500 Jewish businesses were seized by the government. A statement branding the Jews as 'enemies of the state' was read out in the mosques of Cairo and Alexandria."[37] "Jewish bank accounts were confiscated and many Jews lost their jobs. Professionals such as lawyers, engineers, doctors, and teachers were not allowed to work. In 1967, just after the Six

---

36 "The Lavon Affair: Is History Repeating Itself?," *What Really Happened?*, accessed July 13, 2014, http://whatreallyhappened.com/WRHARTICLES/lavon.html. This website has been quoted by many in charging Jews with conspiracy theories, including 9/11.

37 "Jewish Refugees From Arab Lands," *World Heritage Encyclopedia* (2002), accessed May 30, 2016, http://www.worldlibrary.org/articles/jewish_refugees_from_arab_lands.

Day War, Jews were detained and tortured, and Jewish homes were confiscated."[38] We can find narratives by a Jewish doctor named Sachs, such as the following, that yield a sense of loss and longing:

> After the nationalist revolution took place in 1952, one felt less at ease. There were many rules and regulations. There was an established spy system, and one could not get funds out of Egypt. It's quite simple, when my father left Egypt via Port Said, the British and the French occupied the town. They left on a refugee boat for France. My father did not want to leave and abandon his store, but his wife prevailed and they took with them all available cash.[39]

Many such historical narratives display the exile and antisemitism felt by many Jews from Egypt as they moved to places like Israel and the United States. In Liliane S. Dammond, *The Lost World of Egyptian Jews: First Person Accounts from Egypt's Jewish Community in the Twentieth Century*, one finds narratives written by Jews about living in Egypt, experiencing antisemitism, and the return to "Palestine" post- and pre-1952. In some of these narratives, one finds the deep longing for an old Egypt lost to wars and colonialism, where Jews could indeed live much more freely and hold good jobs, where Egyptians were one people and religion was a matter of choice. In Arabic literature, including that of Naguib Mahfouz, we find similar sentiments. Mahfouz, an Egyptian Muslim writer, won the Nobel Prize for Literature in 1988. He wrote a trilogy based on the generational and political developments within Egypt, especially Cairo. He describes the mood of Egyptians during the 1952 rebellion as open and honest—to be Egyptian encompassed Jews and Copts in the same manner that to be American includes Christians, Jews, and Muslims today. The mood that Mahfouz expresses in his writings is clearly critical of the religious versus the scientific, moving away from the idea that Egyptians in power had to be Muslim. As Rasheed El-Enany has pointed out in his work on Mahfouz, "Mahfouz's distaste for religious fundamentalism has not waned with time. In his memoirs, Mahfouz proclaims the course of reviewing political forces active on the scene during his youth: 'the ones I hated from the beginning were the

---

38 Howard Sachar, *A History of Israel* (New York: Alfred A. Knopf, 1979).
39 Dammond, *The Lost World of the Egyptian Jews*, 55.

Moslem Brothers.' He draws a very negative portrait of a prominent leader of the Muslim Brothers movement, Sayyid Qutb (1906–1966), whom he knew personally in his youth at a time 'when Qutb had shown more interest in literary criticism than in active religious fundamentalism (Qutb was in fact among the first critics to draw attention to the budding talent of Mahfouz in the mid-1940s). However, it's important to note how Qutb changed when he was drawn to Islamism."[40]

Mahfouz's work shows the generational differences and changes within the climate of Egypt through his novels but also his own conversations with El-Enany, who succinctly points out that many Egyptians were moving to rejecting the West, which also included rejecting the Jews. In this strain of thinking, the Jew represented the colonial struggle; some Egyptians who struggled with this also implicated Jews, especially in light of the many incidences of mistrust such as the Lavon Affair and the immigration of Jews both into and out of the Middle East. Egyptians felt a sense of being trapped by colonialism, unable to relocate easily if desired, exacerbated by what they saw as the freer movement of Jews, their colonial oppressors. Mahfouz's rejection of fundamentalism and acceptance of a heterogeneous environment also reflects the various encounters that challenged Muslims in the advent of colonialism. This aspect of Egyptian life has been left out of the conversations of Egypt seen only as a "Muslim" country rather than one with Coptic and Jewish inhabitants, as well as being an African indigenous country of historical significance. The challenge of fundamentalism also incorporates the Jew as one of the targets in the fight for independence and religious freedom for Sayyid Qutb, as Tibi points out:

> In *Our Struggle with the Jews* Qutb describes the cosmic war the Muslim people are compelled to fight against the Jews and pays tribute to the youth who joins in that war "not for the sake of any material benefits, but simply to die and sacrifice one's own life." According to Qutb, Muslims have no choice but to fight, because the Jews themselves, whom he describes as the major enemy of Islam since the beginning of its history, want this war.[41]

40 Rasheed El-Enany, *Naguib Mahfouz: The Pursuit of Meaning* (London: Routledge, 1993), 23–24.
41 Tibi, *Islamism and Islam*, 64.

To illustrate Mahfouz's own work further, Kamal, the main character in *Sugar Street,* the last of Naguib Mahfouz's fictional trilogy, becomes the model of a questioning Egyptian identity, one who is critical of religion and the inclusion of others in his culture: "Without any hesitation Riyadh replied, 'All of us Copts are Wafdists. That's because the Wafd Party represents true nationalism. It's not a religious, Turkish-oriented bunch like the National Party. The Wafd is a populist party. It will make Egypt a nation that provides freedom for all Egyptians, without regard to ethnic origin or religious affiliation.'"[42] In Dammond's book, we find this to be true for many Jewish Egyptians. Dr. Sachs writes, "In Egypt it was normal to be known as Jewish. There was certainly less hatred of Jews in Egypt than in Europe ... I was still accepted in Egyptian circles, and I never encountered violence or discrimination. In 1948 there was a rumor that Israelis had dropped a bomb in Cairo, and that triggered a violent demonstration. The mob took to the streets burning and destroying."[43] One can read numerous testimonies of longing for Egypt to be the same as it was pre-1948. Post-1948, Jews were fired from jobs, even placed in internment camps, and the fear of the Germans approaching Cairo and Alexandria compelled many to leave for Europe, the United States, and Israel. In one testimony, Anna Perle writes, "[N]obody knew anything about the Holocaust at the time. It is only after the war that we learned about it. When the Germans arrived in El Alamein, we were frightened. They were only thirty minutes from Alexandria. We heard canon shots and many people took flight. But where was there to go? If the Germans entered Egypt, they would occupy all of it. If we went from Alexandria to Cairo, what was to be gained?"[44] As Jews fled Egypt and the government gained momentum as a nationalist government that opposed Britain and France, one begins to see the rise of antisemitism. Jews were to be hated and feared because they were the enemy not only of the Palestinians but Arabs and their allies. This perception was very successful in causing Egyptians to see the Jews as allying with the colonists, Samuel Huntington's concept of the "clash of civilizations"—or, to put it another way, the struggle between

42 Naguib Mahfouz, *Sugar Street* (New York: First Anchor Book Editions, 1993), 135.
43 Dammond, *The Lost World of the Egyptian Jews*, 54.
44 Ibid.

Islam and the West—which is ironic, since Israel is also included in and perceived as being in the Middle East, but is dominated by the West. As a Muslim, to see oneself as pitted against the West is deeply demeaning and feeds into the idea of colonialism. However, Israel is perceived by Muslims as belonging to the colonial realm. Propaganda literature has brewed for more than fifty years in Egypt and the Muslim world. I focus on Egypt here, but being a South Asian Muslim from Pakistan, a country with one of the largest Muslim populations in the world, I can say that we experience the same stereotypes and hatred of the Jew: the fall guy, the conspirator, and the one who will fight with the European Christian against Muslims.

In Pakistan in the 1800s, there was a community of Jews who had emigrated from India and lived mostly in large urban centers, mainly Karachi. There is not much information available on the current Jewish population in Pakistan, but they are regarded with hatred and suspicion, and believed to be behind every bomb, outbreak of disease, and war in Pakistan. The Jewish community itself is nearly nonexistent in Pakistan in the new millennium, according to the following article:

> In 1893, a B'nei Israel from Bombay, Solomon David Umerdekar, inaugurated the Karachi Magen Shalom Synagogue on the corner of Jamila Street and Nishtar Road, which officially opened in 1912. During these years, the Jewish community thrived.
>
> In 1903, the community set up the Young Man's Jewish Asso- ciation, and the Karachi B'nei Israel Relief Fund was established to support poor Jews. In 1918, the Karachi Jewish Syndicate was formed to provide housing at reasonable rents, and the All India Israelite League, which represented 650 B'nei Israel province of Sind (including Hyderabad, Larkuna, MirpurKhas and Sukkur, as well as Karachi), was first convened – founded by two prominent B'nei Israel, Jacob Bapuji Israel and David S. Erulkar. Karachi became a fulcrum for the B'nei Israel in India, the place where they congregated for High Holiday prayers. There was also a prayer hall, which served the Afghan Jews residing in the city. A 1941 government census recorded 1,199 Pakistani Jews: 513 men and 538 women. So accepted were the Jews of Karachi in these years

that Abraham Reuben, a leader in the Jewish community, became the first Jewish councilor on the Karachi Municipal Corporation.[45]

Furthermore, per a posting on the Yahoo! Groups MidEast News Service Analysis page: "'In 1956 there were demonstrations outside the [Magain Shalome] synagogue [in Karachi] and it was damaged. Most of the remaining Jews left then, and most of them went to Bombay,' said Katz. 'The last caretaker of the synagogue, a Muslim, rescued artifacts from the synagogue— the bima, the ark, things like that—but he doesn't know what to do with them. They're sitting in his backyard, I think.'"[46]

After September 11, 2001, the news in Pakistan was inundated with claims that Jews were behind 9/11 and that it was impossible for Muslims to have committed this crime. Newspapers, family members, and friends in Pakistan assured me that the Jewish attack was not a rumor but the truth.

It is well known that the prophet Mohammad (PBUH) befriended Jews and had a dialogue with them, praised them for their understanding in God as the one God, and ordered Muslims to accept Jews as among the "people of the book." How did "Jew" become a vile word in the streets of Pakistan? How can Pakistanis know Jews? Hatred of the "others" is joined by conspiracy theories that minimize one's own responsibility for terror and instead point a finger at the Jews.

> Nothing illustrates Pakistani newspapers' careless and self-contra-
> dictory attitude than their treatment of 9/11. With the exception of
> a handful of columnists such as Hamid Mir, Saleem Safi, Dr.
> Muhammad Farooq, and Ataur Rahman almost all Urdu newspapers
> continue to proclaim, like an article of faith, that 9/11 was a "drama"
> staged by the Jews. For example, Mr Majeed Nizami, the powerful
> owner of Nawa-i-Waqt, *The Nation* and Waqt TV channel, believes
> that 9/11 was a Jewish conspiracy against the Muslim world

45 Shalva Weil, "A Jewish Presence in Pakistan," accessed December 13, 2016 http://www.jewish-timesasia.org/community-spotlight-topmenu-43/pakistan/544-pakistan-communities/2806-a-jewish-presence-in-pakistan-karachi-in-another-time

46 Ser Sam, "Surprise! There Are Still Jews in Pakistan," *MidEast News Service Analysis* (2010), accessed July 15, 2013, http://groups.yahoo.com/neo/groups/MewBkd/conversations/topics/17888.

(*The Nation*, March 7, 2004). According to him, American newspapers have written that on 9/11 no Jew went to work at the World Trade Center and no one has contradicted this story.[47]

Furthermore, one reads the following about Zionist, Jewish Conspiracies, and one is alarmed at the accusations, which have been confirmed by Al-Qaeda worldwide:

> In its editorial on July 9, 2005, Nawa-i-Waqt wrote that like 9/11 the London bombings could also be the work of pro-Zionist American lobby. "The drama of 9/11 is still a mystery for the world. To date the US has not presented any real, circumstantial and solid evidence against any individual or organization." According to Mian Shahid Nadeem (N.W., Feb. 10, 2010), Waqt TV has convincingly proved that the 9/11 conspiracy was staged by the United States and Israel to occupy the resources of Muslim countries. In an article entitled "Jews, not Muslims, are the enemies of America," Dr. Ajmal Niazi wrote in Nawa-i-Waqt (July 20, 2005), that not a single Jew died in the 9/11 attacks on [the] World Trade Center. Abdus Shakoor Abi Hasan, Nawa-i-Waqt's Kuwait-based correspondent, also made this claim on July 26, 2005. These claims are without any basis in fact. According to Wikipedia's article entitled "9/11 conspiracy theories," at least 270 Jews lost their lives in 9/11 attacks. This article is available on the Internet free of cost.[48]

The story of antisemitism is not restricted to Arab Muslims, but has infected most Muslims, who believe that Jews are aligned with colonial powers and want to exterminate all Muslims.

Leila Ahmed states that prior to 1948 Jewishness was never a "problem" in Egypt, but one finds many Egyptian Jews who would say that they were always outsiders, but nonetheless that Egypt was home to them in several

47 Shakeel Chaudhary, "View Point: 9/11 and Pakistan's Urdu Press," *Pakistan Media Watch* (June 10, 2004), accessed August 10, 2013, http://pakistanmediawatch.com/2010/09/13/view-point-911-and-pakistans-urdu-press/.
48 Ibid.

important ways. It was an ancestral home; they felt they were Egyptians, yet they were required to leave for their own safety. Leila Ahmed's own confession about her friendship with Joyce, a Jewish friend, is telling of how ordinary Egyptians were taken by surprise by the uprooting of many Jews. As she finds out that her friend has to leave for an indeterminate length of time, she believes President Gamal Nasser's proclamation that "the Jews were welcome to stay." "I heard him myself on the radio. Many Jews thought of Egypt as their homeland, he'd said, and they were welcome to stay, but if they did they must be with us all the way and give up their foreign passports and accept Egyptian nationality. That had sounded fair to me. If you lived in Egypt and considered it your home, then you should accept Egyptian nationality. Why not?"[49]

Ahmed points out that hers was a naïve perspective, yet she noticed that, slowly, all the British and Jewish students left her school. This resulted in a tumble in academic standards, and the rise of the need to be "Arab"—to speak Arabic and learn more about Islam at school. Egypt today has managed to create purely Arab perspectives.

So, how are Jews seen by Arabs? Jews themselves, as people, are often lost in the discussion of political agendas and the stand on Israel. Examples in Arab literature portray Jews as assimilated pre-1948. In Naguib Mahfouz's *Palace Walk*, set in the 1940s, one finds the female Muslim characters, denied certain freedoms as Muslim women, envying the Jewish girls who could work in factories. The demise of Egyptian pluralistic education is also related to an intellectual bitterness toward Jews/Zionists and, in turn, toward the West for colonizing and taking control of a cosmopolitan place like Egypt. The world has become narrower. We are suffocated by real-world politics and games of language. Yet how do we academics, intellectuals, and writers, working at our desks or attending conferences, help to create a channel of understanding? I can imagine Edmond Jabès and Naguib Mahfouz, both Egyptian writers and each exiled for different reasons, engaging in conversation with one another as their home, Egypt, confronts the problematic relationship between Jews and Arabs in different ways. They would renounce the superficial categories of Arab and Jew in favor of complicating categorization by calling themselves Pharaonic (see the Afterword).

---

49 Ahmed, *From Cairo to America*, 172–74.

Chapter Six

Muslims and the Memory of a Colonial Holocaust

Not only did such persecution exist where Arabs lived, but Arabs played a role at every level. Some went door-to-door with the Germans, pointing out Jews for arrest. Others led Jewish workers on forced marches or served as overseers at labor camps. They manned the railroads that took bewildered European Jews deep into the Sahara, prepared the gruel that passed for food at torture sites, patrolled the streets of Bizerte, Tunis, and Sousse, armed with guns and clubs, looking for Jewish escapees. Some took these jobs because they needed money to feed their families; others volunteered because they were zealous about their work. Every person's story was different, but the common thread that connected them all was their shared undeniability.[1]

Arabs were not primarily collaborators and certainly not perpetrators of the *Shoah*, but some had knowledge about the labor camps under the Vichy government in countries such as Morocco, Tunisia, and colonized Algeria. It is important that Arabs recognize the historical evidence of such camps in light of the collaboration of Arabs and, more important, the Arab rescue of Jews. The existence of labor and concentration camps in these Arab countries is a testimony to the power and reach of Nazi Germany and the Vichy governments. Colonial occupation in the Arab/Muslim world has also been overlooked in discussions of its history; the evidence

---

1   Satloff, *Among the Righteous*, 160.

of camps in these areas demonstrates challenging circumstances under the colonial forces at local levels.

Shoah through Muslim Eyes is a journey that I hope will connect Arabs to Jews in a different manner. The *Shoah* crept into places where even Jewish survivors had no knowledge; Arab lands. I was surprised when I asked the Jewish survivors whether they knew about the camps in Arab lands and they were shocked by this fact. I wanted to bridge the misperceptions and, as a Muslim, create a point of understanding, if I could point out the terrible onslaught of antisemitism and simultaneously explore how Arabs became implicated in the catastrophe of the *Shoah*. Arabs' role in the *Shoah* was minimum at best, yet the contact and exchange during this time has been a lost story. Arabs were not the perpetrators of the persecution of Jews, nor did they have any similar antisemitic laws that were found in Italy, France, and most especially in Germany. Arabs were in a different predicament, humiliated, powerless, and under colonial rule. However, this journey is about acceptance, sympathy, and attempting to eradicate the myths about Jews.

As a Muslim woman who teaches about the *Shoah* and Islam, I often see many eyebrows raised at the connection of these two very different terms in academia and the arena of politics. How can Muslims have any connections to the *Shoah*? The only connections that we have seen between Muslims and the *Shoah* are things like the image of the Mufti al-Husayni (the Muslim leader in mandatory Palestine 1921–1937) and Hitler sitting together, or the idea that Muslims were complacent about the extermination of Jews in Europe. However, what was being planned was an enormous alliance with the Arab world that relied increasingly on Islamic ideas for propaganda purposes, with Jewish hatred being at the forefront. The famous encounter between Hitler and al-Husayni on November 28, 1941, is recorded as follows.

> Their conversation was limited to an exchange of empty courtesies and the affirmation that they were fighting against common enemies—the British, Jews, and Bolshevism. When al-Husayni asked Hitler for a written guarantee of Arab, and especially Palestinian, independence, the dictator evaded the issue. After al-Husayni's repeated request, Hitler told him that in the current state of war it was too early for these kinds of questions, but asserted his "uncompromising fight against the

Jews," which also included Jews of the Arab lands. Another request for a meeting with Hitler in 1943 was unsuccessful.[2]

The overimagined deep relationship of Arabs and the Nazi party is inaccurate in many ways that create a bigger rift. Arabs were in desperate need of alliances and were fearful of the immigration of Jews into Palestine. In other words, the Arabs and Germans could create an imaginary alliance based on ideology, not religious belief. The "promotion of an alliance with the Islamic world was first and foremost motivated by material interests and strategic concerns, not by ideology."[3]

Another major concern for the German Nazis and their policy toward Muslims was its racism and prejudice. Muslims/Arabs were also seen as racially inferior and of non-European descent. For example, the Arabs secured their position with German Nazis as much as they could, since they witnessed the brutality of the camps in Arab lands under the Vichy-led Nazi Party and knew that this was a racial prejudice that could fall on them as well. Arabs were not in charge, nor were they confident that this colonial-led occupation was going to be in their favor. As Satloff writes:

> Politically, Arabs were not on sure ground either. To many Germans and their European partners, Arabs were only marginally less inferior then Jews. As one German officer said ominously to an Arab enjoying the comeuppance of Jews near Tunis, "Your time will come. We will finish with the Jews then we will take care of you." If indifference meant that Arabs were primarily concerned with securing the means for their own survival—finding food, shelter, work, and so on—and could not spare the effort to act on their natural human sympathy toward their Jewish compatriot, then theirs was an understandable, even legitimate "indifference," born of necessity.[4]

In other words, Arabs were integrated into the Vichy-led occupation and forced to obey orders because they, too, were under an occupation and

---

2 Motadel, *Islam and Nazi Germany's War*, 42.
3 Ibid., 56.
4 Satloff, *Among the Righteous*, 73–74.

threatened by the Vichy, not just in terms of power or force by their own racial composition. The Arabs/Muslims fared no better than the Jews, and if it were up to the Nazis they would kill them as well. Muslims did not know about the death camps, and most Muslims at this time were under colonial rule: the Vichy government of France had taken control of Morocco and Tunisia, and Libya was under direct German rule. Many understand that colonialism took place, but the impact of colonialism on Muslim countries had an enormous impact that is still experienced by Muslims of all backgrounds—Edward Said's *Orientalism* was one of the first books to discuss in depth the stark implications for Muslims under colonial rule. The vast scope of Muslim lands occupied by the British, Dutch, Italians, and Germans is a complex but important story that connects Muslims to the *Shoah*.

In David Motadel's *Islam and Nazi Germany's War*, one finds some jarring historical information on the alliance of Arabs with Nazi Germany, which is worth mentioning and analyzing on an ideological level. As he states:

> On a more general level, this study addresses the relationship between religion and power, specifically, the role of religion as an instrument in world politics and military conflict. It contributes to our understanding of the ways by which governments actively sought to use religion to expand their political influence and to wage wars. Attempts to mobilize religious groups were part of great power politics throughout the nineteenth and twentieth centuries. Religious groups—populations defined along religious lines—were regularly considered powerful political forces that could be utilized.[5]

This ideology was used as a means to an end, the empowering of al-Husayni, focusing on Arab countries, including the Soviet Union, the Germans were able to promote Islamic ideas to convince the Arabs to align with them. The deep and thorough ways in which officials created "Berlin's Muslim Moment" (a chapter in Motadel's book) is often overlooked.

---

5 Motadel, *Islam and Nazi Germany's War*, 9.

As *Shoah* denial and relativism spread into Muslim countries, some Jews and Muslims struggle to keep their history and connections to one another alive by telling stories of past cooperation and faith. However, antisemitism still looms large in Arab and Muslim discourse, as I have discussed in this book, discounting the many positive roles that the two traditions have shared. For the past few years, many Arab and Muslim academics, professionals, and much media have perpetuated antisemitism and the roots of the *Shoah* as a hoax. This went through several phases; for some time, the problem was that the number of Jews killed was disputed, then the roots of denial were later exposed, but the role of the *Shoah* in Jewish, western, and Arab consciousness changed, intensifying over time to more of an antisemitic European model. "'The Jewish Holocaust—a historical lie,' and the 'greatest Zionist lie history had ever known' are but two of the numerous expressions that appeared in the Arab discourse to deny the historical veracity of the Holocaust."[6]

Antisemitism is everywhere, like smog that hangs in the air—thick, dirty, and choking. Even in Karachi, where I was born, the Jews are everywhere, although they have not lived there as a community of any size in several hundred years. Hatred and suspicion of Jews is in the schoolroom, the pulpit, the media, and even at the butcher's shop in the dense Karachi marketplace, where, as I recall, the butcher blamed the spread of bird flu on Jews on a poster as one walked into the Sunday bazaar.

The examination of Muslims and the *Shoah* is a growing field within Holocaust studies, history, and religious studies. Muslims' involvement in the *Shoah* expands and particularizes the genocide of Jews in its infiltration of countries such as Algeria, Tunisia, Morocco, and Libya under the German and collaborationist French Vichy governments. Muslims during this period were in the midst of a crisis resulting from the many pressures of colonialism and World War II, and there were some Arab countries that were sympathetic to Germany.

Both Jews and Muslims had their same respective challenges pre-*Shoah*: Jews were being severely persecuted, and Muslims in fascist-controlled

---

6 Litvak and Webman, *From Empathy to Denial*, 155. See also, for instance, Ahmad 'Abd al-Ghafur 'Attar, *Al-Yahudiyya wal-sahyuniyya* (Beirut: 1972), 152; Rafiq Shakir Natshe, *Al-Isti'mar wa-filistin: Isra'il mashru 'ist'mari* (Aman: 1984), 147; *Al-Jumhurriya*, August 5, 1986; *Al-Bilad*, June 1, 1996; *Al-Sabil*, April 27, 1999.

countries were under colonial rule. Muslim Arabs at this time were going through nationalism and resistance to colonial rule; most Arabs were under colonial rule during the war and many were influenced by fascist and Nazi ideology in their struggle against the Jews, who they identified as western and European, precisely as they were being thrown out of Europe, as discussed in Chapter Five.

> Mufti al-Husayni was a religious authority and at the same time, an Arab nationalist. This fact confuses some scholars and induces them to identify him with political Islam. Even though he acted as a mufti, his ideas were rooted in Palestinian nationalism, not Islamism. Embracing Nazi ideology and submitting to its political leadership, as Husayni did, are things no modern Islamist would have done.[7]

This is a significant comment by Bassam Tibi, in which the lines of Islamic principles become conflated with nationalism and politics. The influence of the fascist, Nazi, and Vichy parties became a powerful tool in the geopolitical actions in the Middle East. Islam has clearly warned of any fascist ideology and to accept all people of difference and faith.

> O mankind! We created you from a single (pair) of a male and a female, and made you into nations and tribes, that ye may know each other (not that ye may despise each other). Verily the most honoured of you in the sight of Allah is (he who is) the most righteous of you. And Allah has full knowledge and is well acquainted (with all things) (Surah 49:13).[8]

Relatively little has been written about how and where Jews and Muslims suffered together and collaborated in this acutely antisemitic period. I want to recall the forgotten histories of Jews and Muslims at this sensitive time through the firsthand narratives of a Tunisian Jew and an Algerian Muslim who were interned in camps in African Arab nations, and examine how

---

7 Tibi, *Islamism and Islam*, 61.
8 Assad, *Message of the Qur'an*, Surah 49.

many Muslims reacted to the persecution of Jews in countries such as Algeria, Morocco, Libya, and Tunisia.

When I am asked by colleagues or friends about what my main focus is as a professor, I respond with "Islam" and "the Holocaust/*Shoah*." They mostly look at me quizzically or with distaste, some with curiosity, and some with disdain. How can a professor have two very distinct and disconnected worlds to live in? I say, why not? As academia narrows its focus and we tend to "specialize" in one area or religion, I think that broadening the focus can only develop our thinking and shift the focus to historical realities and meaningful understanding. The terms "Islam" and "Holocaust" appear to be at odds with each other, according to the usual political and social images of Muslims and the *Shoah*. The contrast is due to the tension caused by Muslim responses that have relativized or denied the *Shoah* in various ways.

After the violence of Judaism's first encounter with Islam, Jews fared better under Islamic rule. Antisemitism became most prevalent in Muslim lands during World War II, with earlier roots in the political actions of the British and the Balfour Declaration of 1917: "During the 1930s, Britain's commitment to the establishment of a homeland for the Jews made in the Balfour Declaration of 1917 came under increasing pressure in the face of Arab opposition to Jewish immigration to Palestine."[9] Violence flared within Palestine in 1929 and most especially in 1936. Why did the Arab world become so seduced by antisemitic propaganda? The Nazis understood the importance of their influence on the Arabs/Muslims, and worked to maintain it. The mechanism by which they were able to influence so many Arabs was the growing resentment of the increasing numbers of Jews migrating to Palestine. Arabs were already resentful of Jews, as they were seen as European enemies and imagined to be more powerful than they were. Shortwave radio broadcasts helped nurture this resentment:

> The Arab propaganda campaign, especially with shortwave radio, was far more extensive than a focus on the Mufti alone would suggest. Fascist Italy broadcast Arabic programs from 1934 to 1943 … In August 1941, a United States Office of War Information (OWI) report estimated that there were about 90,000 shortwave radios in

---

9   Jeffrey Herf, *Nazi Propaganda for the Arab World* (New Haven, CT: Yale University Press, 2009), 8.

the region: 150 in Aden, 55,000 in Egypt, 4,000 in Iraq, 24,000 in Palestine, 6,000 in Syria, 500 in Saudi Arabia, and 40,000 (mostly Jewish) listeners in Palestine. The numbers in Algeria (70,000) and in Morocco (45,770) included many Europeans.[10]

Furthermore, in the 1950s through the 1980s,[11] the military conflicts with Israel and the migration of Arab Jews from Arab countries to Israel, Europe, and the United States created a deeply tense and violent historical memory for Arabs and Jews. The 1990s marked a new phase in Arab *Shoah* denial with the publication of several books, such as Syrian author Muhammad Nimr Al-Madani's *Were the Jews Burned in the Ovens?* (1996), and Yasir Husayn's book entitled *Hitler* (1995), as well as popular Arabic translations of *Mein Kampf.*

> Hitler's book *Mein Kampf* was translated in full into Arabic in 1963 and a second edition was issued in 1995. Earlier, Luis Heiden, a former Nazi propaganda official, had prepared a pocket-sized Arabic translation of *Mein Kampf* that was distributed as a gift to Egyptian army officers. Two abridged translations came out in Beirut in 1974 and 1975.[12]

There is a correlation between the intensity of the role that the *Shoah* played in Jewish consciousness, both in Israel and the United States, and the prevalence of *Shoah* denial in the Arab world. The greater the role played by the *Shoah* in Jewish identity and in western society, the greater the investment of Arab intellectuals in denying it. On the surface, it is confusing as to why Arabs would deny a German crime and a European crime that the perpetrators have repeatedly acknowledged. Imagine it for a moment: the President of Iran denies that the Germans perpetrated a crime that the Chancellor and the President of Germany openly confess. The important question is: what do Muslim scholars, translators, and writers claim to know about German history that the Germans themselves do not know?

---

10 Ibid., 9.
11 Litvak and Webman, *From Empathy to Denial*, 3–6.
12 Ibid., 279.

Shoah denial and relativism fed into the hatred and animosity toward the Jews in the Muslim world; Jews were seen as the allies of the West, the new colonial force aligned with the Europeans and, later, the Americans. *Why are the Jews so important to the Europeans?* This question was asked by the Arabs and Muslims as the mythological images of the Jew came alive in the Muslim world.

Antisemitism in the Arab/Muslim world also figures in political and social realities that have led to *Shoah* denial and relativism, and have produced a selective reading of the history of the Jews that casts them as Zionists (those who align with Israel as a political movement) and as allies of colonialism. Colonial history has also been dismissed in many western curricula, while the memory of colonialism in every Muslim country is still fresh in the twenty-first century. Today, many national borders in Africa, Asia, and the Middle East that were created by twentieth-century colonial forces are collapsing in the turmoil of war. Colonial memory is still fresh and has nurtured a deep resentment in much of the Arab world that has now moved to American frontiers.

Colonialism in Muslim countries and oppression on the part of the Germans, French, British, Italians, and Dutch has resulted in a complex modern Jewish and Muslim history. The history of coexistence and mutual faith-based traditions has been buried under much geopolitics and propaganda. The evidence that Muslims played a role in the *Shoah* (as I discuss later) points to the complicated fabric of post-colonial and post-*Shoah* perspectives. Muslims played many roles during this time—from actively participating in the suffering of Jews to being mere bystanders, occasional rescuers, and, at times, victims themselves.

> Nazi-Germany's Arabic-language propaganda was not primarily the result of the translation of Nazi ideology and canonical texts into Arabic. Although *Mein Kampf* and *The Protocols of the Elders of Zion* had been translated into Arabic before 1939, neither figured prominently in Arabic propaganda in contrast to the propaganda campaign in Germany and Europe. The assertion the Jews 'have always been' and were in 1941 'enemies of Islam' remained a staple of Nazi radio broadcasts that highlighted the Koran's anti-Jewish passages.[13]

---

13 Herf, *Nazi Propaganda for the Arab World*, 5.

Antisemitism in the Arab world is a frequent topic today, as we see Arab/ Muslim leaders politicize, minimize, or outright deny the *Shoah*. It is not only the history of World War II that beckons me to look at the stark reality of Jewish–Muslim relations, but also the historical exchange between Jews and Muslims in Arab/African/Asian lands. The sentimentalized notion that Muslim empires were places where Jews could thrive is contradicted by historical data and documentation that point to mistreatment of Jews in Arab lands. I remember giving a talk about contemporary Jewish–Muslim relations at the Iranian Cultural Center in Los Angeles, whose director is an open and willing peacemaker. However, some of his audience gawked at me as I said that the "golden age" of Jews living under Muslims was not all that golden; Jews and Christians were allowed to participate in their own communities, but were also required to pay punitive taxes and live publicly according to the laws of Islam. I shared the positive stories of Jews living in Arab/African lands during the so-called golden age between the tenth and twelfth centuries, when there was indeed a flourishing of art, architecture, poetry, and language. Major thinkers such as Maimonides, Nachmanides, Moses Ibn Ezra, Solomon Ibn Gabirol, and Judah Halevi could work in an "Islamic civilization in Spain [that] profoundly influenced Jewish art, architecture, leisure activities, and even modes of religious devotion. Andalusia was not alone in such development: Jews in Egypt, North Africa, and Sicily followed the Iberian cues with their own circle of poets."[14] Things changed for Jews in Arab lands, however, with their confinement in the fifteenth century to ghettos or *mellahs,* and many Jews recorded incidences of hatred and mistreatment from the fifteenth century onward.

> Jewish life in Islamic lands entered a long period of decline following the Almohad persecutions (Berber-Muslim dynasty). The military despotisms of Islamic rulers disrupted urban life, and trade declined precipitously. Then, pushed out of international trade by the ascendant seafaring Italian republics, and subjected to increasingly extortionate levies, Jewish communities suffered and decreased in the thirteenth and fourteenth centuries. The Islamic

---

14 Sara Reguer, Reeva S. Simon, and Michael M. Laskier, eds., *The Jews of the Middle East and North Africa in Modern Times* (New York: Columbia University Press, 2003), 7–8.

environment was no longer stimulating to Jewish intellectual life. The great academies of learning in Iraq and Palestine had long ceased to function, destroyed by the decay wrought by invading Mongols and crusaders. Then thousands of Sephardic Jews from Iberia and Majorca came into the region [in the] fourteenth, fifteenth and sixteenth centuries, bringing a renewal of Jewish life.[15]

The audience to which I was speaking at the Iranian Cultural Center seemed surprised to hear that Muslims had not traditionally been open to and nurturing of Jews and others.

As the Palestinian–Israeli conflict continues to widen the gap of misunderstanding and limit dialogue between Jewish and Muslim communities throughout the world, a few Jewish and Muslim "artisans of peace" continue to forge interfaith partnerships and inter-religious dialogues of reconciliation between Israelis and Palestinians. Jewish–Muslim compatibility in the Islamic Spain of the Middle Ages has emerged as their historical reference. We know that Muslims have seen historical periods of power, sophistication, and wealth, as well as those of colonization, poverty, and despair. As Muslims, we have to take account of these facts all the more, as we are under scrutiny in contemporary times in terms of anti-Muslim sentiment. The Iranian audience was disappointed that my understanding of Muslim history was critical, disruptive, and, for them, uncomfortable. Many of these experiences led me to question how I could communicate the historical role of Muslims in the *Shoah*; how could I connect these two communities to something meaningful and engaging?

Historically, the *Shoah* has been well known but insignificant in Arab lands. Today, it plays a pivotal role in the politics of Israel/Palestine. As mentioned in previous chapters, the *Shoah* is read by Arabs and Muslims as an event that was related, and restricted, to World War II, and its magnitude is seen to have been exaggerated by the Jews in order to gain support for the existence and expansion of the modern State of Israel.

---

15 Jane S. Gerber, "History of the Jews in the Middle East and North Africa from the Rise of Islam Until 1700," in *The Jews of the Middle East and North Africa in Modern Times*, ed. Sara Reguer, Reeva S. Simon, and Michael M. Laskier (New York: Columbia University Press, 2003), 1–16.

This is probably the reason that the discussion of the Holocaust in the Arab context always revolves around its political implications, and circumvents the event itself. The scene of the disaster was Europe, and the perpetrators of the extermination acts were Europeans, but the reparations were paid first and foremost in the Middle East by the Palestinians. Arab anti-Zionist stance determined their [Arabs'/ Muslims'] attitude toward the Holocaust, as toward anti-Semitism in general. This stance is not the cause of the Arab-Israeli conflict, but its outcome. Anti-Jewish texts were engaged in the justification of the Holocaust and with its denial as a Zionist hoax—a rhetoric which, among other things, was an attempt to deal with the Zionist instrumentalization of the Holocaust.[16]

The *Shoah* has been seen implicitly as a European event, and the stark reality that Jews were imprisoned, murdered, and persecuted in Arab countries has been overlooked. Yet we must stress that Europeans were responsible for this persecution, carried out in Arab lands under colonial rule, often by Europeans with Arabs in decidedly secondary roles.

Research and scholarly works on Muslims and the *Shoah* range widely, and include such books as Norman Gershman's *Besa: Muslims Who Rescued Jews during World War II*, Fariborz Mokhtari's *In the Lion's Shadow: The Iranian Schindler and His Homeland in the Second World War*, Robert Satloff's *Among the Righteous*, Karen Gray Ruelle's and Deborah Durland Desai's *The Grand Mosque of Paris: A Story of How Muslims Rescued Jews During the Holocaust*, and Joëlle Allouche-Benayoun's *Perceptions of the Holocaust in Europe and Muslim Communities: Sources, Comparisons and Educational Challenges*. Michael Laskier has also conducted research on the condition of Jews in modern Africa in *North African Jewry in the Twentieth Century: The Jews of Morocco, Tunisia, and Algeria*. These are certainly not the only scholarly works that discuss the various aspects of this topic, but they present a good overall portrait of the progression of colonialism, the *Shoah*, Zionism, and Muslim involvement in the sheltering of Jews during World War II. These titles underline the fact that the story of Muslims and the *Shoah* is an important one for

16 Azmi Bishara, "The Arabs and the Holocaust. The Analysis of a Problematic Conjunctive Letter," Zmanim 53 (Summer 1995) in Litvak and Webman, *From Empathy to Denial*, 23.

many reasons; it is significant for Jews from Arab countries, it examines Muslims' roles in the *Shoah*, and, finally, it contributes to the narrative of history, in which witnessing and memory may help nurture mutual understanding of some of the underlying concerns between Jews and Muslims.

The Holocaust, or, as I have chosen to call it throughout this book, the *Shoah*, is significant not only because six million Jews were murdered, but because such evil actions could even be committed by human beings. This lesson is important to me as a Muslim, as it is through others' sufferings that we can often hear the voice of empathy and compassion. As the Qur'an states that we must learn from others, so must we also accept cultural and religious diversity, because we were created as a diverse people.

> We created you from a single (pair) of a male and female, and made you into nations and tribes, that ye may know each other. (49:13) As Muslims, like Bassam Tibi, I would contend that we devote ourselves to the "possibility of pluralism" in the face of what Tibi calls *Islamism,* a political, militant, and in his view, misguided version of Islam. Islamism, Tibi argues, is not supported by careful reading of the Qur'an.[17]

Perhaps Tibi and I, like many Muslim scholars, are constantly attempting to reread, reinterpret, and reengage with Islam, as do our religious counterparts of Judaism and Christianity, who reread some of their basic texts to move toward greater tolerance and acceptance of the other. Islam is a religion that was revealed to the prophet Mohammad [PBUH], who was human, and humans make mistakes; that is why we must not worship prophets in the same way as we worship God. Scholars like me seek to interpret and recognize the whole message of Islam regarding justice and peace, rather than just the verses of the Qur'an that call for certain alliances with others. Translation and interpretation of sacred texts has long been a problem within religious studies. The *Shoah*, however, is not about translation and interpretation, but about allowing the "other" his or her place as a subject of justice and care. To speak about the *Shoah* as a Muslim is a challenge, and to read the testimony

---

17 Leonard Grob and John K. Roth, *Encountering the Stranger: A Jewish-Christian-Muslim Trialogue* (Seattle, WA: University of Washington Press, 2012), 7.

of Muslims who were aware of the circumstances of the *Shoah* and stood by becomes difficult. Jews and Muslims once lived side-by-side in relative peace that was often more harmonious than Jews' experience in Christian lands. But this changed drastically. History demonstrates that Muslims and Jews were separating slowly by the seventeenth century due to the colonization of Arab and African countries by Europeans.

> The Jews remained a minority of diminishing importance in the world of Islam after the seventeenth century. Travelers to the region were struck by the abject poverty and disease rampant in the teeming Jewish quarters. Their golden ages under Umayyads, Abbasids, and the early Ottomans were but a distant memory—if they were remembered at all. As the European powers began to colonize some of North Africa and Arabian ports, the Jews began to look to Europe, hoping that an ascendant European Jewry could offer them the protection they now found wanting. At this juncture historians speak of the end of medieval times and the dawn of the modern era for the Sephardic and Middle Eastern Jews.[18]

The "dawn of the modern era for the Sephardic and Middle Eastern Jews" had a very different trajectory under the Europeans than it had under Muslims. Muslims were themselves weakened and under colonial rule that could not provide much economic or technological strength, so Jews looked to Europe for their livelihoods. For example, France was the only country that gave Jews the option of French citizenship after the French Revolution. Unfortunately, "[g]iven the fierce loyalty many Jews expressed toward France, it is a great irony that—among the three European powers that brought the Holocaust to Arab lands—France was the most eager to persecute Jews in North Africa."[19] France, an important colonial force in North Africa, enforced many antisemitic laws against the Jews in 1940 in the *Statut des Juifs*, which was approved by Algeria and Tunisia; in Morocco, Sultan Muhammad V approved the Moroccan version of *Statut des Juifs*. These laws forced Jews into labor and isolation camps. In 1942, at the Wannsee Conference, plans for the "Final

---

18 Gerber, "History of the Jews in the Middle East and North Africa," 23.
19 Satloff, *Among the Righteous,* 26.

Solution of the Jewish Question" exacerbated the situation for Jews all over the world, including in Northern Africa. The strategy of the Vichy, Italian Fascist, and Nazi colonial regimes in Arab countries included the goal of exterminating Jews from these countries. Generally unaware of the death camps in Europe, local Arabs also had little direct knowledge of Jews being interned in their own countries; Jews, however, were seen as Europeans and not Arabs, which may have made it easier for Arabs to turn a blind eye to their treatment. The Arab image of Jews at this time had already changed from the Arab Jew to the western Jew, who was seen as propelling the Zionist agenda and being allied with the colonizer, Britain.

> [A]n Axis victory in North Africa and the Middle East would also mean an extension of the Final Solution of the Jewish Question in Europe to the 700,000 Jews living in the Arab world ... Accordingly, the Nazi regime presented itself both as a supporter of Arab anti-imperialism aimed at British and as a friend to the Arabs and Muslims based on common values and a common hatred of the Jews and Zionism.[20]

Any cooperative history between Jews and Muslims at this point was suppressed in the language of politicians who used religion to pit the two groups against one another. Jews and Muslims who had lived together for some time were now both threatened with division by colonialism. Even books such as Jeffrey Herf's *Nazi Propaganda for the Arab World* and Robert Satloff's *Among the Righteous*, which concisely discuss Arabs/Muslims and the *Shoah*, fail to see how the pressures of colonialism played into these events. There was colonialism and the fight for nationalism, but the deeper issue was the insistence of Germany in aligning with Muslims in Arab and Eastern fronts. "After all, German propaganda for North Africa and the Middle East promoted a clear image of the Third Reich as a friend of Islam, and the army was eager to preserve this on the ground.[21]

The impact of colonialism can be found in a concise book by Sven Lindqvist, in which he begins with a narrative of intimate insights regarding

---

20 Herf, *Nazi Propaganda for the Arab World*, 57.
21 Motadel, *Islam and Nazi Germany's War*, 120.

the deep psychological and social impact of colonialism, focusing on Joseph Conrad's work on colonialism.[22] Lindqvist writes:

> The way of life of primitive peoples is so wholly adapted to climate and nature that sudden changes, however innocent and even useful they may seem, are devastating. Radical changes such as the privatization of land that had previously been public property, disturb the basis of a whole way of life.[23]

Furthermore, Edward Said's *Orientalism* demonstrated how many native Muslims, especially Arabs, were described by the colonial perspective rather than having their own narrative. This colonial presence for years tainted the perceptions and distorted the relationship with the Muslims and European powers, an important aspect of history that many do not take into account as being the cause of the many problems arising in Muslim countries regarding control of government, oppression, freedom, and identity of specific Muslim countries.[24] Furthermore, pre–World War II, Germany was also very anxious about the Russians and the role that they could potentially play in the arena of war and the axis of enemies. Many Muslims lived under communism and, like many, they were threatened if they practiced their religion. Many Muslims were also secular, but some were religious, and the Nazi party saw them as a population, like the Arabs, to be radicalized against the allies and Russians. The SS was primarily the motivator of much of the propaganda, consisting of anti-Bolshevik and anti-Jewish messages, targeted to Eastern Muslims in Europe. As David Motadel makes clear, "cases of violent suppression of the Muslims and their faith in the Soviet Borderlands and occupied territories were to be used as leverage to discuss the Soviet Union as an enemy of Islam."[25]

---

22 Joseph Conrad, *Heart of Darkness* (London: Dover Thrift Editions, 1990). This novel narrates the journey of the main character, Marlow, through the Congo, and his spellbound power over its inhabitants. It is a pivotal work of fiction whose story is based on the cruelty and power grabbing of the colonization of Africa, one of the many examples of colonialism.

23 Sven Lindqvist, *Exterminate All the Brutes: One Man's Odyssey into the Heart of Darkness and the Origins of European Genocide,* trans. Joan Tate (New York: The New Press, 1992), 143.

24 Please see Edward Said, Leila Ahmed, and Akbar Ahmed for more on colonialism, its impact on Muslim identity, women, and pluralism.

25 David Motadel, *Islam and Nazi Germany's War,* 67.

On the other hand, anti-US and anti-British messages were also used. This propaganda that Herf discusses is analyzed on an even deeper level in Motadel's work, which presents in detail the harsh conditions of colonialism and the way in which Muslims could be swayed with promises of freedom of religion. Colonialism had already eradicated Islamic systems of rule, language, culture, and community, and it seemed that the Germans could help Muslims regain some piece of their identity. Nonetheless, the antisemitism that was propagated has become a deepening reality for many Muslims today.

"The reawakening of Islam meant the strengthening of anti-Bolshevik forces. ... In practice, the SS began to employ Eastern Muslim formations and provided its soldiers with special religious care and religiously charged political indoctrination and in 1944 also opened a mullah school in Dresden for the education of filed Imams. ..."[26]

The story of colonialism reemerges when the discussion of Jewish relegation to Arab camps surfaces in Muslim and Jewish narratives; the two minor narratives of Jews and Muslims that I discuss emerge within their own specific situations and witnessing. In other words, Jewish and Muslim identity struggled immensely through the time of the fall of the Ottomans in 1922, colonialism, the oppression of native Arab/Muslim/Jewish narratives, and finally the *Shoah*.

Many Jews who had fled Germany in 1938 to 1939 were later captured in France and interned in camps in Arab lands. The Arabs who fought against the colonists and attempted to overthrow the colonial forces also ended up in camps in the Sahara, in some cases alongside Jews.

> The camp at Hadjerat-M'Guil was opened on 1 November 1941, as a punishment and isolation camp. It contained 170 prisoners, nine of whom were tortured and murdered in conditions of the worst brutality. Two of those murdered were Jews, one of whom had earlier been in a concentration camp in Germany but had been released in 1939 and had fled to France. This young man's parents had become refugees in London. On learning of their son's murder in the Sahara, they committed suicide.[27]

---

26 Motadel, *Islam and Nazi Germany's War*, 53.
27 Martin Gilbert, *Atlas of the Holocaust* (New York: William Morrow and Company, 1988), 56.

These and other stories emerge about Jews in camps in Tunisia and Morocco, and personal narratives and testimonies have been given by Jews like Frederic Gasquet. In *La Lettre de Mon Pèere: Une Famille de Tunis dans L'enfer Nazi*, he discusses the difficult plight of his family as he discovers that his grandfather, father, and uncle were taken from Tunisia and imprisoned at Dachau, then beheaded for espionage at Torgau, Germany. His grandfather, Jo Scemla, had befriended a Tunisian Muslim man, Hassen Ferjani, who was a Nazi collaborator who betrayed Scemla's family. (Ferjani was later tried by the Allies and imprisoned for fourteen years.) This story about a Jewish family from Tunisia attempting to escape the French and then the Nazis both in Europe and in Tunisia exemplifies the reach of the *Shoah* into Arab lands. Gasquet's memoir contains a letter from his father, Gilbert Scemla, to his wife, Lila, that conveys the deepest feelings of a Jew facing his own beheading along with his father and brother: "I do not want anything of the ones who have condemned us; they have taken their own path. Revenge never serves anyone. I do not want anything from those who denounced us and brought us here as we tried to escape. However, they deserve death."[28] Scemla goes onto say, "I leave everything to God and history to take care of the rest. Another civilization will be born. However, I will not have even a glimmer of such a world.[29] This memoir is mentioned in Robert Satloff's book, as Satloff seeks a member of Ferjani's family and tries to find out exactly what happened. Satloff travels to Tunisia and meets Ferjani's nephew, Mustapha Ferjani.

> We then launched into the story of Hassen and the Scemlas. Was Hassen Ferjani a German informant? At first, Mustapha temporized. There were "two versions" of the story, he explained. According to one version, it was just the Scemlas' bad luck to have been stopped by the Germans. If it had been another day, with another guard manning the checkpoint or more traffic on the street, the Scemlas would have escaped and no one would ever have heard of his uncle. According to the second version, Hassen was, in fact, an agent

---

28 Frederic Gasquet, *La lettre de mon père: Une famille de Tunis dans l'enfer Nazi*, trans. Mehnaz Afridi (Paris: Le Felin, 2006), 58.

29 Ibid.

provocateur acting on behalf of the Germans, a cunning man who arranged the entire scheme to trap the hapless Scemlas.[30]

If Hassen Ferjani did turn in the Scemlas, did he appreciate the consequences of his actions? Did he know that the three Jewish men were going to be imprisoned? Was he aware of the concentration camp, Dachau? Did he know that these men, whom he called friends, would be executed by the Germans? There is no evidence that the extent of Nazi actions against Jews were transparent to people in Arab countries—in this case, Tunisia. However, Arabs were clearly aware of the existence of concentration, slave labor, and military camps in their own countries.

Ferjani eventually returned to Tunisia and ran a fabric store. He was one example of the many Arabs/Muslims who were influenced by perhaps the strong European antisemitism or desperation for money and enterprise that began to emerge in Arab and Muslim countries in the twentieth century, especially after the establishment of Israel in 1948. This raises some questions about the *Shoah* and whether Muslims were aware of Axis actions against Jews across Europe and Africa. Even though Germany did not occupy North Africa, leaving it to the Vichy and Italians, they still had influence through their propaganda.

> By 1948, compassion toward the Jews had faded in both the official and the public discourse, giving rise to additional motifs: 1) the Arabs were not responsible for the Holocaust; and 2) if they would pay the price of the Holocaust, it would be a tragedy no less serious than the Holocaust ... The diversity of voices was substituted by a more monolithic discourse that increasingly used the Holocaust as a tool in rhetoric of conflict.[31]

Antisemitism in Muslim communities was fueled by geopolitical factors during both World Wars. Whether it can be blamed on the Zionist movement, European oppression, or Jewish alliances with the West, antisemitism has persisted alongside the many myths about Jews, Judaism,

---

30 Satloff, *Among the Righteous*, 94.
31 Litvak and Webman, *From Empathy to Denial*, 57.

and the *Shoah*. As noted earlier, the genocide of the Jews that took place in Europe also played out in many other parts of the world. The admission of these historical facts would create a place of exchange and mutual respect for Jews and Muslims in our time. As the genocide of Jews and others in Europe has been accepted even by the Germans themselves, I ask why we Muslims deny it. Have we denied the Bosnian death camps? No. Have we denied Armenia? Yes. Have we rescued our brothers and sisters in Darfur, Sudan? No. The *Shoah* is not an isolated event, but it was unprecedented in scope, reaching even into the Arab world.

In *The Historiography of Genocide*, the debate over the definition of the term "genocide" is reviewed from its first coining by Raphael Lemkin[32] to the United Nations Convention on Genocide, 1948.

> In the present convention, genocide means any of the following acts committed with intent to destroy, in whole or in part, a national, ethnical, racial or religious group, as such:
>
> 1. Killing members of the group;
> 2. Causing serious bodily or mental harm to members of the group;
> 3. Deliberately inflicting on the group conditions of life calculated to bring about its physical destruction in whole or in part;
> 4. Imposing measures intended to prevent births within the group;
> 5. Forcibly transferring children of the group to another group.[33]

Muslims did not participate directly in the Nazis' Final Solution to murder all Jews. Many Muslims had no knowledge of such horrific acts of murder that occurred in European death camps. However, Muslims were bystanders as Jews were persecuted, forced to work in labor camps, and executed by the colonial forces in their countries. Martin Gilbert's *Atlas of the Holocaust* is a valuable resource that maps the locations in which the Nazis established

32 F. Chalk, "Redefining Genocide," in *Genocide: Conceptual and Historical Dimensions*, ed. G. Andreopoulos (Philadelphia, PA: University of Pennsylvania Press, 1994), 48.

33 Ann Curthoys and John Docker, "Defining Genocide," in *The Historiography of Genocide*, ed. Dan Stone (New York: Palgrave Macmillan, 2005), 14.

camps. One map is entitled "Slave Labor Camps of the Sahara, 1941–42." Gilbert's explanation underneath the map is telling:

> In April 1940, more than 15,000 Jews were serving in the French Foreign Legion, hoping to fight against Nazi Germany. But with the German conquest of France in June 1940 they were first "demobilized," then interned, and finally sent to labour camps in French North Africa ... Many of these Jews were refugees from Germany and Austria who had been in France at the outbreak of war.[34]

Jews were taken from what they perceived as safe havens to camps where they were tortured and killed.

In 1940, Morocco was ruled by Vichy France. However, Sultan Muhammad V issued an order as the official leader that he would not implement certain antisemitic laws. Islam forbids the passing of laws based on race, and "the Vichy government had declared people Jewish if their parents were Jewish, regardless of whether they themselves professed to be Jewish."[35] The sultan asked for two amendments to the laws: first, that Jews in Morocco be defined by religious choice, not ethnicity; and second, that Jewish institutions, such as schools and communal Jewish life, not be constrained. These acts have made him a respected figure, but according to Yad Vashem's criteria one can only be recognized as Righteous Among the Nations if one's life was at risk, and there is little evidence that the Sultan's life was at risk.

> Toward the end of 2006 a new publication, Robert Satloff's book *Among the Righteous: Lost Stories from the Holocaust's Long Reach into Arab Lands*, ignited a debate over the Sultan's role in the events of the 1940s and his behaviour toward the Jewish minority. Satloff's aim was to find Arab rescuers of persecuted Jews in North Africa. He proposed naming the Tunisian Khaled Abd Al-Wahab a *Righteous Among the Nations* in Yad Vashem. To date about 50

34 Gilbert, *Atlas of the Holocaust*, 56.
35 "Among the Righteous": Lost Stories of Arabs Who Saved Jews During the Holocaust," American Council for Judaism, accessed October 23, 2016 http://www.acjna.org/acjna/articles_detail.aspx?id=487

Muslims, most of them from Turkey and the Balkans, have been honoured as *Righteous*, yet there is not a single Arab among them. The potential nomination of the first Arab and the question of whether there were more Arabs who had helped their Jewish fellow citizens gave rise to the idea that the former Moroccan king Mohammed V be also honoured as *Righteous*.[36]

Satloff argued that Muhammed V and others were risking their lives to save Jews, a story that could be told in the Arab world with pride.

> In private, Muhammad V offered vital moral support to the Jews of Morocco. When French authorities ordered a census of all Jewish-owned property in the country, the Jewish leadership feared this was the precursor to a general confiscation. Secretly, the sultan arranged for a group of prominent Jews to sneak into the palace, hidden in a covered wagon so he could meet them away from the prying eyes of the French.[37]

Satloff states that "[b]y virtually all accounts, the mass of Arabs neither participated in nor actively supported the anti-Jewish campaign that European Fascists brought to North Africa."[38] Witnesses in the Northern African internment camps relate how some Arabs helped Jews, some colluded with the Vichy regime and the Nazis, and most stood by with apathy. Satloff's argument is that the Arabs were trying to protect their jobs. Tunisians, Moroccans, and Algerians are still hesitant to discuss this tragedy in light of the founding of Israel in 1948. The lingering silence of both the culpable and the righteous ones who rescued Jews and protected them during the *Shoah* remains an untold story.

In 2012, I was invited to be a consultant at the United States Holocaust Memorial Museum in Washington, DC by Victoria Barnett. We have discussed

---

36 Sophie Wagenhofer, "Contested Narratives: Contemporary Debates on Mohammed V and the Moroccan Jews under the Vichy Regime," *Quest: Issues in Contemporary Jewish History* (November 2012): 4.
37 Satloff, *Among The Righteous,* 110.
38 Ibid., 74.

building curricula for *Shoah* education involving multi-faith groups. I was also fortunate to have a look at their archives and spend some time talking with Aomar Baum, a researcher there who studies Moroccan attitudes toward Jews. I asked him if there was an account of a Muslim at a camp in the Sahara during the *Shoah*. He said that there was one document that was at the University of Paris, and he had not read it. I was fortunate enough to obtain it through the library of Manhattan College, where I teach, with the help of Amy Handfeld, and had it translated with the help of a student, Miruna Barnoschi. This is an invaluable document, which we hope to publish. This account was written in 1965 by Mohammed Azerki Berkani, an Algerian Muslim man whose memoir is entitled *Three Years of Camps: A Year of Concentration Camp, Two Years of the Disciplinary Center; Djenien-Bou-Rezg Sud-Oranais (1940–1943, Vichy Government)*. This memoir discusses his torture by the Vichy regime for dissention and participation in the Algerian Nationalist movement and ENA Start of North Africa (Algerian Nationalist Organization, established 1926). Berkani recounts the stories of activists within France who went to Algeria to fight for Algerian independence, but more important, he describes the concentration camps where he was tortured and persecuted. He begins his memoir with the following: "I would like to let the readers know about the three years that my Muslim friends and Europeans spent, like me, in this cruel camp, now impossible to forget."[39] As he describes the various camps and their infrastructure, it is clear that there are different sections:

> First they put all the people together—Muslims and Europeans— in the same section and in the same room, but just a few days before our arrival, they were separated, the Muslims in the first section, and the Europeans including the Israelis [Jews??? There were not Israelis then] in the second section. We arrived on the 27th of June 1940 and the camp had been opened since the 1st of May [with]in the same year. The first contingents arrived there [on] the 15th of May 1940.[40]

---

39 Mohammed Arezki Berkani, *Three Years of Camps: A Year of Concentration Camp, Two Years of the Disciplinary Center; Djenien-Bou-Rezg Sud-Oranais (1940–1943 Vichy Government)*, trans. Miruna Barnoschi and Mehnaz Afridi (Koudia: Setif, 1965), 8.

40 Ibid., 9.

Berkani's experience exemplifies the severe punishment that Arabs experienced under the Vichy and German governments, especially if they were nationalists; participation in the rebellions in Algeria and Morocco resulted in internment in concentration camps, where Jews were also interned. Jews who were caught in Arab lands from all over Europe, and some who were in camps in both Morocco and Tunisia, were eventually sent back to Europe to be killed. Berkani's memoir testifies to the various parties and races that were persecuted by Vichy and the Germans. Berkani encountered several officers who commanded the camp, but he has specifically traumatic memories of one officer. He writes that "[t]he arrival of Lieutenant Dériko was a terrible time for the prisoners. He transformed the camp into a center of discipline. He came [in] the month of April 1941 and left in 1943."[41] While other camp commanders would at least question prisoners suspected of stealing before meting out punishment, Dériko would punish for any disobedience or infraction. Berkani relates his relationship with Jewish fellow internees under Dériko's command: "He was always looking for new ways to create tension between the monitored prisoners. He demolished a wall that separated the first section (of the prison) from the second and added four or five bedrooms to the first section. In the past, these rooms (had) belonged to the second section."[42] Dériko clearly attempted to encourage ethnic tensions among those interned in the camps: "He gathered the Jews of the camp, who were previously mixed with the Europeans, and separated them from the French, or rather from the Europeans. This cursed Dériko prepared further provocations once again. Europeans were separate, the Arabs were separate, and the Jews too were separate. The Jews became part of the first section."[43] He was able to push the different sections into a bigger section within the prison. Those interned were aware of Dériko's divisive tactic:

There is no doubt that Dériko did this with the intention of seeing the Jews cut down and killed by the Muslims,[44] since the Jews were not numerous. But the Jews realized his goal; the Arabs too realized the same thing. Commander Dériko expected that there would be fights between Arabs and

---

41 Ibid., 35.
42 Ibid., 43.
43 Ibid., 44.
44 Berkani uses the terms Muslims and Arabs interchangeably.

Jews, but the opposite occurred: a friendly understanding spread between the two communities. Never could one have believed that the Arabs and the Jews in the first section of the camp would become real friends, even brothers. Whether you wish to believe it or not, they were moreover brothers in hunger, in suffering, in misery, in punishment/pain etc. ... in Dériko's camp.[45]

In Berkani's memoir, Jews and Arabs, usually portrayed as enemies, are in similar positions and, significantly, are victims in both Algeria and France. Berkani's story continues to give an account of the sufferings of the various groups together in the camp.

Growing evidence in the literature that the *Shoah* is connected to Jewish–Muslim relations is unavoidable. Sansal's *The German Mujahid*, mentioned earlier in this work, examines a young Arab's confrontation with his German father's role in the Nazi party as an SS guard:

> One question drives me mad: Did papa know what he was doing in Dachau, in Buchenwald, in Majdanek, in Auschwitz? I can't think of him as a victim anymore, as some fresh-faced innocent unwittingly infected by evil. And even if he was, there comes a moment, a split second, some event, however trivial, some unexpected, fleeting series of terrible images which lead to realization, doubt, revolt... My father tortured and killed thousands of people who never did him any harm and he got away scot-free.[46]

Sansal's novel relates a Muslim boy's anxiety about his father's German past and his Islamic future. A novel that confronts the Holocaust in the context of Algeria and Islamic fundamentalism echoes Berkani's own struggle within Algeria during World War II.

During the *Shoah*, there were also many stories of Muslims rescuing and sheltering Jews. These stories range from Albania to Morocco, Turkey, Iran, Sarajevo, and Tangiers. Muslims who risked their lives to hide Jews to save their lives are also part of the history of Muslims and the *Shoah*. The stories of faith, cooperation, and witnessing reflect the historical reality of how Muslims reached out to Jews and understood that they were being persecuted

---

45 Ibid., 45.
46 Sansal, *The German Mujahid*, 88.

on religious grounds. Many Muslims who aided Jews used their knowledge of Islamic codes of social justice to fight for protection and help at a time when Jews were being persecuted. The one predominantly Muslim country in Europe, Albania, managed to save all its Jewish citizens during the *Shoah*.[47] Albania was 70% Muslim and 30% Christian. In Norman H. Gershman's *Besa: Muslims Who Saved Jews During World War II*, there are many narratives of Albanian Muslims who saved Jews because of their own understanding of Islam. As one of the rescuers asserts:

> We lived in the town of Elbasan. I was twelve years old, and my two other brothers are younger. It was just a few steps from here that our father sheltered six Jews in a stone house much like the one we lived in. It is in the Koran that in the name of God we help all humans. They were Raphael Camhi, Chaim Isaac and Leon Isaac, with his wife and two children. The Isaac family spoke Serbo-Croatian, as did our father. In 1945, they all left for Yugoslavia. Leon Isaac came back for a visit in 1948. He and his family were living in Macedonia. To show his gratitude for saving the lives of his family, he wanted to give my parents a restaurant in Macedonia and offered to pay all their expenses for ten years. Our mother did not want to live in Macedonia so we stayed in Elbasan. After 1949, we lost contact with the Isaacs. The communists then imprisoned our father. We have never sought recognition, but we are glad for this opportunity to have our father remembered. It is in the Koran that in the name of God we help all humans.[48]

In most European countries, Jews were transported to camps, but Albania, Morocco, Turkey, and Iran are a few of the countries from which one hears

---

47 "Albania, the only European country with a Muslim majority, succeeded in the place where other European nations failed. Almost all Jews living within Albanian borders during the German occupation, those of Albanian origin and refugees alike, were saved, except members of a single family. Impressively, there were more Jews in Albania at the end of the war than beforehand" ("Besa: A Code of Honor," *Yad Vashem*, accessed December 2014, http://www.yadvashem.org/yv/en/exhibitions/besa/introduction.asp).

48 Norman Gershman, *Besa: Muslims Who Saved Jews During World War II* (Syracuse, NY: Syracuse University Press, 2008), 35.

stories of Muslims risking their own safety to help Jews. Under the Vichy government, Morocco and Tangiers opened labor camps where they interned Jews; here, too, there were stories of Jews being rescued by Muslims. In Albania, Muslims changed the names of Jewish families and hid them in their homes as Nazis hunted for them. In Tangiers, a Muslim man named Khaled Abdul Wahab[49] hid a family in his house while he entertained SS guards, risking his life. Since the establishment of Yad Vashem, 21,700 people have been awarded the title of Righteous Among the Nations,[50] 60 of whom have been Muslims. Even though Muslims are now so often identified with Holocaust denial, there were many Muslim initiatives to save Jews during the *Shoah*.

Ulkumen Selahattin, a Turkish diplomat, is among those Muslims recognized as being named Righteous Among the Nations by Yad Vashem. Despite his diplomatic status, which should have granted him immunity— recall that Turkey was neutral—he was recognized as risking his life because his wife and daughter were killed. This was a courageous act, as the final result was that he lost his beloved ones. This rescue story demonstrates the historical significance and complicated nature of the actions of people in some Muslim countries that were embroiled in World War II. Many Jews born in Turkey lived in places such as Rhodes, and when Italy captured the island from Turkey in 1912, many Jews consequently opted for Italian citizenship and gave up their Turkish identities. When the Germans took control of the island in 1943, the Jewish community despaired, and many fled, leaving about 1800 Jews on Rhodes. Selahattin was Turkish consul-general on the island, and helped about 50 Jews by asserting that they were still Turkish nationals; since Turkey was a neutral country, the Germans left these Jews unharmed.

> Responding to the appeal of Mathilde Turiel [Jewish *Shoah* survivor], and other beneficiaries who survived thanks to Ulku-men's magnanimity and courageous action, Yad Vashem awarded the Righteous title to the retired Turkish diplomat, in 1989 ... Fifty

---

49 Satloff, *Among the Righteous*, 126.
50 *Yad Vashem is World* Center for Holocaust Research, Documentation, Education, and Commemoration in Israel. It has awarded the title of Righteous Among the Nations to hundreds of people who rescued Jews and risked their lives during the *Shoah*.

Jews state, "I am alive thanks to him; had he not intervened—I would not be alive." ... further proof of how public servants in various capacities could, if they wished, reinterpret existing laws and regulations in such a way as to make it possible for Jews to elude capture and death at the hands of the Nazis.[51]

Another example of public servants intervening to protect Jews appears in the book entitled *In the Lion's Shadow: The Iranian Schindler and His Homeland in the Second World War*. This discusses the life of a junior Iranian diplomat named Abdol Hossein Sardari in France, who saved hundreds of Iranian Jewish families by challenging the Third Reich's racial laws and turning Nazi logic into a Mosaic law. This created Mosaique law. Sardari argued that Iranian Jews were not Semites, but from Aryan stock, and asserted that while their religion was based on the teachings of Moses, they were not racially Jewish.

> [Sardari] introduced his argument with some historical background, presenting an overview of Iran's population as predominantly Muslim, yet inclusive of the Shiites, Sunnis and Mosaique [Iranian followers of Moses; Jews]. The latter were indistinguishable from the rest in culture, language and even their observance of national and cultural celebrations ... The Mosaique, he emphasized, did not speak Yiddish, nor did they celebrate separate holidays. Furthermore, they did not have any similarities with European Jewry. Their nationality was Iranian and their race, as was the case with all Iranians, Aryan. The group's distinction, he argued, had historic roots unrelated to racial inferences. The Mosaique mixed and married with fellow Iranian Muslims and were engaged in each and every profession. Their common names were typical Muslim names. They resembled the *Djougoutes* of Afghanistan or Boukhara or Turkistan—all of Iranian origin.[52]

---

51 Mordecai Paldiel, *Saving the Jews: Amazing Stories of Men and Women Who Defied the "Final Solution"* (Rockville, MD: Schreiber Publishing, 2000), 144–45.

52 Fariborz Mokhtari, *In the Lion's Shadow: The Iranian Schindler and His Homeland in the Second World War* (Gloucestershire: History Press, 2011), 95.

The many rescues that took place and that are still being uncovered link to narratives like Berkani's regarding the camps in which many thousands of Jews were persecuted in Arab lands during the *Shoah*. The *Shoah* is a brutal lesson for all humanity, not for just the Jews; but Muslims must accept that the main target was the Jewish community, and must invite openness about the suffering of Jews in Nazi hands as well as on Muslim soil after 1948.

Finally, I want to relate the compelling story of the Indian Muslim Noor Inayat Khan, which demonstrates how we can become people of faith and justice for others, especially in unique circumstances.

> [Khan] was a wartime British secret agent of Indian descent who was the first female radio operator sent into Nazi-occupied France by the Special Operations Executive (SOE). She was arrested and eventually executed by the Gestapo. Noor Inayat Khan was born in 1914 in Moscow to an Indian father and an American mother. She was a direct descendant of Tipu Sultan, the eighteenth-century Muslim ruler of Mysore. Khan's father was a musician and Sufi teacher. He moved his family first to London and then to Paris, where Khan was educated and later worked writing children's stories. Khan escaped to England after the fall of France and in November 1940 she joined the WAAF (Women's Auxiliary Air Force). In late 1942, she was recruited to join SOE as a radio operator. Although some of those who trained her were unsure about her suitability, in June 1943 she was flown to France to become the radio operator for the "Prosper" resistance network in Paris, with the codename "Madeleine." Many members of the network were arrested shortly afterward, but she chose to remain in France and spent the summer moving from place to place, trying to send messages back to London while avoiding capture."[53]

As with many stories during the *Shoah*, many victims were betrayed, stories shared by many. It was thus with Khan; the mistrust of a French woman took Khan's life away:

---

53 "Noor Inayat Khan 1914–1944," *BBC* (2014), accessed May 9, 2016, http://www.bbc.co.uk/history/historic_figures/inayat_khan_noor.shtml.

In October, Khan was betrayed by a French woman and arrested by the Gestapo. She had unwisely kept copies of all her secret signals and the Germans were able to use her radio to trick London into sending new agents—straight into the hands of the waiting Gestapo. Khan escaped from prison but was recaptured a few hours later. In November 1943, she was sent to Pforzheim prison in Germany, where she was kept in chains and in solitary confinement. Despite repeated torture, she refused to reveal any information. In September 1944, Khan and three other female SOE agents were transferred to Dachau concentration camp, where on September 13 they were shot.[54]

She too was a hero, murdered by the same killers as the Jews. She was my heroine as a Muslim woman as well. She fascinates me—it is her courage that I can look up to and remember the many heroes that rescued one another in a great time of turmoil and uncertainty. A Muslim who worked for the rescue for Jews, hoping some day that she could help the victims escape—instead, she became a victim with other Jews in the same camp.

---

54 Ibid.

Afterword

Debate on the nature and proper role of Islam is of course steeped in a sense of the past, in memories of what Islam has been and how it has operated in society over a period of fourteen centuries. These memories are not mere shadows; they shape discussion and conflict in very direct ways. No group or tendency in contemporary Islam says that it aims to create something new. Rather, each claims—and surely believes—that it is trying to recapture the essence of the pure Islam that once existed. It is memory that identifies goals and purposes within the debate.[1]

As a child saturated with the stories of the prophet Mohammad [PBUH] and Islam, growing up in Western Europe, my mind was chock full of wonderful nuances of the East and West. The stories that surrounded me were full of glimpses of supernatural events and miraculous twists of fate, all of which created an indelible feeling in a young, impressionable girl. The luminous feeling that there was something larger than the galaxy transported my mind to imagine and feel God and Islam in a very intimate yet incomprehensible way. Intimacy and distance are the terms I use to describe my feelings about the mere knowledge and intuition of faith and God.

---

1 Stephen R. Humphreys, *Between Memory and Desire: The Middle East in a Troubled Age* (Berkeley: University of California Press, 1999), 10.

As a child, I would lie by my tiny bedroom window that framed the sky. Whenever I wanted to shift my tiny bed around the room to make it feel new, I stared into the sky, seeing what I imagined were figures of prophets, stories of miracles, and, at times, a glimpse of God. These stories were "other" and "different" from the ordinary European life that I lived at school and elsewhere. European stories about the Greeks, Romans, discovery, invention, and the Christian Church ornamented the culture around me. Europe, especially Switzerland, was breathtaking, but was very different from the interior of my home. My home life was replete with the words of the Qur'an, the smell of fried bread, and the sounds of old Indian and Pakistani singers from the 1950s and 1960s. I held the outside world at bay, but respected it and its difference throughout my Islamic education and upbringing. The indelible imprint of Islam for me was about the stories of the prophet Mohammad (PBUH) and the magnificent history of Islam. The story of Mohammad's (PBUH) escape from the Quraysh tribe, when he was protected by a spider, has kept me from killing spiders all my life. I was amazed at the spider that wove its web so quickly over the opening of the cave in which Mohammad (PBUH) was hiding that his enemies could not conceive of anyone having just entered it, and so passed by. Another story tells how a woman would throw rubbish at the prophet every day as he walked to the mosque, while he would silently walk by and not say a word. One day, when she was not there, he inquired after her and was told that she was sick. He went to visit her, and she was so taken aback that she accepted him as the prophet and the one God. The wondrous story of Mohammad's (PBUH) ascension to heaven amused me the most, as I saw him as a gentle negotiator meeting with all the great prophets. He negotiated with Moses for the right and reasonable number of prayers prescribed for Muslims.

The love story of Khadija and Mohammad (PBUH) gave me the power as a young girl to set my sights on a feminism that, for me, existed within Islam, and not in the patriarchal Pakistani culture of cocktail and tea parties that my parents attended. Memories of praying and fasting the day before Eid-ul-Fitr, at Lake Geneva where we lived, come back as sweet memories of new clothes, the smell of almond halva, and a hope that my parents would give a large gift of money to me as a reward for my observance during Ramadan. The prayers that my father conducted in the apartment in

Pfaff-Hausen, in the company of perhaps 100 Muslims, and my father leading Eid prayers as my mother made 200 *parathas* (a type of fried bread), are ingrained in my memory. My memories of Islam and the special place it occupied in the mind of a young girl growing up in the West are good, solid. I find myself bewildered equally at idealistic or vilifying memories of Islam.

The process of writing this book has opened up new thoughts and questions in my mind about memory and how we see the past, present, and future. Recently, someone asked me about the goal of my book, and I responded that I was fatigued by antisemitism and Islamophobia in the world, and I thought that the book might offer hope to Muslims, a different perspective. I do not know if this book will have a great impact, but it might help to create a dialogue about the pain and suffering of the "other." My personal goal is to present historical facts, but also to look at memory as clearly and honestly as possible, in a way that is not simply nostalgic or senti-mental. Memory has its own issues in post-*Shoah* literature. The memory that I discuss regards the Muslim mind and the inflated collective memory of an ideal era of early Islam under the prophet Mohammad (PBUH), and the celebrations of great empires lost and forgotten. How do we remember the past? What do we glorify? Do we read our own history? These questions lurk beneath the substance of this book as gaps of repression that I hope will be reawakened. The reawakening can be painful and disappointing, I know, but can also offer the possibility of change. Memory is a major concern in many communities, kept alive by religious and secular commemorations that enliven the mind with ontological and epistemological works of identity, faith, and nationality. A celebration of one's identity steeped in historical and sacred scriptures is lived through holidays and festivals in both Judaism and Islam. Suffering, exile, and the births of communities are remembered throughout Jewish and Muslim history, but the memory of the "other" can be forgotten in the process of strengthening one's own identity. Leila Ahmed speaks about the sweetness of this memory:

> I remember it as a time, that era of my childhood, when existence itself seemed to have its own music—a lilt and music that made up the ordinary fabric of living. There was a breath of the wind always, and the perpetual murmur of trees; the call of the *karawan* that

came in the dusk, dying with the dying light; the reed-piper playing his pipe in the dawn and, throughout the day, the music of living: street-vendors calls; people passing in the street, talking; the clip-clop of a donkey; the sound of a motor car; dogs barking; the cooing of pigeons in the siesta hour.[2]

Memory that we construct with our own traditions may obstruct the many important facets of understanding and change. Survivors of the *Shoah* and other genocides have to deal with memories of suffering and torture. The question of memory for Muslims and Jews remains an important one that needs rethinking and, more important, a critical lens that might allow some room for nostalgia to be seen in perspective.

As a child, my first visual images of Islam were of Anthony Quinn riding a horse through Arabia and his encounter with the prophet Mohammad (PBUH) in the movie *The Message*. The music and the skillful actors relayed a beautiful image of the birth of Islam. Visually, this was stimulating and, as I recall, I was so proud to have the movie as a reference for where my ancestors came from and how Islam was such a peaceful and humanitarian religion. The film explored early Islam's attempts to eradicate racial and gender inequality, especially female infanticide, and the idea of democracy and fairness in an age when social contracts were seldom honored, especially between different tribes and people of different faiths. I would lie in bed as my mother would tell me stories that the *Hadiths* recounted about the great and kind prophet who brought to humanity the message of God for the third time to "the people of the book." I would dream of his face and try to decipher the stories about his henna-colored hair, the glow in his face, and his imprints on historical figures. I idealized this time, place, and prophet whose tradition I felt so proud to inherit as a Muslim girl. Still proud and much older, I am also more knowledgeable about the time and the many challenges that Mohammad (PBUH) and his companions faced.

Memory is an important aspect of Islam, as is the remembering of God, the prophet, and the traditions. *Dhikr*, the practice of reciting God's name over and over again, was part of the many religious gatherings I would attend, and

---

2 Leila Ahmed, *A Border Passage: From Cairo to America—A Woman's Journey*, New York: Penguin, 2000, 47.

the thought of how to remember God's many different names and characteristics was filling up my mind. I would sit with women holding a rosary (or as we call it, *Tazbi* in Urdu) in my hand, pushing each bead as I recited the different names of God, or I would set aside a few minutes every night after *isha* prayers to recite His name a hundred times. What was I doing, and why? A feeling of closeness and a lapse of memory are what come to mind—to meditate by occupying one's mind with words detached from images until a state of otherworldliness descended. I would lose myself in the memory of God and the prophet Mohammad (PBUH). These memories are ones that are very close to me even now as I repeat these exercises, especially throughout Ramadan, which is a period for cleansing oneself and a reflective month of abstinence, and, at the end, a feeling of accomplishment. However, my remembrance of God does not begin with Islam, but spans from the time of Abraham to the present, where God has existed everywhere and in every time. The memory lapses into ponderings of historical nostalgia and reflects on the context of the early years of Islam, when we imagined that life was perfect, but the period of early Islam was hardly perfect. This is where perhaps memory and Islam need to be examined and reconsidered in terms of identity.

> Humiliated memory thus forces us into an unnatural relation with
> the past, because the knowledge it imparts crushes the spirit and
> frustrates the incentive to renewal.[3]

Many wonderful books have been written on the prophet Mohammad (PBUH), with depictions of his life in Mecca and Medina, but he too experienced opposition, resistance, and war. Prophet Mohammad (PBUH), who sealed the prophecy for Muslims, is revered, and the *Hadiths* (stories of the prophet) have been told over and over and used to help settle disputes when the Qur'an and the four major schools of Islamic thought do not suffice. However, the nostalgia for Mohammad's (PBUH) time carries with it some issues and concerns. The first issue is how and why Muslims revere him to the point of idolatry. The second is how this period was a very difficult one and that the "first Muslims" were as warlike as others at this time.

---

3 Lawrence Langer, *Holocaust Testimonies: Ruins of Memory* (New Haven, CT: Yale University Press, 1991), 79.

The issue of idolatry is deeply serious in Islam. As Muslims, we are commanded by God to worship only him, and have no images of him or of the prophets. Image-making has been an issue in the past few years, as in the case of the Danish cartoon controversy, which aroused anger in the more zealous Muslims. The Danish cartoons of prophet Mohammad (PBUH) not only mocked him but physically depicted him and his image. This is forbidden in Islam, as it is in Judaism. However, making images of God, prophets, or other Qur'anic figures is banned by Islam because, in Islam, we are to believe that our human capability in relation to God is limited. Even considering the complexity of the human mind, it does not have the capacity to understand what is unimaginable, such as God and God's creation. The more common issue that one encounters in many Muslim-majority countries is that of the celebration of Mohammad's (PBUH) birth and his past as a sacred glorification, which in itself is forbidden.

Hence, as I wrote this book, I wanted to take account of the different shifts of power and memory, and how these dimensions bring us to think about the reality of the *Shoah* and the role of Muslims. I have to admit that I remain befuddled by the many misperceptions about Arabs and Muslims and their direct role in the *Shoah*, including images of Muslims depicted as Nazis with the Hazdar (a Bosnian division of the SS). The close connections of Bosnian Muslims to Nazis in the proliferation of right-wing images of Hitler inspecting their uniforms, and the Nazi salute in the image on Jeffrey Herf's book, are true and horrific to me as a Muslim, and a lot of it makes clear how the role of Arabs in the Second World War created murky misunderstandings between Muslims and Jews. A handful of Muslims are now involved in *Shoah* research around the world, but few have access to the kind of information on the *Shoah* that would promote understanding, which is a central issue between Muslims and Jews. Memory is an integral part of post-*Shoah* literature and it is my duty as a Muslim to remember the victims of the *Shoah*, and to understand that the "person remembering and those trying to make sense of Holocaust testimony are struggling with problems that emerge from differences in experiences, interests, and expectations."[4]

---

4 Jurgen Matthaus, ed., *Approaching an Auschwitz Survivor: Holocaust Testimony and Its Transformations* (Oxford: Oxford University Press, 2012), 3.

A world that has gotten narrower perhaps needs some opening through a fictionalized dialogue that I have created in a world of Egyptian Jew and Muslim:

Edmond Jabès: One needs to have wandered a lot, to have taken many paths, to realize, when all is said and done, that at no moment one has left one's home.

Naguib Mahfouz: Wandering in the alleyways of Cairo, leaving one's home and never having traveled far, one can also see far, it is a matter of who we are ...

Edmond Jabès: I was exiled from my home, your home where you live, dwell, and wander in the alleyways, is there no room for me?

Naguib Mahfouz: Home is a matter of identity, and what is Egypt? There has been much discussion concerning our identity. It is said that we are of Pharaonic, not Arab, descent, that we are northerners and not Africans, or that we are Mediterranean peoples who have no roots in Asia. In my opinion, our homeland is the source of our identity, something that has nothing to do with race. Egyptians represent an integral culture, formed by races of different civilizations—Arabs, Sudanese, Turks, and Moors, as well as ancient Egyptians. The common denominator has been our homeland, which has made one people of migrants of many races and civilizations, fusing their traits to form our national and cultural identity.

Edmond Jabès: But if everything common is in the homeland, why am I in exile? The longing for the desert leaves me with traces and imprints of my prophet Moses, and allows me to have a nostalgic longing that can create animosity against the Arab.

Naguib Mahfouz: Nobody is an Arab, as I have said, the new Muslim movement has scarred our homeland as this or that, we lived among Copts and Jews in harmony—we elected Christian leaders and worked side by side with Jews.

Edmond Jabès: But wherever I look today in Cairo, there are no Jews, the synagogue's dilapidated and no more *harat al-yarud* (Jewish Quarter in Medieval Cairo). I am haunted by a cult of old memories of my own; I was a member of the Jewish cosmopolitan culture, and this compelled me to write and stay connected to Egypt.

Naguib Mahfouz: A homeland, yes, to you, yet you claim Israel as one too, in spite of the Palestinians. Can we understand this to be a twofold issue? I am of the mind that if Cairo is your city, then Jerusalem is yours too!

Edmond Jabès: We Jews have wandered and home was everywhere. We wanted a home, a paradise, a longing, and we made it so after we lost millions and still are in danger of losing what I call the true home, which is the visibility and invisibility of writing. The power of writing letters is to rewrite the world. When nomads wandered the earth, I cry out with the indelible cry of Auschwitz: the splintering word within every word and the piercing cry that is the unhealable wound of language.

Naguib Mahfouz: I am sad for the Jews and I am sad for the Arabs; how can we understand that religion and land are not a right, but a matter of where we land? We have become possessive and lost the intellectual bent that ethics is the ultimate answer and political justice the way ... alas, Jabès, we will someday connect in new generations, but I hope that it will be through literature.

Bibliography

Adler, Margot. "Islamic Center Near Ground Zero Sparks Anger." NPR. Accessed July 15, 2010. http://www.npr.org/templates/story/story.php?storyId=128544392.

Afridi, Mehnaz. "Elmau & Dachau: A Muslim's Testimony." *Jewish Journal* (2007). Accessed March 15, 2015. http://www.jewishjournal.com/articles/page2/elmau_dachau_a_muslims_testimony_20071005/.

Afridi, Mehnaz. "The Role of Muslims and the Holocaust." Oxford University Press (2014), Accessed October 23, 2016. http://www.oxfordhandbooks.com/view/10.1093/oxfordhb/9780199935420.001.0001/oxfordhb-9780199935420-e-005

Afridi, Mehnaz. "Jews and Muslims: Collaboration through Acknowledging the *Shoah*." In *Judaism, Christianity and Islam: Collaboration and Conflict in an Age of Diaspora*, edited by Sander L. Gilman, 35–54. Hong Kong: Hong Kong University Press, 2014.

Agamben, Giorgio. *Remnants of Auschwitz: The Witness and the Archive*. Translated by Daniel Heller-Roazen. New York: Zone Books, 1999.

Ahmad 'Abd al-Ghafur 'Attar, *Al-Yahudiyya wal-sahyuniyya* (Beirut: 1972), 152. Quoted in Meir Litvak and Esther Webman, *From Empathy to Denial: Arab Responses to the Holocaust* (New York: Columbia University Press, 2009), 155.

Ahmed, Leila. *A Border Passage: From Cairo to America—A Woman's Journey*. New York: Penguin, 1999.

al-Arabi, Ibn. *The Tarjuman al-Ashwaq*. Translated by Reynold A. Nicholson (sacred-texts.com: 1911) [Islam World's Greatest Religion, Durood–e-ibrahim].

Accessed May 1, 2016. https://islamgreatreligion.wordpress.com/2009/04/12/durood-e-ibrahim/.

Al-Bilad, June 1, 1996. Quoted in Meir Litvak and Esther Webman, *From Empathy to Denial: Arab Responses to the Holocaust* (New York: Columbia University Press, 2009), 155.

Al-Jumhurriya, August 5, 1986. Quoted in Meir Litvak and Esther Webman, *From Empathy to Denial: Arab Responses to the Holocaust* (New York: Columbia University Press, 2009), 155.

Allouche-Benayoun, Joëlle and Gunter Jikeli. *Perceptions of the Holocaust in Europe and Muslim Communities: Sources, Comparisons and Educational Challenges.* New York: Springer Dordrecht Heidelberg, 2013.

Al-Madani, Nimr. *Were the Jews Burned in the Ovens?* Beirut: Al-Manara, 2001.

Al-Sabil, April 27, 1999. Quoted in Meir Litvak and Esther Webman, *From Empathy to Denial: Arab Responses to the Holocaust* (New York: Columbia University Press, 2009), 155.

Amichai, Yehuda. *The Selected Poetry of Yehuda Amichai.* Translated by Chana Bloch and Stephen Mitchell. Berkeley: University of California Press, 1996.

"Among the Righteous": Lost Stories of Arabs Who Saved Jews During the Holocaust," American Council for Judaism. Accessed October 23, 2016. http://www.acjna.org/acjna/articles_detail.aspx?id=487

Ansary, Tamim. *Destiny Disrupted: A History of the World through Islamic Eyes.* New York: Public Affairs, 2009.

Antepli, Abdullah. "After Abraham, Before Peace: Navigating the Divides." *Islamic Monthly.* Accessed July 30, 2014. http://islamicommentary.org/2014/07/after-abraham-before-peace-navigating-the-divides/.

Arendt, Hannah. *Eichmann in Jerusalem: A Report on the Banality of Evil.* New York: Penguin, 1963.

Assad, Muhammad, trans. *The Message of the Qur'an.* Gibraltar: Dal-al-Andalus Publishers, 1980.

Baker, Leonard. *Days of Sorrow and Pain: Leo Baeck and Berlin Jews.* New York: Oxford University Press, 1980.

Bartov, Omer, and Phyllis Mack. *In God's Name: Genocide and Religion in the Twentieth Century.* New York: Berghahn Books, 2001.

Bauer, Yehuda. "Holocaust and Genocide Today." *Yad Vashem.* Accessed October 6, 2013. http://www.yadvashem.org/yv/en/education/international_projects/chairmanship/yehuda_bauer_genocide_today.pdf.

Baymeh, Mohammad A. *Intellectuals and Civil Society in the Middle East: Liberalism, Modernity and Political Discourse.* London: I. B. Tauris Co. Ltd., 2012.

Berenbaum, Michael. *After Tragedy and Triumph: Modern Jewish Thought and the American Experience.* Cambridge: Cambridge University Press, 1990.

Michael Berenbaum, "Holocaust European History." Accessed October 24, 2016. https://www.britannica.com/event/Holocaust

_____. *The World Must Know: The History of the Holocaust as Told in the United States Holocaust Museum.* New York: Little Brown and Co., 1993.

Berenbaum, Michael, and Fred Skolnik, eds. *Encyclopaedia Judaica.* 2nd ed. Detroit: Macmillan Reference USA, 2007.

Berkani, Mohammed Arezki. *Three Years of Camps: A Year of Concentration Camp, Two Years of the Disciplinary Center; Djenien-Bou-Rezg Sud-Oranais (1940–1943 Vichy Government).* Translated by Miruna Barnoschi and Mehnaz Afridi. Koudia: Setif, 1965.

Berkovits, Eliezer. "Faith after the Holocaust." In *A Holocaust Reader: Responses to the Nazi Extermination*, edited by Michael L. Morgan, 96–102. New York: Oxford University Press, 2001.

"Besa: A Code of Honor." *Yad Vashem.* Accessed December 2014, http://www.yadvashem.org/yv/en/exhibitions/besa/introduction.asp.

Blanchot, Maurice. *The Writing of the Disaster.* Translated by Ann Smock. Lincoln and London: University of Nebraska Press, 1986.

"Bob Barboza & Renee Firestone in Los Angeles." Accessed October 23, 2016. https://www.youtube.com/watch?v=uZ7MXsa6Mqg

Browning, Christopher R. *Collected Memories: Holocaust History and Postwar Testimony.* Madison: The University of Wisconsin Press, 2003.

_____. *Ordinary Men: Reserve Police Battalion 101 and the Final Solution in Poland.* New York, Harper Perennial, 1992.

Chalk, F. "Redefining Genocide." In *Genocide: Conceptual and Historical Dimensions*, edited by G. Andreopoulos, 47–63. Philadelphia, PA: University of Pennsylvania Press, 1994.

Chaudhary, Shakeel. "View Point: 9/11 and Pakistan's Urdu Press." *Pakistan Media Watch* (June 10, 2004). Accessed August 10, 2013. http://pakistanmediawatch.com/2010/09/13/view-point-911-and-pakistans-urdu-press/.

Chemseddine, Anwar. "The Arabs View of the Holocaust is Indeed Troubled." *Legacy Project.* Accessed July 12, 2010. http://www.legacyproject.org/index.

php?commentID=1&page=comment_detail&sympID=1 (URL no longer active)

Cohen, Mark R. *Under Crescent and Cross: The Jews in the Middle Ages.* Princeton, NJ: Princeton University Press, 1994.

____. "When Jews and Muslims Got Along." *Huffington Post.* Accessed January 15, 2015. http://www.huffingtonpost.com/mark-r-cohen/when-jews-and-muslims-got-along_b_4964469.html.

Conrad, Joseph. *Heart of Darkness.* London: Dover Thrift Editions, 1990.

Curthoys, Ann, and John Docker. "Defining Genocide." In *The Historiography of Genocide*, edited by Dan Stone, 9–41. New York: Palgrave Macmillan, 2005.

Dajani, Daoudi Mohammed S., and Robert Satloff. "Why Palestinians Should Learn about the Holocaust." *The New York Times.* Accessed November 2013. http://www.nytimes.com/2011/03/30/opinion/30iht-edsatloff30.html?_r=0.

Dammond, Liliane S. *The Lost World of the Egyptian Jews: Firt-person Accounts from Egypt's Jewish Community in the Twentieth Century.* New York: Universe, Inc., 2007.

Davidson, Ivan, and Derek J. Penslar. *Orientalism and the Jews.* Boston: Brandeis University Press, 2005.

"'Death to the Dictator' Chant Protestors as Ahmadinejad Denies Holocaust." *The Guardian* (September 19, 2009). Accessed June 14, 2010, http://www.theguardian.com/world/2009/sep/18/opposition-protests-iran-quds-day.

"Declaration of the Church to Non-Christian Religions Nostra Aetate Proclaimed by His Holiness Pope Paul VI on October 28, 1965." The Holy See, Daily Bulletin of the Holy See Press Office. Accessed November 15, 2013. http://www.vatican.va/archive/hist_councils/ii_vatican_council/documents/vat-ii_decl_19651028_nostra-aetate_en.html.

"Denmark in the Holocaust." *Encyclopedia at USHMM.* Accessed July 8, 2014. http://www.ushmm.org/information/exhibitions/online-features/special-focus/rescue-of-the-jews-of-denmark.

Devil Came on Horseback, The. Directed by Ricki Stern and Anne Sundberg. New York: Break Thru Films, 2007.

Diner, Hasia. *We Remember with Reverence and Love: American Jews and the Myth of Silence after the Holocaust, 1945–1962.* New York: New York University Press, 2009.

Drakulić, Slavenka. *S: A Novel about the Balkans*. New York: Penguin, 2001.

_____. *They Would Never Hurt a Fly: War Criminals on Trial in the Hague*. New York: Viking, 2004.

"Eichmann Trial." United States Holocaust Memorial Museum. Accessed July 2, 2104. http://www.ushmm.org/wlc/en/article.php?ModuleId=10005179.

El-Fadl, Khaled Abou. "Speaking, Killing and Loving in God's Name." *The Hedgehog Review* (Spring 2004). Accessed January 15, 2015. http://www.scholarofthehouse.org/skiandloingo.html.

"Elie Wiesel: The Museum Deeply Mourns the Passing of Elie Wiesel, Holocaust Survivor, Nobel Laureate, and International Leader of the Holocaust Remembrance Movement." United States Holocaust Memorial Museum. Accessed October 28, 2016. https://www.ushmm.org/wlc/en/article.php?ModuleId=10007176

Encyclopedia of Mass Violence. Accessed May 12, 2016. http://www.massviolence.org/Shoah.

Esposito, John L., and Dalia Mogahed. *Who Speaks for Islam? What A Billion Muslims Really Think*. New York: Gallup Press, 2007.

"Fact Sheet: Jewish Refugees from Arab Countries," Jewish Virtual Library. Accessed October 23, 2016. http://www.jewishvirtuallibrary.org/jsource/talking/jew_refugees.html

Faiz, Faiz Ahmed. "No Sign of Blood." In *Against Forgetting: Twentieth Century Poetry of Witness*, edited by Carolyn Forche, 524–525. London: Norton, 1993.

Fine, Ellen S. *Legacy of Night: The Literary Universe of Elie Wiesel*. Albany, NY: State University of New York Press, 1982.

Franke, Patrick. "Minorities: Dhimmis." In *Encyclopedia of Islam and the Muslim World*, edited by Richard C. Martin. Vol. 2, 451–52. New York: Macmillan Reference USA, 2004.

Frankel, Jonathan. *The Damascus Affair: "Ritual Murder," Politics, and the Jews in 1840*. Cambridge: Cambridge University Press, 1997.

Freeman, Joseph. *Job: The Story of a Holocaust Survivor*. St. Paul: Paragon House, 1996.

Garman, Emma. "'The German Mujahid,' by Boualem Sansal." Accessed October 24, 2016. http://www.wordswithoutborders.org/dispatches/article/the-german-mujahid-by-boualem-sansal

Gasquet, Frederic. *La lettre de mon père: Une famille de Tunis dans l'enfer Nazi.* Translated by Mehnaz Afridi. Paris: Le Felin, 2006.

Gerber, Jane S. "History of the Jews in the Middle East and North Africa from the Rise of Islam Until 1700." In *The Jews of the Middle East and North Africa in Modern Times*, edited by Sara Reguer, Reeva S. Simon, and Michael M. Laskier, 1–16. New York: Columbia University Press, 2003.

Gershman, Norman H. *Besa: Muslims Who Saved Jews During World War II.* Syracuse, NY: Syracuse University Press, 2008.

Gilbert, Martin. *Atlas of the Holocaust.* New York: William Morrow and Company, 1988.

_____. *Dearest Auntie Fori: The Story of the Jewish People.* New York: HarperCollins, 2002.

Gilman, Sander. *Multiculturalism and the Jews.* New York: Routledge, 2006.

"Gisela Glaser." HGI Manhattan College. Accessed July 7, 2014. http://www.hgimanhattan.com/gisela_glaser/.

Grob, Leonard, and John K. Roth. *Encountering the Stranger: A Jewish, Christian, Muslim Trialogue.* Seattle, WA: University of Washington Press, 2012.

Grossman, David. "Uri, My Dear Son." *The Observer* (August 19, 2006). Accessed January 4, 2014. http://www.theguardian.com/world/2006/aug/20/syria. comment.

Heberer, Patricia, and Jurgen Matthaus. *Atrocities On Trial: Historical Perspectives on the Politics of Prosecuting War Crimes.* Lincoln, NE: University of Nebraska Press, 2008.

Herberg, Will. *Protestant—Catholic—Jew: An Essay in American Religious Sociology.* Chicago: University of Chicago Press, 1960.

Herf, Jeffrey. *Nazi Propaganda for the Arab World.* New Haven, CT: Yale University Press, 2009.

———, ed. *Anti-Semitism and Anti-Zionism in Historical Perspective Convergence and Divergence.* New York: Taylor & Francis, 2008.

Humphreys, Stephen R. *Between Memory and Desire: The Middle East in a Troubled Age.* Berkeley: University of California Press, 1999.

Husayn, Yasir. *Hitler.* 1995. Quoted in Meir Litvak and Esther Webman, *From Empathy to Denial: Arab Responses to the Holocaust* (New York: Columbia University Press, 2009), 155.

"Influence of Islamic Thought on Maimonides, The." *Stanford Encyclopedia of Philosophy*. Accessed October 2013. http://plato.stanford.edu/entries/maimonides-islamic/.

"Introduction to the Holocaust." United States Holocaust Memorial Museum. Accessed June 10, 2013. http://www.ushmm.org/wlc/article.php?lang=en&ModuleId=10005143.

"Iraq: ISIS Abducting, Killing, Expelling Minorities." Human Rights Watch. Accessed July 20, 2014. http://www.hrw.org/news/2014/07/19/iraq-isis-abducting-killing-expelling-minorities.

"Islamic Terror Attacks on Christians." Accessed April 10, 2015. www.thereligionofpeace.com/Pages?ChristianAttacks.htm.

Ispahani, Farahnaz. *Purifying the Land of the Pure: Pakistan's Religious Minorities*. New York: HarperCollins, 2015.

Jabès, Edmond. *The Book of Questions: Volume One; The Book of Yukel, Return to the Book*. Translated by Rosemarie Waldrop. Middletown, CT: Wesleyan University Press, 1991.

Jacobs, Steven L., and Mark Weitzman. *Dismantling the Big Lie: The Protocols of the Elders of Zion*. Los Angeles: Simon Wiesenthal Center, 2003.

"Jewish Refugees From Arab Lands." *World Heritage Encyclopedia*. 2002. Accessed May 30, 2016. http://www.worldlibrary.org/articles/jewish_refugees_from_arab_lands.

Jikeli, Gunther. *European Muslim Antisemitism: Why Young Urban Males Say They Don't Like Jews*. Bloomington, IN: Indiana University Press, 2015.

Johnson, Hannah. *Blood Libel: The Ritual Murder Accusation at the Limit of Jewish History*. Ann Arbor, MI: University of Michigan Press, 2012.

Kassam, Zayn. "Whom May I Kill?" In *Encountering the Stranger: A Jewish, Christian, Muslim Trialogue*, edited by Leonard Grob and John K. Roth, 24–37. Seattle, WA: University of Washington Press, 2012.

Khan, Saniyasnain, Ed. *Tazkiyah Made Simple*. New Delhi: Goodword Books, 2014.

Kocaman, Aylin. "Zionism Means Something Different for Some Muslims." *The Jerusalem Post*. Accessed July 7, 2014. http://www.jpost.com/Opinion/Op-Ed-Contributors/Zionism-means-something-different-for-some-Muslims.

Kujawsky, Paul. "Bosnia Genocide Unrolls in Scrolls of Shame." *Jewish Journal*. Accessed October 22, 2016 http://www.jewishjournal.com/opinion/article/bosnia_genocide_unrolls_in_scroll_of_shame_20080806

Langer, Lawrence. *Holocaust Testimonies: Ruins of Memory.* New Haven, CT: Yale University Press, 1991.

Laqueur, Walter. *History of Zionism: From the French Revolution to the Establishment of the State of Israel.* London: Tauris Parke Paperbacks, 2003.

____. *The Terrible Secret: Suppression of the Truth about Hitler's "Final Solution."* Boston: Little Brown and Company, 1980.

Laskier, Michael M. *Egyptian Jewry under the Nasser Regime: 1956–1970.* New York: Taylor & Francis, 1995.

____. "Egyptian Jewry under the Nasser Regime: 1956–70." Accessed October 29, 2016. http://www.hsje.org/Egypt/Egypt%20Today/egyptian_jewry_under_the_nasser_.htm#.WBT05fkrLIV.

____. *North African Jewry in the Twentieth Century: The Jews of Morocco, Tunisia, and Algeria.* New York: New York University Press, 1994.

The Lavon Affair: Is History Repeating Itself?" *What Really Happened?* Accessed July 13, 2014. http://whatreallyhappened.com/WRHARTICLES/lavon.html.

Levin, Marc. "Protocols of Zion." *Thinkfilm Productions.* Accessed May 12, 2016. http://worldfilm.about.com/od/documentaryfilms/fr/protocolsofzion.htm.

Lewis, Bernard. *The Jews of Islam.* Princeton, NJ: Princeton University Press, 1984.

____. "The New Anti-Semitism: First Religion, Then Race, Then What?" *American Scholar* (2004). Accessed October 23, 2016. https://theamericanscholar.org/the-new-anti-semitism/#.WA0O5uArLIU.

Lindqvist, Sven. *Exterminate All the Brutes: One Man's Odyssey into the Heart of Darkness and the Origins of European Genocide.* Translated by Joan Tate. New York: The New Press, 1992.

Lipstadt, Deborah. *Denying the Holocaust: The Growing Assault on Truth and Memory.* New York: Plume Books, 1994.

____. *America and the Memory of the Holocaust, 1950–65. Modern Judaism.* Vol. 16. New York: Oxford University Press, 1996,

Litvak, Meir, and Esther Webman. *From Empathy to Denial: Arab Responses to the Holocaust.* New York: Columbia University Press, 2009.

Mahfouz, Naguib. *Sugar Street.* New York: First Anchor Book Editions, 1993.

Mark, Jonathan. "Muslim Woman to Lead Holocaust Center." *Jewish Week.* Accessed January 2014. http://bovinabloviator.blogspot.com/2011/03/manhattan-college-gets-religionsort-of.html.

Martin, Richard, and Abbas Barzegar. *Islamism: Contested Perspectives on Political Islam.* Stanford: Stanford University Press, 2010.

Massad, Joseph. "Semites and Anti-Semites, That Is the Question." *Al-Ahram.* Accessed December 10, 2016. http://www.campus-watch.org/article/id/1455.

Maswadeh, Ahmed. "Why Should We, Palestinians, Learn about the Holocaust?" *Jerusalem Post.* Accessed November 9, 2015. http://www.jpost.com/Opinion/Why-should-we-Palestinians-learn-about-the-Holocaust-399168.

Matthaus, Jurgen, ed. *Approaching an Auschwitz Survivor: Holocaust Testimony and Its Transformations.* Oxford: Oxford University Press, 2012.

Meyer, Michael A. *Ideas of Jewish History.* New York: Behrman House Press, 1974; Detroit: Wayne State University Press, 1987.

Middle East Media Research Institute TV Monitor Project. Accessed May 3, 2016. http://www.memritv.org/.

Mokhtari, Fariborz. *In the Lion's Shadow: The Iranian Schindler and His Homeland in the Second World War.* Gloucestershire, UK: History Press, 2011.

Motadel, David. *Islam and Nazi Germany's War.* Cambridge, MA: The Belknap Press of Harvard University Press, 2014.

Muslim, Imam. *Sahih Muslim, Kitab al-Fitan wa Ashrat as-Sa'ah*, Book 41. Translated by Abdul Hamid Siddiqui. Accessed June 2, 2016. http://www.theonlyquran.com/hadith/Sahih-Muslim/?volume=41.

"Noor Inayat Khan 1914-1944." *BBC* (2014). Accessed May 9, 2016. http://www.bbc.co.uk/history/historic_figures/inayat_khan_noor.shtml.

Oz, Amos. *In the Land of Israel.* New York: Harcourt Brace Jovanovich, 1983.

Paldiel, Mordecai. *Saving the Jews: Amazing Stories of Men and Women Who Defied the "Final Solution."* Rockville, MD: Schreiber Publishing, 2000.

"Palestinian Professor: No Regrets over Taking Students to Auschwitz." *The Guardian.* Accessed July 15, 2014. http://www.theguardian.com/world/2014/jun/13/palestinian-professor-resigns-students-auschwitz.

"Poet of the Arab World." *The Guardian.* Accessed November 20, 2013. http://www.theguardian.com/books/2002/jun/08/featuresreviews.guardianreview19.

Powers, Samantha. *A Problem from Hell: America and the Age of Genocide.* New York: Basic Books, 2002.

Miranda Prynne, "Holocaust Commission launched by Prime Minister," *The Telegraph*, Accessed October 29, 2016. http://www.telegraph.co.uk/history/10599278/Holocaust-Commission-launched-by-Prime-Minister.html

Quilliam Foundation, The. Accessed November 18, 2013. http://www.quilliam-foundation.org/.

Rafiq Shakir Natshe, *Al-Istiʿmar wa-filistin: Isrāʾil mashru ʾistʿmari* (Aman: 1984), 147. Quoted in Meir Litvak and Esther Webman, *From Empathy to Denial: Arab Responses to the Holocaust* (New York: Columbia University Press, 2009), 155.

Reguer, Sara, Reeva S. Simon, and Michael M. Laskier, eds. *The Jews of the Middle East and North Africa in Modern Times*. New York: Columbia University Press, 2003.

Rose, Jacqueline. *The Last Resistance*. New York: Verso, 2007.

Roth, John K. "Reflections on Post-Holocaust Ethics." In *Problems Unique to the Holocaust*, edited by Henry James Cargas, 169–81. Lexington, KY: University Press of Kentucky, 1999.

Ruelle, Karen and Deborah Desais. *The Grand Mosque of Paris: A Story of How Muslims Rescued Jews During the Holocaust*. New York, Holiday House, 2010.

Sachar, Howard. *A History of Israel*. New York: Alfred A. Knopf, 1979.

Said, Edward. *Orientalism*. New York: Vintage Books, 1978.

Sam, Ser. "Surprise! There Are Still Jews in Pakistan." *MidEast News Service Analysis* (2010). Accessed July 15, 2013. http://groups.yahoo.com/neo/groups/MewBkd/conversations/topics/17888.

Sansal, Boualem. *The German Mujahid*. Cathedral City, CA: Brunswick Press, 2009.

Sarna, Jonathan D. *When General Grant Expelled the Jews*. New York: Random House, 2012.

Sarwar, Ghulam. *The Children's Book of Salah*. London: The Muslim Educational Trust, 1998.

Satloff, Robert. *Among the Righteous: Lost Stories from the Holocaust's Long Reach into Arab Lands*. New York: Public Affairs, 2006.

Schweitzer, Frederick M. *Antisemitism: Myth and Hate from Antiquity to the Present*. Gordonsville, VA: Palgrave Macmillan, 2005.

Shavit, Ari. *My Promised Land: The Triumph and Tragedy of Israel*. New York: Penguin Random House, 2013.

Shermer, Michael, and Alex Grobman. *Denying History: Who Says the Holocaust Never Happened and Why Do They Say It?* Berkeley: University of California Press, 2002.

"Muselmann." Shoah Resource Center, International Center of Holocaust Studies. Accessed May 12, 2016. http://www.yadvashem.org/odot_pdf/Microsoft%20Word%20-%206474.pdf.

"Six Day War." *Encyclopedia Britannica*. Accessed July 2, 2014. http://www.britannica.com/EBchecked/topic/850855/Six-Day-War.

"Son of Nazi/SS Faces Holocaust Survivor from Auschwitz." Accessed October 23, 2016. https://www.youtube.com/watch?v=7razS3QPDDg

Stahl, Jeremy. "Where Did 9/11 Conspiracies Come From?" *Slate*. Accessed May 2, 2016. http://www.slate.com/articles/news_and_politics/trutherism/2011/09/where_did_911_conspiracies_come_from.html.

Stannard, David E. "The Dangers of Calling the Holocaust Unique." *The Chronicle of Higher Education* (August 2, 1996). Accessed August 2012. http://chronicle.com/article/The-Dangers-of-Calling-the/96089/.

Stern, Yoav. "Founder of Holocaust Museum in Nazareth Invited to Tehran." *Haaretz* (November 17, 2006). Accessed December 12, 2006. http://www.haaretz.com/hasen/spages/789142.html.

Sutzkever, Avrom. "Frozen Jews." Accessed May 2, 2016. http://www.auschwitz.dk/id6.htm.

Tibi, Bassam. *Islamism and Islam*. New Haven, CT: Yale University Press, 2012.

_____. "Public Policy and the Combination of Anti-Americanism and Anti-Semitism in Contemporary Islamist Ideology." *The Current* (Cornell University) 12 (Winter 2008): 123–46.

Ul Qadri, Muhammad. "Rights of Minorities in Islam." Accessed December 20, 2013. http://www.minhaj.org/english/tid/8850/Rights-of-minorities-in-Islam/.

Wagenhofer, Sophie. "Contested Narratives: Contemporary Debates on Mohammed V and the Moroccan Jews under the Vichy Regime." *Quest: Issues in Contemporary Jewish History* (November 2012): 4.

Weil, Shalva. "A Jewish Presence in Pakistan." Accessed December 13, 2016. http://www.jewishtimesasia.org/community-spotlight-topmenu-43/pakistan/544-pakistan-communities/2806-a-jewish-presence-in-pakistan-karachi-in-another-time

Weiss-Wendt, Anton. "Problems in Comparative Genocide Scholarship." In *The Historiography of Genocide*, edited by Dan Stone, 42–70. New York: Palgrave Macmillan, 2008.

Wiesel, Elie. *Night*. New York: Bantam Books, 1982.

Yanover, Yori. "Relatives of Egyptian Righteous Gentile Refusing Yad Vashem Award." *The Jewish Press*. Accessed March 20, 2014. http://www.jewish-press.com/news/breaking-news/relatives-of-egyptian-righteous-gentile-refusing-yad-vashem-award/2013/10/20/.

Yehoshua, A. B. Translated by Hillel Halkin. *The Liberated Bride*. New York: Harcourt, 2003.

Yusuf, Ya'qub Abu, and Abdul Hamid Siddiqui, eds. *Kitab-Ul-Kheraj*. Lahore: Islamic Book Center, 1979.

Index